THE GENIUS

OF

DESPERATION

The Schematic Innovations That Made the Modern NFL

Doug Farrar

FOREWORD BY LOUIS RIDDICK

Praise for *The Genius of Desperation*

"Doug Farrar is my favorite NFL writer. I always look forward to reading Doug's work because of his dedication as well as the massive amount of research he conducts for all of his projects. His love for football and his proclivity for preparation have never been more evident than in *The Genius of Desperation*, in which Doug explains the design of many of the great innovations in football tactics, as well as who created them, and where, and why."

—**Tony Khan, Jacksonville Jaguars senior vice president of football administration and technology**

"If you love football—whether you have been in it your entire life or are a fan who appreciates the chess match of the game—you must read this book." —**Joe Banner, former Philadelphia Eagles president and Cleveland Browns CEO**

"Irrespective of your level of knowledge and understanding of the game of football, you will benefit from and enjoy reading this book. It's a book that can serve as a tome, if you will. It can and should sit on the office shelf of many." —**Amy Trask, CBS Sports/former CEO of the Oakland Raiders**

"As someone who knows Paul Zimmerman well, I can tell you Dr. Z would love this book." —**Peter King, NBC Sports**

"If you're a football geek, this book is for you. If you're a fan of good writing and journalism, this book is also for you." —**Mike Freeman, Bleacher Report**

"I have never read a sports book that does such a seamless job of synthesizing statistics and the personalities who bring the numbers to life. In a series of vignettes that span NFL history, Farrar shows how desperation is the true mother of invention." —**Dave Zirin, sports editor for *The Nation***

THE GENIUS OF
DESPERATION

THE GENIUS OF DESPERATION

THE SCHEMATIC INNOVATIONS THAT MADE THE MODERN NFL

DOUG FARRAR

TRIUMPH
BOOKS

Library of Congress Cataloging-in-Publication Data

Names: Farrar, Doug (Football writer), author.
Title: The genius of desperation : the schematic innovations that made the modern NFL / Doug Farrar.
Description: Chicago, Illinois : Triumph Books LLC, [2018]
Identifiers: LCCN 2018016981 | ISBN 9781629375793
Subjects: LCSH: Football—United States—History. | National Football League—History. | Football—Defense. | Football—Offense.
Classification: LCC GV954 .F37 2018 | DDC 796.332/64—dc23 LC record available at https://lccn.loc.gov/2018016981

This book is available in quantity at special discounts for your group or organization. For further information, contact:

Triumph Books LLC
814 North Franklin Street
Chicago, Illinois 60610
(312) 337-0747
www.triumphbooks.com

Printed in U.S.A.
ISBN: 978-1-62937-579-3
Design by Meghan Grammer
Play Diagrams by Doug Farrar and Lindsey Schauer

For Laura

- CONTENTS -

- FOREWORD -

The NFL is a copycat league. If I have heard that phrase once, I have heard it a thousand times since my days as a professional player came to an end in 1999. But if you take a journey back in time and study the history of this great game on the professional level, it becomes clear that the game would not be what it is today if it merely was about duplicating what was successful for others. What has taken place is a continuous evolution borne out of necessity, a point-counterpoint dynamic between offensive and defensive schemes, strategies, and tactics.

It all began in earnest in the 1950s when the legendary Paul Brown basically created the blueprint for how the game of football would be played for the next 65-plus years. Football legends—Vince Lombardi, Tom Landry, Sid Gillman, Hank Stram, Al Davis, Bill Walsh, and Bill Belichick—all took from what Coach Brown started, and coaches today continue to look for the next tactical advantage that will give them a leg up on the competition and take the game into the future and beyond.

When Doug Farrar first approached me about writing the foreword for this masterpiece that he has so carefully put together, it quickly became apparent what my contribution should be. I played safety for Belichick when he was the head coach of the Cleveland Browns in the early 1990s, and, though he was known as a defensive mastermind coming off the success he had with the New York Giants as defensive coordinator in the mid-to-late '80s, it was not until after my playing career was finished that I truly realized what I had been exposed to. Between Belichick and a man named Nick Saban (you may have heard of him), who was Belichick's defensive coordinator/defensive backs coach with the Browns, I had received the best training in the history of the game at my position. They were ahead of the game then and they remain ahead of the game now.

The '90s were a time when offensive football was exploding by way of spread concepts that threatened the field horizontally and vertically, and there were quarterbacks in the league who could light up the scoreboard in a hurry. Dan Marino, Steve Young, Jim Kelly, Warren Moon, and John Elway were all at the top of their game during this time and all destined for the Hall of Fame, and men like Belichick and Saban had to come up with ways to slow them down on a weekly basis. Pre-snap disguise and defensive schematic innovations became points of emphasis for us at the Browns. Things as simple as playing left and right safety instead of strong and free safety in our base and nickel/dime packages so quarterbacks could not get a pre-snap read on our coverage rotations in the secondary were part of the disguise element. The use of pattern matching within zone concepts, which was essentially giving the illusion of playing traditional spot-drop zone coverage at the snap but instead matching up man-to-man as the routes developed down the field, was part of the schematic innovation. With option routes/route conversions becoming more and more standard within NFL offenses being quarterbacked by future Hall of Famers, evolution was necessary or else things were going to get out of control.

The individual player profiles on the defensive side of the ball began to change as well. A greater emphasis was put on speed, lateral agility, and short area quickness when it came to coverage defenders on the second and third level of the defense, as offenses wanted to spread you out and get their best athletes isolated one-on-one in space. If you could not play pass coverage at a high level on third down against legitimate No. 1 wide receivers like Jerry Rice, Andre Rison, Isaac Bruce, and Andre Reed, who were taking the league by storm, then your role began to diminish as a defensive coverage player and players better suited to do so saw their playing time increase. It was what the game demanded, leading to increased specialization. It was what had to be done. Adapt or die.

The Genius of Desperation takes you on a comprehensive, chronological journey of how the game of football has become what we know and love it to be today. What it all came down to in the end was finding a way to win games, finding a way to move the ball more effectively on offense and score points, and finding a way to get off the field on third down and keep teams out of the end zone on defense. That's what the game has always been about, and what it will always be about. It just has been done differently over time, and if you want to know why, this is the book for you.

—Louis Riddick
ESPN NFL analyst

- INTRODUCTION -

"Vision without execution is hallucination."
—Thomas Edison

If necessity has been the mother of invention throughout the history of professional football, it could also be said that desperation is the father. It's entirely rare for any football innovation to occur without an owner, general manager, coach, group of players, or single player up against the wall and looking for a way to succeed. The schematic history of the pro game can be broken down into a series of if-this, then-that scenarios, in which one opponent had the upper hand, and another opponent created a mismatch more through a resoundingly original concept than through the improvement of personnel. Especially in-season, the improvement of personnel is a tough proposition. Generally speaking, one either has the horses to make it go or one does not. And when one does not, there is a base necessity for innovation.

I could give all kinds of examples, but for in-season desperation, it's tough to beat the circumstances that brought the Wildcat formation into NFL prominence. The 2008 Miami Dolphins had a rookie head coach in Tony Sparano, a first-year quarterbacks coach in David Lee, and a veteran quarterback in Chad Pennington who was intelligent but relatively noodle-armed. Sparano had replaced Cam Cameron, who led the 2007 Dolphins to a franchise-worst 1–15 mark. The 2008 Dolphins didn't start out much better, losing their season opener to the New York Jets by a 20–14 mark and getting trounced by the Arizona Cardinals 31–10 in Week 2.

It was on the plane home from University of Phoenix Stadium that the Dolphins—in a fit of desperation—did what so many teams before them did: they threw out the traditional NFL paradigm, said, "To hell with it," and let invention carry the day. Sparano talked with Lee and asked him to detail the Wildcat formations Lee had used as the Arkansas Razorbacks offensive coordinator the year before. In a nutshell the Wildcat had three basic plays, and each had a running back taking the snap from center and the quarterback flanked wide right. *Steeler* has the running back move from left to right after the snap and taking the ball from the quarterback. The running back then blasts off to the right behind a pulling left guard, an unbalanced offensive line, and an H-back either between and behind the two right tackles or just outside the right tackle to block. *Power* is a fake to the running back in the *Steeler* formation, which leaves the quarterback to (hopefully) blow through any one of four different holes to the right. In *Counter* a fake leaves the defense biting on *Power*—only to watch helplessly as the quarterback runs left through a huge open cutback lane.

That was the idea anyway. The Dolphins knew that they were too undermanned to beat teams head-to-head and, with the underwhelming Ted Ginn and Greg Camarillo as their leading receivers that season, they weren't going to outgun anyone through the air. So they turned instead to a series of option plays that go back decades in their various iterations and decided to debut them against the New England Patriots. New England head coach Bill

Belichick has seen just about every offense and defense there is, and his defenses are known for their flexibility and versatility. But against three basic option plays, that multiple and disciplined defense was left gasping for air. "When they get settled, they're pretty fundamentally sound as a defense," said Miami running back Ronnie Brown, who ran for a franchise-record four touchdowns in the game as the Wildcat's point man. "So we wanted to give them something to adjust to."

That they did, and the normally uber-disciplined Patriots were aghast that they were helpless to stop such a simple series of concepts in a 38–13 loss that set the Dolphins on a path to a highly unlikely AFC East title. "I don't know why in the world we couldn't stop that play. They just came in and beat our butts," Patriots safety Rodney Harrison said. "You've got a bitter taste in your mouth. The only way to get rid of that bitterness is to come in and work hard. You get bitter and you get better."

Getting bitter is a natural response to adversity; getting better has its base in the ability to see beyond a problem that has been created through whatever circumstance. Perhaps the most famous adaptation to adversity in NFL history is what happened after Cincinnati Bengals quarterback Greg Cook suffered a severe shoulder injury in his rookie season of 1969. The fifth overall pick in the 1969 AFL-NFL draft out of Cincinnati, Cook was widely regarded as having the potential to be one of the best quarterbacks in NFL history. The Bengals' offensive coordinator at the time, Bill Walsh, was charged with getting Cook ready for the pro game right away. It didn't take long for things to unravel dramatically. Tackled on his throwing shoulder in the third game of his NFL career by Kansas City Chiefs linebacker Jim Lynch, Cook tore his rotator cuff in the process. He took cortisone shots and played through the pain, but there was no surgery that would bring him back to full strength like there is now. He finished his rookie campaign with 106 completions in 197 attempts for 1,854 yards, 15 touchdowns, 11 interceptions, and had the first in a series of surgeries after the season. Doctors were also contending with the fact that Cook had a partially detached biceps muscle, and Cook attempted a grand total of three passes in the remainder of his NFL career. Cook led the AFL in completion percentage, passer rating, and yards per attempt in 1969, proving that even as a halfway broken rookie quarterback he had special skills. But none of that mattered now.

With the knowledge that Cook would be out for the 1970 season, Walsh and head coach Paul Brown had to make do with Virgil Carter, who had completed a total of 143 passes in two seasons with the Chicago Bears before the Bengals acquired him. Carter was a journeyman at best. But he's an important footnote in football history in that his limitations forced Walsh to create entirely new concepts for his team. "Carter was able to go through his progressions quickly and throw on the go, not blessed with a big arm, but accurate," *Sports Illustrated*'s Paul Zimmerman wrote in 2001. "So, Walsh crafted an offense to suit him, a horizontal offense with a lot of motion and underneath routes and breakoff patterns, an attack that now goes by the misnomer 'West Coast Offense.'"

It was a misnomer because the offense that Walsh later made famous in San Francisco was created in the Midwest, but that's of little consequence. Walsh had a vision that included shorter passes—essentially, using the passing game as a rushing attack much of the time—and a series of advanced route concepts that almost always left a man open against any defense. And in an era when quarterback mobility was seen by most as a glaring negative, Walsh had Carter roll out of the pocket—not to gain rushing yards, but to open throwing lanes and buy time for route concepts to open.

It worked from the start, and the rest, of course, is history. Carter had completed less than 50 percent of his passes with the Bears, but he led the NFL in completion percentage in 1971 with a 62.2 mark. Soon after the Bengals selected Ken Anderson out of tiny Augustana College in Ohio in the third round of the 1971 draft, Walsh discovered that Anderson possessed the intelligence, mobility, and ability to work within the structure required by this new offense. In a career that ended in 1986, Anderson led the NFL in completion percentage three times, passing yardage twice, yards per attempt twice, and passer rating four times. His success in Cincinnati went far beyond Walsh's tenure there—Walsh lost a power struggle with Brown after the 1975 season—but the concepts were the same. After a year with the San Diego Chargers as an assistant and two more at Stanford as the head coach, Walsh went on to perfect his system with an underrated quarterback named Joe Montana at the helm. Back when the NFL was paraded around as a game of power running with occasional long passes mixed in, Walsh was derided for his offense at the start. "When what is now known as the 'West Coast Offense' was being developed, it was summarily dismissed by many people as nothing more than 'nickel and dime,'" Walsh wrote in his seminal book, *Finding the Winning Edge,* in 1997. "They argued that, as an offensive system, the West Coast Offense was developed out of a 'desperate' attempt by a team to counteract its lack of overpowering personnel. History has shown that these individuals were glaringly mistaken."

Well, that's a bit of revisionist history, and his detractors weren't entirely wrong, though they missed the point in this case. Walsh said more than once that had Cook stayed healthy, the Bengals would have thrown the ball deep more because of Cook's ability to do that at a very special level. Walsh had to counteract a lack of talent at his most important position and he did have to re-scheme his offense out of desperation to a degree. Where Walsh differentiated himself from the rank and file was in his comprehensive understanding of how his system could not only beat the game, but also revolutionize it—and how to pass that understanding along to his players. "Teams, which attempt to adopt the West Coast Offense and to duplicate its success solely by copying the schematics and the blocking schemes, are taking a fragmented approach to installing such a system," he wrote. "In order to fully understand the West Coast Offense, a number of factors concerning the parameters of the system must be considered."

Walsh then went into some of those parameters, including the schematic complexity his players could reasonably handle; whether the scope of the offense is appropriate to a team's specific personnel; the requirements for installing the system; the practical application of the offense on gamedays; the adjustments in assignments, techniques, and schemes required through a game; and the defensive alignments and schemes most applicable to beat various offenses.

In the end the difference between the Wildcat and the West Coast Offense was diversity. Although the Wildcat had just a handful of base concepts that could be expanded upon to various degrees (which is why it petered out of the NFL in a few short years), the West Coast Offense embodied an entirely new way of seeing the game. Sparano and Lee were bailing out of a sinking boat; Walsh was building a new breed of ship. But each innovation came from luck and desperation—whether their inventors preferred to admit it or not after the fact—and given the ways in which the NFL has expanded as a schematic entity, that's absolutely par for the course.

Yes, there had been precedents to a short passing game that stretched the field in different ways, but it took Walsh to put it all together in ways that revolutionized the NFL, thus forcing opposing defensive coordinators to invent their own counter-checks and checkmates. And yes, there had been all kinds of option offenses run at varying levels of success through the league's history, but it took these three plays to upend one of the smartest football coaches ever to walk the Earth.

The T Formation forced the defenses of the old 7-Diamond and 6-2-2-1 to adapt to the 5-3-2-1. Halfbacks catching passes caused a change to the Eagle and Stack Defenses. More complex passing formations led to the Umbrella and 4-3 defenses, and extra receivers led to the advent of nickel and zone defenses. Personnel realities and the constant need for innovation led to the rise of the 3-4 defense. The West Coast Offense had teams taking a closer look at the zone blitz and the 46 Defenses. Multiple defensive fronts were created to counter more complex offenses, and the game today reflects a schematic diversity never seen before.

As former NFL quarterback and current ESPN analyst Ron Jaworski wrote in *The Games That Changed the Game*, "Today, defenses must be ready for exotic personnel changes on every snap. Defenses of old were four down linemen, three linebackers, and four defensive backs. Now, you can have three linemen, five linemen, or no linemen. You can have two guys with their hands on the ground or four with their hands on the ground. One play later, you get no one with his hand on the ground! You can have five defensive backs, or six, or even eight! That's 20th century football."

Not to mention 21st century football. And whether these concepts are long-lasting or short-form transitions, they form the history of professional football that goes beyond—and to a degree underneath—the game we see in the current era on Sundays, Mondays, and Thursdays. In this book we'll examine the NFL's history of schematic innovation and detail the work of a great many gifted—and desperate—men.

CHAPTER 1

BEGINNINGS
The NFL from 1920 through 1949

> *"Find out what the other team wants to do.*
> *Then, take it away from them."*
> —George Halas

When a group of executives met in 1920 to officially form the American Professional Football Conference—what became the National Football League in 1922—the game was a leather-helmeted, three yards-and-a-cloud-of-dust, war of attrition for the most part. The T formation and the single-wing were the dominant formations in football and saw stacked defensive fronts to counter the ground game. In 1932, the first season for which there are official statistics, Arnie Herber of the Green Bay Packers led the league with 34 completed passes on 104 attempts for 639 yards, nine touchdowns, and nine interceptions. It wasn't until 1939 that any passer attempted more than 200 throws, and in that season, both Parker Hall of the Cleveland Rams and Davey O'Brien of the Philadelphia Eagles did it. For his efforts Hall was rewarded with nine touchdowns and 13 interceptions, while O'Brien had six touchdowns and 17 picks.

In its early decades, the NFL's strategy was brutish and basic. Don Hutson of the Packers ran the first option routes and could be considered the first truly modern receiver because of his ability to get free with speed and agility in a route tree that—while hardly advanced at today's level—got the job done. In 1942 Hutson caught 74 passes for 1,211 yards and 17 touchdowns, which represented an inconceivable series of numbers at the time. Pop Ivy of the Chicago Cardinals ranked second that year with 27 receptions. The first truly organized passing game took the league by storm as the men in charge of the league narrowed the ball over the years to make it less like a rugby ball and more like the instrument we see today.

Selected sixth overall out of TCU in the 1937 NFL Draft, Sammy Baugh of the Washington Redskins led the league in his rookie year in attempts (171), completions (81), passing yards (1,127), and…interceptions (14). Baugh was a great thrower for his era, but he plied his trade in an unfavorable passing era. He did throw for three touchdowns to beat the Bears in the 1937 NFL Championship, but it wasn't until 1945 that he put up a condensed version of what might be considered a modern passing season. That year he completed 70.3 percent of his passes—a record that stood until Ken Anderson of the Cincinnati Bengals broke it in 1982—with 11 touchdowns and four interceptions. Passing efficiency would not be the name of the game for several decades. Even into the 1960s and 1970s, quarterbacks were inclined to hurl the ball deep to receivers running basic route concepts against rudimentary defenses.

When Baugh came into the NFL, he had to fight an uphill battle to get his passing acumen on the field. In doing so he helped change the game forever. "Ray Flaherty was our coach when I got to Washington and he was a pretty typical coach for the time," Baugh told *The Sporting News*. Flaherty admonished Baugh to remember that in the pros receivers expected their quarterbacks to be accurate with "none of those wild heaves you see the college boys throw."

Baugh remembered the following conversation. "They tell me you're quite a passer," Flaherty said.

"I reckon I can throw a little," Baugh replied.

"Let's see it. Hit that receiver in the eye."

"I cocked an eye toward Wayne Millner, who was running a little buttonhook pattern, and I turned to Flaherty and said, 'Which eye?'"

Flaherty, who Baugh remembered as a "mean-hot-tempered sonofabitch," didn't question Baugh too much after that. The Redskins ran the single-wing at the time, but Baugh's skill allowed them to tweak the system from tailback-based to quarterback-based. "What we did with the single-wing in Washington was to add the wrinkle of passing early in downs and controlling the clock. That's what we did at TCU, and that's really all I knew how to do."

Glenn "Pop" Warner invented the single-wing in the earliest days of the 20th century and implemented it to perfection when he coached the Carlisle Indian Industrial School. Warner used sweeps, spins, and reverses, as well as the first real iteration of the forward pass, to befuddle opponents, who never quite knew whether a pass, run, or punt was coming at them. Warner then expanded his single-wing concept to a double-wing when he put two receivers to one side. (The single-wing idea can still be seen in certain power sweep and Wildcat plays.) The double-wing was in many ways the precursor to the shotgun formation. The inevitable triple-wing put three receivers to one side and was as close as anybody got to a spread offense in the game's early days.

Steve Owen's A formation had a heavy line to one side and the backs strong to the other side. Knute Rockne invented what was called the "Notre Dame Box." In this formation players would shift from the standard T Formation into a power formation designed with heavy blocking for end runs. And there was the ubiquitous T Formation, which spawned more innovations at the NFL level than any early formation—and most of it from two Bears coaches, Ralph Jones and Clark Shaughnessy. Indeed, when we turn to the idea that the old game has shaped the new game, one football mind—Shaughnessy's—did more to establish concepts that are still seen today than anybody else.

Clark Shaughnessy: The NFL's Forgotten Innovator

The most innovative coach of the pre-Paul Brown era did the most to forward professional football to the game it is today. "I always looked upon Clark Shaughnessy as a conscientious idealist who might better have followed the trail of Father Flanagan of Boys Town," football historian Roger Treat told *Sports Illustrated*. "He may never be entirely happy in the jovial thuggery of pro football, where every man has a little assassin in him."

Shaughnessy was a head coach for just two seasons at the NFL level with the Los Angeles Rams in 1948 and 1949. His NFL experience began more than a decade before, when he first spoke to Chicago Bears owner George Halas at a civic dinner in 1935. Shaughnessy was the University of Chicago's head coach and he told Halas that he had watched several Bears games that season and that he had some ideas regarding the use of the T formation that might open things up for Halas' team. Named this because there are three running backs behind the quarterback in the shape of a T, the formation allowed the quarterback to drop back to pass, gave different rushing options, and offered new sleights of hand.

But knowing it needed to be tweaked, Halas rearranged the place cards at his table so he and Shaughnessy could sit together, and heard him out. Halas had been working with the T formation since his freshman year at the University of Illinois in 1914, but it was time for new ideas. As happens with any static offensive scheme, defenses had figured out the T. Shaughnessy told Halas that he had some additional elements—"hidden-ball stuff, but with power"—to try out.

Halas had already employed one T formation innovator—Ralph Jones, Halas' freshman coach, who Halas later hired to coach Chicago's offense. Jones widened the offensive line and backfield splits to make the formations less compressed and more open. He also put a man in motion pre-snap, so the quarterback could hand off to one of his backs or drop back to pass, and the man in motion element added a degree of defensive uncertainty. Jones was also credited as the first coach to put together gameplans. Jones and his staff assembled specific offensive and defensive plays and drilled their players all week on those concepts above all others. He also brought a system of terminology to the game, numbering the gaps and creating basic play calls. This is where the current gap-numbering system began. Jones numbered the gaps from 0—between the center and left guard—to 9—outside the strong side of the formation. If the right halfback was aligned in the 4 spot, was supposed to run between the center and the right guard (or the 2 gap), the left halfback was motioning pre-snap from the 3 gap, and the snap count on two, the play call might be "42-32." Basic, but effective.

It wasn't until Paul Brown came to the NFL in 1950 that there was a truly universal and organized system for offense and defense that would resemble the modern game. Brown's offensive philosophies set the league on its collective ear, and defensive adjustments to those strategies—including by Brown himself—took the NFL into a new and more recognizable era.

But in the pre-Brown era, Shaughnessy moved the game ahead as much as anybody. "Football is a science to me, the maneuvering of men to attain an objective. It is very comparable to military strategy," Shaughnessy said in the book, *The Wow Boys*. "So when George Halas didn't laugh at me or my theories, I naturally warmed up to him. He didn't make fun of me and he was willing to listen. So when I'd make a suggestion, he'd listen and we'd discuss it. As I propounded some of those pet theories of mine, he would take them, try them out. Some results were apparent."

Halas invited Shaughnessy to his office to hear more and was sufficiently impressed. He offered Shaughnessy a consultant position in 1937, paying him $2,000 per year. In 1940 Shaughnessy's refinements to the T took over both branches of football—the Bears used it to demolish the Washington Redskins in the NFL championship game, and Shaughnessy's Stanford Indians went 10–0 on the season. "[The T] is simply, clearly, definitely, and completely a breakaway from the old power game based on blocking," Shaughnessy wrote in a 1942 article for *Esquire*. "Concealment of the ball by the quarterback turning around instantly, as in the early days, sets the stage for a finesse, deceptive, speed type of attack."

For Shaughnessy his "deception attack" was all about opening things up. He compared it to the advent of airplanes and light tanks in war, "making it very difficult, if not impossible, for a wide front of fixed positions to be held effectively." He also made boxing analogies, comparing his T formation to "the left jab of a boxer— the man in motion and the faking of backs to the feints, and the fullback plays to the real punch. The pass plays should be used as the unexpected sock."

In Shaughnessy's T the motion man forced defenses away from static placements and formations, forcing at least one defender to follow the moving offensive player. In addition he wanted quarterbacks to throw more than they had in previous iterations of the T formation. At the University of Chicago, Shaughnessy didn't have the players to make his advanced concepts go, so his ideas were hypothetical when he brought them to Halas. But Halas saw the genius in the man and his ideas. "Before we began collaborating," Halas said, "our T formation had two major weaknesses, which enabled other clubs in the league to get too familiar with our ball carriers. One trouble was we only had two end runs…thanks to Shaughnessy, we have 22 maneuvers around the ends—touchdown plays. Second, the majority of our plays went to the side of the line of the man in motion. Shaughnessy designed ground-gainers that run to the side opposite to the man in motion. These counter plays were honeys."

They were, and the counters were most effective in that 1940 championship. Four weeks before, the Redskins had beaten the Bears 7–3, and Washington owner George Preston Marshall famously called the Bears "crybabies." That bulletin board material certainly had an impact on the 73–0 score in the return matchup, but it was Shaughnessy's counters—not to mention three interceptions returned for touchdowns—that made the difference on the field. "We were a pretty tense bunch," Bears legend Bulldog Turner, a rookie in 1940, told famed sportswriter Red Smith. "Shaughnessy relieved the tension. He made the pregame talk, and you've never seen anyone so calm. 'You can beat the Redskins,' he said, 'and here's how.' He outlined a play we had charted as our second of the game. 'It might go for a touchdown the first time.' Somehow, we believed him."

What Shaughnessy had on the Redskins that day was his team's reactions to Washington's predictable defenses. At the time the Redskins shifted their linebackers to the man in motion, so Shaughnessy devised counter plays that would take those linebackers out of the play. The second play of the game did indeed go for a touchdown, though it wasn't the triumph of the counter one might think. Fullback Bill Osmanski took the ball from Sid

Luckman and ran to the front side. Osmanski actually ran through the wrong hole but was able to spring free after end George Wilson blocked two Redskins defenders downfield. And the 73–0 score was hardly all about Chicago's offense—the Bears intercepted eight passes from three different Redskins quarterbacks, returning three of them for touchdowns. But the intricacies of Shaughnessy's T did get noticed and did catch on over time. "After the Bears beat the piss out of us in that '40 Championship game…well, you could literally see the game changing before our eyes," Baugh said. "By the next season, almost everybody in football started messing with the T. Since then about every form of pro-style offense has been a cousin of the T. The triple option, the wishbone, the veer— you name it. So, whenever you see what Johnny Unitas and Fran Tarkenton and Dan Marino and John Elway and all those great passers were able to do, you can trace it back to 73–0."

The Bears then went on one of the most remarkable runs in league history. From 1940 through 1943, they amassed a 37–5–1 record that remains the best four-year span in NFL annals. They won three of the four NFL championship games and had a perfect 11–0 season wiped out with a 14–6 loss to the Redskins in 1942. Those teams that converted to Shaughnessy's version of the T formation had the advantage of the players he had taught that same formation at Stanford. Halas drafted fullback Norm Standlee, halfback Hugh Gallerneau, and quarterback Frankie Albert, though Albert signed instead with the San Francisco 49ers of the All-America Football Conference. Philadelphia Eagles head coach Earle "Greasy" Neale put his charges in the Shaughnessy T early on and took four Stanford players in 1941 alone. Through the 1940s both college and pro teams adapted to the more open and versatile version of the T formation, and this was the first example of a Shaughnessy design becoming the norm in the game.

It was not to be the last.

In 1948 Shaughnessy signed on with the Rams as an advisor to head coach Bob Snyder. During the 1948 preseason, Rams owner Dan Reeves was so impressed with Shaughnessy's football acumen that he made Shaughnessy the head coach. At first Shaughnessy ran the same formations he always had, but during that first season, he realized that speed runner Elroy "Crazy Legs" Hirsch would be a better receiver than a running back. He converted Hirsch to a flanker and thus created the three-receiver formation as a base offensive concept.

With that offensive design, quarterbacks Bob Waterfield and Norm Van Brocklin, and a group of track-fast receivers, Shaughnessy's Rams went from fourth to second in points scored and ranked first in points scored in each of the three seasons thereafter. Shaughnessy was gone after the 1949 season. (The Rams lost the 1949 NFL Championship to the Eagles as Neale foiled Shaughnessy with the Umbrella Defense.) But he had, in effect, built the bones of the modern passing offense.

Shaughnessy wasn't done. He returned to the Bears as Halas' schematic advisor and defensive specialist. In that capacity he shut down the early version of the shotgun formation so well that the shotgun would not return to prominence in the NFL for decades. 49ers head coach Red Hickey—another eccentric innovator—had his quarterbacks running all manner of option stuff against static lines and for a few weeks in the 1950 season he seemed to have the NFL by the tail.

Shaughnessy's counter was both old school and new school. He put middle linebacker Bill George at the middle guard position, something the league hadn't used in years. With George playing to the center's shoulder and blasting through the line of scrimmage on nearly every play, Hickey's shotgun quarterbacks couldn't run through their options. Shaughnessy also devised a 5-3-3 base defense that presented multiple fronts and was very tough to diagnose, let alone stop. At times the Bears brought pressure with seven at the line; at other times they'd drop linemen into coverage to deal with the short passes prevalent in Hickey's offense.

As had been the case throughout Shaughnessy's career, it was a triumph of preparation and innovation. According to *Sports Illustrated*'s Tex Maule, Shaughnessy analyzed 49ers tape for more than 100 hours and was still refining his defensive strategies the morning of the game. Shaughnessy set up different defenses for different quarterbacks—a passing defense for Josh Brodie, a run defense for Billy Kilmer—as Hickey alternated his passers. "The Bear defense was keyed to the situation, not the player," was how Maule put it. That's a fair summation of Shaughnessy's genius and why his innovations were so resonant. He was at the apex of situational football strategy, which would define the NFL far more in the 1950s and beyond.

CHAPTER 2

THE GAME COMES OF AGE
The NFL in the 1950s

"Boy, this is gonna be one terrific day, so you better live it up because tomorrow you'll be nothing."
—James Dean as Jim Stark in *Rebel Without a Cause*

P hiladelphia Eagles coach Earle "Greasy" Neale had already opened up the structure of NFL defenses by moving to a four defensive back system, taking linemen and linebackers out of the formation to better counter the increase in passing numbers. But when the Cleveland Browns came into the NFL in 1950, they immediately made a serious statement by beating Neale's defense with several of Paul Brown's innovations—the passing pocket, the draw play, and short passes to the side to control the ball. Brown made a superstar out of quarterback Otto Graham and was the NFL's first real modern-age coach. Many of his inventions—the applied use of game film, the first true college scouting network, and the first complex playbooks—are still in effect today in full but with technologically superior versions.

The New York Giants used several different concepts to deal with these more explosive offenses. Head coach Steve Owen used more defensive backs and linebackers who could drop back into coverage. Then, the team hired two able assistants—Vince Lombardi as the team's offensive coordinator and Tom Landry as the team's defensive coordinator—in 1954. Lombardi's schematic innovations will be covered more in the 1960s chapter, but Landry's application of the 4-3 defense turned the Madison Avenue Giants into the first team with a defense that was well-known to the general public.

As the decade ended, one renegade coach proved to be decades ahead of his time with the implementation of a formation that would become the NFL's primary quarterback placement in 2017 and beyond.

Paul Brown

The playbook as it stands today. The coaching staff. The draw play. Dropback pass blocking. The face mask. Studying game film to understand and exploit opponent tendencies and weaknesses. The elimination of pro football's color barrier. The list of innovations brought to pro football by Paul Brown is unmatched, especially in the postwar era, which is why his .672 winning percentage in 25 years of coaching in the pro game tells only half the story. "There's nobody in the game that I have more respect for than Paul Brown. His contributions from the game to the way it's played, to protective equipment and the playbook, every film breakdown, every meeting," Bill Belichick said in *A Football Life: Paul Brown*. "Fifty years later, we're all still basically doing the same thing."

Had he just been a great schematic mind, Brown would still have been an easy Hall of Famer based on the results—a 213–104–9 mark with the Cleveland Browns and Cincinnati Bengals, all four championships in the history of the All-America Football Conference, and three NFL championships with the Cleveland Browns—not to mention his ability to make the expansion Bengals

competitive soon after their entry into the American Football
League in 1968.

Wherever he coached, Brown was a success, and it was primarily because he saw ways to do things that no other coach could.
He started at Massillon High in Ohio and at Ohio State and took
the head coaching position with the Browns of the All-America
Football Conference in February of 1945. *Chicago Tribune* sports
editor Arch Ward proposed the league the year before, and Brown
was offered $17,500 per year to coach the Cleveland team—more
than any other football coach at any level. Brown also received
an ownership stake in the team and a stipend as his military time
was winding down; he had served as the coach of the Great Lakes
Naval Training Station team in 1944 and put up a 9–2–1 record.

The Browns were the AAFC's dominant force. Their four
championships included an undefeated season in 1948. Brown
brought several future Hall of Famers to the Browns, including
quarterback Otto Graham, running back Marion Motley, and
tackle/kicker Lou Groza and refined his search for talent among
those players he had coached and become aware of during his
Massillon and Ohio State days. The league folded in part because
the Browns were so clearly the class of the league, and after the
1949 season, the Browns, Baltimore Colts, and San Francisco
49ers entered the National Football League. Brown finally had a
chance to ply his trade against the best in the business.

The 1950 Browns showed just how far ahead of everyone
else Brown really was. In one season he took down the two-time
NFL champions, maneuvered his way around the origins of a new
defense that would become the league's standard for the next three
decades after his offense had helped to force its creation, and took
down the most prolific offensive team in the league's history in
the NFL championship game. Overall, not a bad little season. It
started with one of the greatest upsets in NFL history.

Week 1, 1950: Cleveland Browns 35, Philadelphia Eagles 10

NFL commissioner Bert Bell wasted no time in setting up a stern test for the new kids. The four-time AAFC champs began their NFL journey with an opener against the two-time NFL champion Philadelphia Eagles, a tough, old-school team with a dynamic rushing attack led by Steve Van Buren and a defense that had shut out the Los Angeles Rams in the previous championship game 14–0. The Eagles had allowed the fewest points and scored the most in 1949, so this game was a clear message to the best team in the AAFC: you may have been a big fish in a small pond, but the NFL is the ocean. "If you could feel cocky before a game, we felt cocky," Eagles running back Bosh Pritchard told NFL Films. "This was a team from what we thought was maybe a bush league…but they weren't."

According to Pritchard, Eagles head coach Earle "Greasy" Neale didn't scout the Cleveland Browns before the game. He apparently thought Paul Brown was little more than a high school coach and that the Eagles wouldn't have to do much to beat Brown's team. "I played for Greasy for quite a few years," quarterback Tommy Thompson said. "He made very, very few mistakes, but I believe he made a mistake on [not] scouting this ballclub."

Well-schooled in motivational tactics, Brown used pregame articles debasing his team's readiness to face the Eagles as bulletin board material. "That was our motivation," Browns running back Marion Motley said. "When we got to Philadelphia, reading [these] newspaper[s] for two weeks, we were ready to hit anything the Eagles had."

The Eagles shouldn't have been oblivious to Brown's strategy, which was made quite public. The September 7, 1950, edition of *The Philadelphia Inquirer* had a story from sports reporter Frank O'Gara, who spoke with "an unusually unreliable source, who doesn't wish to be identified." This source, or O'Gara himself, posited that "the Clevelanders are of the opinion that quick passes, chiefly of the hook variety, will riddle the Eagles' revolving defense and set up victory in the long-awaited football classic."

Brown's gameplan was indeed to rattle Neale's defenses with flare passes to his backs and deep passes down the sidelines. Neale, Philadelphia's head coach since 1941, had devised his "Eagle" defense through the 1940s with a five-man line, two linebackers, and the first four-man secondary. It worked well enough against NFL offenses, but Brown had done the scouting Neale hadn't. He theorized that if he expanded the offensive line spacings and put his halfbacks in motion and out to catch passes to either sideline, Neale's linebackers would have to move out of the middle of the field. Brown had tried this a bit against the Detroit Lions in the preseason "only briefly so as not to tip our hand," said Brown in *PB: The Paul Brown Story*, "but each time their defense reacted as we had hoped." Sending left halfback Alex Bumgardner in motion to pull a linebacker out of the middle was a key component of this strategy.

This left a huge middle gap wide open for slants and crossing patterns. Brown also implemented a double-wing formation with two receivers to one side, forcing single coverage from Neale's defensive backs. Brown cited one mismatch in particular—Eagles cornerback Russ Craft trying to cover halfback Dub Jones one-on-one.

The second part of the Browns' strategy showed just how clinical Brown could be when diagnosing an opponent's personnel and strategies. He theorized that since Neale's defensive linemen were taught to line up outside opposing offensive linemen, moving his offensive linemen farther and farther apart as the game went on would naturally place the defensive linemen farther apart from each other. This would set up Philadelphia's defensive line for the Motley draw plays by widening the splits and leaving the linebackers alone to deal with Motley at the second level—not a pleasant proposition for any linebacker. Motley ran 11 times for 48 yards, becoming more of a factor in the second half when Brown wanted his offense to control the ball. "I'll never forget Alex Wojciechowicz looking around for his defensive tackles and suddenly signaling for time out," Brown wrote. "We could hear him yelling at his tackles to stay close. They made the mistake—as the Lions did—of lining up on our offensive linemen instead of taking their normal spacing from the ball and they never adjusted to it. I couldn't help thinking back to our first game at Ohio State against Missouri and how we saved the day by keeping our normal spacing."

Jones ran six times for 72 yards and caught five passes for 98 yards and a touchdown. He was the most obvious personification of a Browns offense that caught the Eagles' championship defense off guard. Graham completed 21-of-38 passes for 346 yards and three touchdowns, Mac Speedie led all Browns receivers with seven catches for 109 yards and a touchdown, and the Browns had a cakewalk over the NFL champions with a 35–10 score.

To put that achievement in perspective, imagine if the score of Super Bowl I had been reversed and that the AFL's Kansas City Chiefs had beaten the NFL's Green Bay Packers 35–10 and you'd have an idea of just how shocking Cleveland's win was. The Browns beat their old AAFC rivals, the Baltimore Colts, 31–0 in the second week of the 1950 season, racking up 475 yards of total offense and allowing just 219. Then, it was time to welcome the New York Giants to Cleveland Municipal Stadium in the Browns' first NFL home game. What awaited them was a defensive wrinkle they didn't expect.

Week 3, 1950: New York Giants 6, Cleveland Browns 0

Steve Owen started his NFL career in 1924 as a guard for the Kansas City Blues and then played tackle for the Hartford Blues, Cleveland Bulldogs, and Kansas City Cowboys during the next couple of years before he was sold to the New York Giants for $500 in 1926. This was typical of the NFL's itinerant roots in 1964. Owen became a co-player/coach in 1930 along with Benny Friedman and was named the singular head coach the next season and guided the Giants for the next 23 years on a handshake agreement with team owner Tim Mara.

Owen finished his coaching career with a 153–100–17 regular-season mark and a 2–8 playoff record, taking the NFL championship in 1934 and 1938. He was a constant innovator through his career. But the Hall of Famer is perhaps best known for his adjustments to Brown's defense in 1950 and the creation of the modern defense. He had a great defensive roster that season led by an all-time secondary, which benefited from the AAFC's dissolution.

The New York Giants were awarded three defensive backs from the AAFC's New York Yankees franchise—safety Otto Schnellbacher, who was placed with future Hall-of-Famer Emlen Tunnell, and two cornerbacks: Harmon Rowe and a rangy kid from Mission, Texas, named Tom Landry. Owen and Landry, who had been named defensive captain, developed what would be called "the Umbrella Defense" because the defense opened like an umbrella. It was a combination of the 5-2-4 and the 5-3-3 and it allowed for more flexibility because of the six-man front that had two defensive guards, two defensive tackles, and two defensive ends outside. But the ends were actually linebackers able to either stay at the point of attack or drop into coverage.

The Browns didn't complete a single pass in the first half, and Otto Graham completed just 12 passes in 30 attempts for

127 yards, no touchdowns, and three interceptions. Brown's team experienced its first NFL loss 6–0.

What had beaten Graham and the Browns—despite all their innovations—was the first instance of the 4-3 defense, which would become the NFL's base defensive formation from the 1950s through the mid-1970s and remains an option for coaches today. It represented Owen's genius and was the first obvious manifestation of Landry's historic ability to innovate and communicate schemes to his players. Owen drew the new defense up on the board, handed his chalk to Landry, and told the kid to explain it to his teammates. "They called it the Umbrella Defense because it had the effect of an umbrella opening," Landry said in *The Last Cowboy*. "It worked very well. Emlen played next to me. We sort of worked things out on our own on the field. Graham didn't complete a pass on our defense in the first half. We intercepted three. We had both Speedie and Lavelli double-covered."

In the second half, Paul Brown tried rolling Graham out and throwing quick passes underneath the ends, who were dropping back. The Giants responded by blitzing their ends and playing tighter coverage with their cornerbacks.

When the two teams met again on October 22, the Giants came out with a base nickel defense—very rare for the period. Owen and Landry played a 5-1-5 set against Brown's weapons, intercepted three more Graham passes, and became the only team to beat the Browns twice in 1950. In addition to the base nickel concept, Owen had Tunnell play more of a roving defensive halfback position to help coverage to either side based on the alignment and route concepts. It may have been the first example of a free safety on an NFL field and presaged the zone defense, in which players reacted more to areas than opponents.

As the 1950 season went on, Brown started toying with those teams that weren't unfurling Umbrella Defenses against them. In the December 3 rematch with the Philadelphia Eagles, he wanted to prove a point that his team was more than just an aerial attack. So the Browns didn't throw a single pass all day and still beat Earle Neale's team 13–7. The 1950 Browns finished the regular season with a 10–2 record and beat the Giants for the first time in the divisional playoff by an 8–3 score. "This game ranks as the greatest I've ever seen, even greater than our opening victory over the Eagles," Brown wrote, "because of the remarkable array of players—nearly a dozen now in the Hall of Fame aside from many others who belong there—and some of the most astonishing plays ever recorded in pro football history."

After defeating the Giants, they prepared for their first NFL championship game, and it was against a formidable opponent— the point-a-minute Los Angeles Rams. As Brown also pointed out, the game was a writer's delight. The Browns were the new kids who had twice beaten the two-time NFL champions through entirely different methods and they were playing a team that had left Cleveland a few years before. Brown's challenge in this game was to counter a Rams team with two fabulous quarterbacks in Bob Waterfield and Norm Van Brocklin and the fastest group of receivers anyone had ever seen. "Five players who could run the 100 in less than 10 seconds," Brown said.

The story didn't start well for the Browns. The Rams had Glenn Davis fake a block to force linebacker hesitation, and then Davis shot out of the backfield and up the left sideline. Waterfield hit a wide-open Davis downfield, and he ran untouched into the end zone. With 27 seconds gone in the game, the Rams had their first touchdown, and this looked like it could be a rout.

Cleveland responded with a drive in which Graham ran the ball three times and tied the score with a 27-yard pass to Dub Jones. The two teams traded punches back and forth, but in the end, it was Graham's efficiency—he completed 22-of-33 passes for 298 yards, four touchdowns, and one interception—that made the difference, while Waterfield threw four interceptions to the Browns' 5-3-3 base defense. Brown's team wrapped up their first NFL championship in their first NFL season with a 30–28 victory.

There is no equivalent in league history for what the Browns did in their first NFL year—the newcomers forced every other team to adapt to them. Cleveland played in every league championship game until the 1955 season, winning it all in 1954 and 1955. It was clear that not only did the Browns field a tremendous series of teams, but that Brown himself also had set the pace as the NFL's prime innovator.

Brown coached the Browns through the 1962 season. He was fired by owner Art Modell on January 7, 1963. Modell and Brown had gone head-to-head over who ran the team. Brown had enjoyed uncontested decision-making power over strategy and personnel since the AAFC days, but when Modell bought the team in 1961, that started to change.

Brown returned to the game in 1968 with the expansion Cincinnati Bengals and took his new team to the playoffs in three seasons over an eight-year stretch before retiring as a head coach soon after the 1975 season. Brown stayed with the franchise as team president, helping the Bengals to two Super Bowls in the 1980s. The Bengals lost both of those Super Bowls to the San Francisco 49ers led by Bill Walsh, Brown's former offensive coordinator. Walsh had a large sense of revenge through those two Super Bowls. (Brown had passed on Walsh for the head coach position in 1976 and allegedly bad-mouthed Walsh throughout the league so he wouldn't get a similar position elsewhere.)

That wasn't uncommon. For all of Brown's brilliance, he could be autocratic and unfeeling to his players. He came from an era in which players did what they were told without question or argument and endured into an era when that was no longer true. His complicated personal history aside, Brown gave more to pro football than anyone else. More of what he imagined exists in the NFL than any other individual, and that will remain his legacy.

The 4-3 Defense: Sam Huff and the Middle Linebacker as Rock Star

"No single assignment in the field of sport is more demanding than playing a linebacker post in professional football. It requires an almost impossible blend of abilities: size enough to step into a hole in the line and stop a 230-pound fullback head-on, speed enough to cover the league's fast ends or halfbacks traveling at a full head of steam." *Sports Illustrated*'s Tex Maule wrote that about New York Giants middle linebacker Sam Huff in November of 1958. It speaks—to the need for the position in an increasingly complex NFL, the ways in which Tom Landry schemed the position, and how Huff played it—that 50 years later everything said then is still true about the modern middle linebacker.

The true 4-3 defense really started when the Giants selected Huff in the third round of the 1956 draft out of West Virginia, and Landry (then the team's full-time defensive coordinator) saw in Huff the player who would expand his defense beyond the adjustments he and head coach Steve Owen had made earlier in the decade to deal with Paul Brown's offensive motions and formations. "This new middle linebacker position required a combination of lineman and defensive back abilities," Landry said in Huff's 1988 autobiography *Tough Stuff.* Landry was looking for a player who could stuff the run and move through gaps with the power of the old middle guard but cover running backs and tight ends out of the backfield and off the formation. In addition, as the defensive playcaller on the field, the middle linebacker had to be smart enough to be an extension of his defensive coordinator on the field.

It was a tall order to be sure, but Huff was perfectly qualified. He had played middle guard in college, and in Huff's first training camp, the Giants alternated him between his old position and the new. Once he moved back from the line and was able to see the offense more clearly and the entire field more peripherally, the Giants' defense—and all subsequent NFL defenses—changed immediately.

Huff was staying with several other players at the Excelsior Hotel in the West Side of Manhattan, and Landry visited Huff frequently to go over concepts to put the pieces together. "That's how we developed the 4-3 defense." Huff wrote. "We'd have the inside 4-3 where the defensive tackle would shut off the middle and the linebackers would pursue to the outside or we'd go to the outside 4-3, where the tackle would angle outside, and I would come up the middle or catch the play from behind. All the years we played, that's all I ever did."

Having a point man in the center of the defense solved the problems Brown exploited with his routes across the middle of the field and it opened defensive concepts exponentially over time. As Tampa-2 and Cover-2 defenses developed decades later and nickel defenses became the new normal in the 2000s, the middle linebacker as the position was denoted would decrease in importance. But what Landry and Huff started was a necessary adaptation to the increase in offensive diversity and effectiveness. It was also one of the first of many Landry innovations—from the 1950s through the decades to come—that would make it clear that he was one of pro football's all-time great thinkers.

Air Red: Hickey Brings the Shotgun and the Alley-Oop

Howard Wayne "Red" Hickey was one of the most prominent offensive innovators of his time, though he wasn't much of a motivator as a head coach. As the San Francisco 49ers' head man from 1959 through 1963, Hickey brought new and effective schemes to his team, and to great effect, but the percentage of players who did not approve of his old-school methods of communication was quite high. "He tore that team apart," end Gordie Soltau said in *Founding 49ers: The Dark Days Before the Dynasty.* "He called me in and said, 'I want you to retire, but I want you to be one of my coaches,' I told him, 'I don't mind you retiring me, but I could never coach for you.'"

"I had absolutely no respect for him," said legendary 49ers right tackle Bob St. Clair. "He'd yell and scream at you and everyone else." St. Clair remembered Hickey being chased around the locker room by running back Joe Perry once, saying that, "Joe was going to beat the hell out of him." Another time Hickey held up a newspaper, detailing a story in which the player had been named in a paternity suit, saying "St. Clair, you're a disgrace to the 49ers and you don't respect me."

St. Clair's response? "You got that half-right."

But Hickey was responsible for one minor and one major schematic innovation. The minor one was the alley-oop, a jump-ball strategy that made a star out of receiver R.C. Owens. The major one—because it's the prominent offensive formation in the NFL today—is the shotgun. The Green Bay Packers had used a version of what became the shotgun with a short punt formation years before, but that was more of a trick play unintended to be used on every snap. This was different. Hickey told the players in his sales pitch that the 49ers would use it on every play against the Baltimore Colts' dominant defense. "We were looking for an equalizer," Hickey told *High Point Enterprise* in 1975. "We had

Baltimore coming up and couldn't match them man-for-man. They had John Unitas, Gino Marchetti…people like that. And we were hurting. Y.A. Tittle was out with an injury. So, I called a team meeting and told the players what we were going to do. They were quiet, thinking the old man had flipped his wig."

Hickey premiered his version of the shotgun against the Detroit Lions in the third week of the 1961 season, alternating quarterbacks John Brodie, Billy Kilmer, and Bobby Waters. Hickey implemented some basic option principles with the quarterback either running the ball himself or handing to the back alongside him. The 49ers beat the Los Angeles Rams 35–0 the next week, and even those players who did not get along with Hickey felt that he was obviously on to something. "It was great blocking for it." St. Clair said. "Hickey would tell us the guard had to be a yard away from the center and the tackle two yards away from the guard. One time in practice, he blew the whistle and came out with a measuring tape, shouting, 'Don't move. Don't move.' Then he'd tell us we weren't the right distance apart."

Perhaps the pinnacle of Hickey's short-lived shotgun domination came in a 38–24 Week 5 win against the Minnesota Vikings. Kilmer ran 20 times for 115 yards and four touchdowns. Waters added 60 yards and a rushing touchdown on nine carries. The next week against the Chicago Bears proved to be the shotgun's undoing—or at least Hickey's version of it. As St. Clair later recalled, Chicago defensive coordinator Clark Shaughnessy had a fool-proof plan to stop it. "Shaughnessy decided to put two guys over the center, and two guys over the guard." St. Clair said. "With the shotgun you were one blocker shy, and one of the Bears' linemen would always get through because there was no one to block him."

Bears owner George Halas had come up with this tactic as he reviewed his old playbooks from the 1930s, essentially turning

Bill George into a middle guard and creating a blitz package that this shotgun team couldn't stop. With a few exceptions, the San Francisco shotgun died on October 22, 1961. Hickey used it a few times after that, but he did not develop it further as a schematic concept that could aid his offense. It would take years for the shotgun to return to the NFL and even more time before it was taken seriously.

The notion of rotating quarterbacks further illustrates the limitations of Hickey's shotgun. He was deploying his quarterbacks as point men in base option formations, where the quarterback's ability to throw well at multiple depths and decipher defenses was not as important. For coaches who viewed the quarterback position as the way to undress any defense, rotating men at what was becoming the most important position in football must have seemed to be utter madness.

Back in the AFL days, San Diego Chargers head coach Sid Gillman once prepared his team to use the shotgun against the Buffalo Bills when he became aware that the field at Buffalo's War Memorial Stadium was going to be a mess. "In my judgement the shotgun is the best formation for slush and mud, which prevent the rushing linemen from gaining traction and getting to your thrower," Gillman told the *Terre Haute Tribune*. "If the center can get the ball back accurately, the passer has far more time than he would working from the T [formation]."

But in that game, Gillman saw that his plays from under center were working and scrapped the shotgun, which stayed dormant for the most part until 1975 when Hickey, then a scout for the Cowboys, persuaded Tom Landry to bring it back into vogue. Landry had already tried rotating his quarterbacks in 1962 with Eddie LeBaron and Don Meredith and in 1971 with Craig Morton and Roger Staubach but then reverted to the one-quarterback system both times. He had also used the shotgun years before it became a fundamental part of his offense in the mid-1970s. Landry told the *Los Angeles Times* before the 1975 season: "What it does is enable the quarterback to have an extra second or second-and-a-half to read the defense."

Landry was open to innovation and had the ability to tinker successfully with schematic concepts that eventually put the shotgun on the right track. Under him and with Staubach as its purveyor, the shotgun became less a schematic conceit and more a way to improve the quarterback's vision and ability to absorb information. "The spread gives me more freedom, more maneuverability," Staubach said. "Your ability to see the defense is better, and all your receivers are in position to put quicker pressure on the defense, too."

The Cowboys completed 54-of-117 passes for 814 yards, four touchdowns, and five interceptions from the shotgun in 1975. Those aren't exactly efficient stats, but the 1970s weren't an efficient time for quarterbacks, and Dallas used the shotgun primarily as a passing-down endeavor, throwing downfield against defenses spread out to defend the pass through multiple zones. The most famous shotgun play of the Cowboys' 1975 season was Staubach's 50-yard game-winning touchdown pass to receiver Drew Pearson late in the fourth quarter of Dallas' 17–14 victory against the Minnesota Vikings in the divisional round of the playoffs. The Cowboys' version of the shotgun faded away in the late 1970s as Staubach got older—he retired in 1979—and other teams weren't initially fond of the idea as a base concept. Washington Redskins fans once booed the formation when the Cowboys ran it, and Rams linebacker Isiah Robertson said, "It's a rinky-dink formation. It'll catch up to them before the season is over."

"It's one of those 50-50 things," Philadelphia Eagles quarterback Ron Jaworksi told *The Philadelphia Inquirer* in 1980. "It has its good points and its bad points. Personally, I enjoy dropping back and looking for receivers. I don't know how appealing it's going to be until we get to working with it. The center's blind snap, that's the biggest thing. Lining up back there, you know you're going to feel the heat. But the idea of being back there and being set is probably an advantage. You can feel the pressure a little better rather than dropping back, setting up, and throwing."

As most NFL teams looked to install variants of Bill Walsh's West Coast Offense through the 1980s and 1990s, the shotgun stayed dormant as Walsh and his acolytes operated primarily out of single-back, I, offset I-formations, and the old pro set backfield with the quarterback under center and a halfback and a fullback on either side of him a few yards back. It wasn't until the new millennium came around that the formation became anything more than a novelty designed for long yardage plays.

As defenses became more advanced and quarterbacks needed better immediate vision to grasp what they were facing—not to mention the need to get quick passes out to deal with different kinds of rushes and stunts—the shotgun became a valuable offensive adjunct and then the default formation.

According to Football Outsiders' charting data, NFL teams ran shotgun just 7.1 percent of their offensive formations in 1989, which is as far back as their data goes. In 2000 it wasn't much different—just 12.8 percent. The insertion of spread-option quarterbacks and corresponding spread-option schemes made the difference. Use of the shotgun bumped up from 13.3 percent in 2004 to 15.9 percent in 2005 to 19.4 percent in 2006. These were the three years that the Atlanta Falcons led the NFL in rushing with the option-variable backfield of Michael Vick, Warrick Dunn, and T.J. Duckett.

The 2007 Patriots, who set an NFL record with 589 points scored in the 2007 regular season, were the first modern team to run more than half their plays out of the shotgun formation. They added slot receiver Wes Welker and speed receiver Randy Moss that offseason, expanding their own offense with deep passing concepts. As has been the case through the new millennium, the rest of the league took New England's lead. The NFL's shotgun percentage increased every season from 2007 through 2016, and the 2016 49ers coached by former Oregon head coach Chip Kelly (a consultant to Bill Belichick through the years when the Patriots were most interested in spread formations and concepts) ran the shotgun on 99 percent of their snaps. The shotgun started as a gimmick and turned into the way things were.

Shotgun Usage

Year	Percentage of Offensive Formation
2007	27.2
2008	31.8
2009	36.4
2010	37.7
2011	40.7
2012	47.4
2013	58.7
2014	60.7
2015	62.2
2016	64.4
2017	58.5

Brown and Landry helped to define the NFL in a schematic sense in the 1950s. In the 1960s professional football would split itself in two, the NFL would face its most skilled rival, and the resulting merger would make the game more diverse and interesting than it had ever been.

CHAPTER 3

ROCKETS IN THE AIR
The AFL Takes Flight

"If you don't like what's being said, change the conversation."
—Jon Hamm as Don Draper in *Mad Men*

There had been other American Football Leagues attempting to compete with the National Football League before the iteration founded by Lamar Hunt in 1959, but the versions created in 1926, 1936, and 1940 fizzled out quickly. The All-America Football Conference lasted from 1946 through 1949 and sent three franchises to the NFL upon its dissolution. The World Football League lasted just two seasons from 1974 into 1975. The United States Football League lasted one season longer from 1983 through 1985, and the most those two leagues could do was to offer more money to NFL players and delay the status of NFL draft picks.

Only Hunt's creation was able to take on the NFL at its own level, forcing a merger in 1966 after just seven seasons. Hunt and seven other businessmen formed the league at the end of the 1950s with franchises in Dallas, Denver, Los Angeles, New York, Houston, Buffalo, Boston, and Oakland. At first the AFL was stocked with NFL castoffs, though several of those players went on to legitimate

Hall of Fame careers. Over time, the AFL gained an advantage over its more storied opponent by reaching into small black colleges to mine talent and doing away with the known quota rules NFL teams had adopted regarding the number of black players on any team and which positions they could play. The AFL would thus become a beacon of meritocracy—less because of an overriding civil rights mind-set and more due to simple necessity—and the speed with which the younger league was able to close the gap in quality of play forced the NFL to adjust its own racial thoughts.

From the start the AFL went with more of a wide-open passing game; defenses and run games—dependent on the choreography of players who had worked together for years—didn't generally exist at a premium level in the new league. In 1961 Houston Oilers receiver Charley Hennigan caught 82 passes for a ridiculous 1,746 yards, a mark that still ranks sixth all time in pro football history. Elroy "Crazy Legs" Hirsch had gained 1,495 receiving yards for the Los Angeles Rams' wide-open offense in 1951, but no modern receiver would exceed Hennigan's mark until 1995, when both Jerry Rice and Isaac Bruce did.

As the league advanced, rushing attacks and defenses caught up. Multiplicity became the name of the game. While NFL coaches and play-designers were, for the most part, stuck in the ideology that you line up with a few plays and out-execute your opponent, the AFL was more diverse. Years before the 3-4 was a base defense in the NFL and hybrid fronts became the order of the day, multiple AFL coaches were running three-man fronts and moving their linebackers around in ways no NFL coach had thought to do. Putting men in motion, designing route combinations that could beat defenses all over the field, pinning receivers off at the beginning of their routes with aggressive man-on-man coverage—all of these concepts were advanced more in the 10 years of the AFL's history than through the previous 40 years of NFL play.

Many coaches would ply their trade in the new league, but it was Sid Gillman and Hank Stram—the only two men who were head coaches of their teams through the league's history—who personified the AFL's progression from a gimmick-laden league with dubious fundamentals to a group of teams that would meet, and eventually exceed, the NFL's standards. At the heart of it all were a series of schematic innovations, a primary reason the AFL's decade is one of the most fascinating in pro football history.

Sid Gillman: Father of the Modern Passing Game

It can be said of Sid Gillman that there was the passing game before him and the passing game after him. And the passing game after him is the modern one. When you see a running back flare out from the backfield to the slot, a tight end line up away from the formation, a slot receiver running a deep seam route, or a coach teaching his players using the three-digit system—and you see all of those things in the modern NFL—you are seeing Gillman's innovations and perfections. When you see the West Coast Offense run like a precision ballet with the routes timed perfectly from quarterback to receiver, you are seeing the development of Gillman's geometric concepts. "Much of what I did I got from Sid Gillman 20 years ago," head coach Bill Walsh told *Sports Illustrated*.

When a running back motions from the backfield to the slot or a receiver goes in pre-snap motion to help the quarterback discern what kind of defense he's facing, these are ongoing iterations of ideas Gillman worked through before many of the current participants were alive.

When you see a spread offense use the entire field horizontally pre-snap, you are seeing the natural outgrowth of Gillman's aggressive football philosophy developed during a time when the forward pass was still viewed with anything from trepidation to outright disgust in various quarters. "The field is 100 yards long and 53 yards wide," Gillman said in *The Games That Changed the Game*. "We're going to use every damn inch of it and force the other guy to defend all of it."

Put simply, Gillman is the father of the modern passing game, and his relative anonymity outside of the circles of hardcore football geeks and coaches at every level is a shame. But those who know Gillman's effect on the game—and in many cases on their own lives—will tell you what he really meant to the game and its strategic history. "Sid Gillman was the father of modern-day passing," Oakland Raiders coach/owner Al Davis told *The New York Times*. "It had been thought of as vertical, the length of the field. But Sid made it horizontal. Sid used the width of the field."

Cerebral quarterback Ron Jaworski had Gillman as his Philadelphia Eagles offensive coordinator during his Super Bowl season of 1980. "Nobody could make adjustments on the fly like Sid," Jaworski wrote in *The Games That Changed the Game*. "When the Eagles walked into the halftime locker room, Sid already had everything we needed on the chalkboard: fronts, coverages, hints, indicators. I believed in him so much that I just knew the changes we made during halftime were going to work. He was unmatched in his ability to figure out the opponent's gameplan and recognize what a team was trying to do to us that day. The 1980 season was my finest in the NFL. I posted my best stats, was named Player of the Year, and got the Eagles to their first Super Bowl. None of this would have been possible without Sid Gillman. To this day I still hear his voice in my head when I think of the core principles of the passing game."

From his time with the University of Miami (Ohio) to the University of Cincinnati; to the Los Angeles Rams of the NFL; to the Los Angeles and San Diego Chargers of the AFL; to the Houston Oilers of the AFC; to his time as a well-regarded assistant with the Dallas Cowboys, Chicago Bears, and Philadelphia Eagles, Gillman was always looking for a schematic advantage. More often than not, he found one, though the results were not always what he imagined.

Gillman played for Ohio State head coach Sam Willaman in the 1930s, and it was Willaman's multi-faceted offense that formed the basis of Gillman's ideology. A fanatic for motion pictures, the young Gillman found a job as a movie theater usher and would cut the football highlights out of movie newsreels to take them home to study on his own projector. This began an obsession with game film and the study of opponent tendencies that followed him throughout his life. Long after he retired from coaching until his death in 2003, he watched game tape and took calls from all kinds of coaches—at all levels of the game—who asked the offensive genius for pearls of wisdom.

Gillman had a 20-year stint as a college coach, culminating in his time as the head coach at Miami of Ohio from 1944 through 1947 and at Cincinnati from 1949 through 1954. In 1955 he was hired to replace Hampton Pool as the head coach of the Rams at the tail end of the team's point-a-minute legacy. Gillman brought in his own philosophies and led the Rams to the NFL title game in his first season but struggled over the next four seasons as the Rams' talent pool dissipated. Even in 1959 when the Rams finished with a 2–10 record, Gillman's offense still ranked second in the league in points.

Fired after the 1959 season, Gillman was available to take an offer from Los Angeles Chargers owner Barron Hilton in time for the AFL's inaugural season. Gillman accepted the offer, took over as general manager as well, and set about revolutionizing the professional passing game in the new league.

The AFL needed a schematic template for its passing game, and as time went on, it became clear that Gillman's concepts ruled the roost. Acolytes like Davis and Walsh took Gillman's ideas and made them their own—Davis did so more with the deep passing game, and Walsh did so with the geometric, horizontal aspects of the playbook—but it was Gillman who combined theory and philosophy into an entirely new package. Together, Gillman and the AFL reached unexpected heights.

There were route concepts and combinations before Gillman, of course, but even the most elevated passing games before Gillman joined the Chargers consisted primarily of isolation routes in which the receiver was tasked to get open using his physical abilities—speed, strength, and elusiveness—against mostly man-on-man coverage. Gillman's concepts were far more advanced and predated the proliferation of zone and hybrid defenses, and when those more complicated defenses came along, Gillman's insistence that receivers should work together to overwhelm defenses before and after the snap set the tone.

Moreover, Gillman's passing game set up his run game and vice versa. With his early Chargers teams, he had Keith Lincoln and Paul Lowe in his backfield, and when defenses arrayed themselves against the Chargers' receivers, Lincoln and Lowe presented the impossible problem uncommon in professional football at that time: who do you cover and who do you tackle? "The theory was to pass, screen, draw, and trap," Gillman told *The NFL Today*. "We felt that if we could pass successfully, we could run the draw play, which you see so often. Then, we could force a heavy rush and then we could have the trap play, where you let [a defender] come in and you hit him with the cross-block. There's 50 different kinds of screens—the late screen, the slip screen, the speed screen—and we had all of those and we could score."

Gillman's 1981 Eagles playbook showed an impressive complexity of routes for every potential receiver—a level of complexity that would be impressive in today's game. Gillman had installed most of that into the Chargers' playbooks in the 1960s, and no defense was quite ready for it all—especially early AFL defenses that were often low on combined talent. "I always felt before Paul Brown," Gillman told the *Chicago Tribune*, "coaches just rolled the ball out onto the field."

Whether that was true or not, Gillman's approach represented a series of masterful steps forward. As much of a stickler as he was for the precision of a route, Gillman sometimes referred to routes as "feelings" and he wanted his receivers to react within structure to what a defender did. Defined and designed openings were Gillman's purpose, but the best of his receivers were allowed to freelance to a degree as long as it worked. This was a prelude to the option routes of the Run-and-Shoot era that you see in every modern passing offense, but it was as if it came from outer space back then.

Because the AFL is categorized primarily as a let-it-rip league with the deep pass as the main attraction, some have typecast Gillman too narrowly as a go-route and post-route play designer. He was that to be sure, but through his time in the AFL, Gillman expanded his passing game horizontally as much as he did vertically. More specifically, he did so geometrically.

The Field Balance Theory

In 1964 Sid Gillman sent assistant coach Tom Bass to a coffee shop to meet with a San Diego State math professor to discuss geometry in general—specifically, potential geometry of routes. Gillman had the notion that every route could be perfectly explained and executed with a pre-planned set of angles: the angle of the route to its breaking point when the receiver cuts, the angle of the route after the cut, and the angle from the quarterback's release point to the point of the catch. "We thought about it, and if you look at [passing] patterns, they are all geometrically designed," Bass told *The (South Carolina) Post and Courier.* "Basically, the only objective we had was to try to make sure when we ran the pass routes that the ball was in the air the same amount of time so that we could time out our passing game."

Well, that wasn't the *only* objective. Timing was one part of it, but rhythm was an equal and crucial component. If the quarterback and his receivers understood the exact depth and length of routes, and the quarterback had all those different depths in his head, he could rely on the gameplan and trust his timing. The quarterback could throw with more anticipation, passing the ball to a spot where the receiver hadn't yet travelled, and that level of trust would set up a rhythm of completions in the quarterback's head. "We really wanted to make the quarterback throws all the same," Bass said. "If you are at the left hash mark, and the throw is to the right sideline, that is the toughest throw. The ball is in the air quite a while. But if you bring the right-side receiver in four yards closer to the center of the field, the flight time of the ball is almost exactly the same [as a throw to the receiver on the left side]."

Gillman and Bass put the angles together and made their players understand the concept, and Gillman took things a step further by assigning different names to different areas of the field.

So when Gillman talked about filling the space of the field with as many targets as possible, he wasn't referring to some kind of random, happenstance collection of receivers. He was literally creating a new dimension in football, in which route concepts were designed and complementary at an entirely new level.

With the timing and geometry set, Gillman's quarterbacks would also throw to their running backs, who would frequently motion to the slot from the backfield pre-snap. Defenses had to face as many as five receivers, and in the days of the two-back, two-receiver, one-tight end formation, that was fairly revolutionary. If this sounds a lot like the West Coast Offense Bill Walsh developed as Paul Brown's offensive assistant with the Cincinnati Bengals from 1968 through 1975 and perfected as head coach of the San Francisco 49ers from 1979 through 1988, that's no accident. Walsh was Al Davis' running backs coach in 1966 and he later called his AFL tenure the foundation of his offensive philosophy. He was exposed to Gillman's passing concepts, which Davis adopted unapologetically when he left Gillman's employ as his receivers coach from 1960 through 1962 and took over the Oakland Raiders in 1963. "It was a fully dimensional approach," Walsh said in *The Genius*, "utilizing the backs and tight ends much more extensively than other offenses. A typical NFL team might have three or four patterns for the halfback, but the Raiders' system had as many as 20, and even they didn't use anything close to Gillman's whole playbook. To develop an understanding of it took time, but once learned, it was invaluable."

Although the passing concepts of the NFL in the 1960s did include single and dual crossing routes and some basic option route concepts, Gillman's theories regarding route concepts were more complex. His acolytes include many of the most talented play designers and theorists in NFL history. "All our terminology—and the terminology Bill Walsh took with him when he left here—came from Sid, plus a lot of the coaching points and much of the offense," Davis told *Sports Illustrated*'s Paul Zimmerman. "Sid's idea was to spread the field and get everyone into the pattern. He liked the quick strike, the relentless attack down the field, same as Bill Walsh. The quick strike to Lance Alworth, where he breaks a short pass for 60 yards, the quick strike to Jerry Rice, same thing. But then we got away from that and started holding the ball longer, looking for the big one."

Gillman had a clear numeric system for the routes assigned to his receivers, tight ends, and running backs, and that was important because he was using the backs and tight ends as much or more as any other coach and definitely in different ways. A defense facing a Sid Gillman offense might see a two-back set and a tight end aligned to the formation—only to have one or both backs motion into the slot or out wide, and the tight end peeling away to the slot.

Against the elementary 4-3 defenses of the day and even against the AFL's occasional 3-4 and nickel hybrid formations, it was a lot to deal with. And as was later the case with Don Coryell's systems with the St. Louis Cardinals and San Diego Chargers and Mike Martz's system with the "Greatest Show on Turf" St. Louis Rams, the play calls were comprised of the single-digit route numbers combined—from left to right, first the outside receivers and then the inside receiver. All of those systems were close imitations of what Gillman invented decades ago.

In Gillman's system an *866* call, for example, would have the left outside receiver (or X receiver) run an 8 route (a deep post), while the outside right Z receiver would run his version of the 6 route (a deep, breaking in-route), and the inside Y receiver would run a 6 route, also a deep, breaking in-route. The route calls to the strong side were always orchestrated together. If the middle number was 0 or the middle number wasn't called, that told the inside receiver (the Y receiver) to block. If the Y receiver's rusher didn't rush on an even-numbered route, he was to run a delayed straight route. If the rusher didn't rush on an odd-numbered route, the Y receiver was to run a delayed short check-down route to provide another easy read for the quarterback.

Gillman's routes were highly complex for any era, and the responsibilities extended to every position. There were 24 different routes for halfbacks and fullbacks and a series of mirrored flares, in which the two backs run routes in tandem. The depth and speed of the route was dependent on the protection. Combination routes with protection adjustments for running backs don't always happen in today's NFL—never mind the AFL of the 1960s.

His crossing routes were incredibly diverse and effective. In the flare series, a running back would run a flare pattern outside the backfield, while there was at least one crossing route and slant or post combination. The dual series had two wide receivers running the same route from either side. If he had two receivers breaking from the double or dual series concept based on an audible, the quarterback would simply call the weakside route in the combination first and so on. Gillman would rely on his quarterbacks to be smart enough to audible based on the defense and he would rely on his receivers to make quick decisions to alter their routes while running them based on coverage. Two decades before the Run-and-Shoot brought multiple option routes to the NFL, Gillman was already setting the pace.

Gillman's route release concepts had their roots in his and Bass' geometric studies. "A release is a movement made by a WR while running the stem of a route on the way to the BREAKING POINT," he wrote in his 1981 Eagles playbook. Gillman defined the breaking point as a designated spot downfield in line with the receiver's basic alignment position. The breaking point was the spot where the quarterback knew his receiver was going to be. The receiver could vary his line to the point or work a double move in, but it was of paramount importance that the receiver got to that point so that the quarterback knew just where he would be. This allowed the quarterback to throw with confidence and anticipation.

Now, multiply that single route concept by as many as five potential receivers trained to ply their routes and breaking points in specific horizontal areas of the field and you start to understand how difficult these passing concepts were to defend. "His passing system was a lot different from ours," former Chiefs tight end Fred Arbanas, who was coached by Gillman in AFL All-Star games, said in the book, *Uncrowned Champs*. "He spent a lot more time on it, with different routes, alternate routes, and ways of screening off linebackers and safeties to break the other guys free on patterns. He wouldn't just show us stuff on the blackboard, though. He would tell us all the reasons why they would work at different times in the game and when to work the screening plays. In those days the defensive backs could knock you around all over the place until the ball was in the air. Sid's screen patterns for his receivers helped break those guys away from you, especially for me because the middle backer would drop off and give you a shot to knock you off a pattern, but the way he set up those screens broke us free."

John Hadl, Gillman's quarterback in San Diego from 1962 through 1971 who led the NFL in passing yards three times during that era, said that an education in the passing game under Gillman was like nothing he could have imagined. "I played for the Rams, Packers, and Oilers after the Chargers and can't remember any of their plays," Hadl said, according to *Uncrowned Champs*. "But the ones we ran in Sid's scheme were so drilled-in through repetition that I can still call them in my sleep. He really taught me how to study and develop a gameplan. The way he was, always so precise in his passing game, was so far ahead of his time. He kept notebooks of pass route descriptions, drawings of each pattern and what everyone else was doing. He was really a master at understanding the game and he wanted his quarterbacks to know it all. He had our receivers screening, like setting picks in basketball, for each other to get space between the defender and our primary receiver or throw flares to spots they vacated when they followed another guy over the middle. We'd send two backs out in a five-man route with each going in different directions. He even had [Keith] Lincoln and [Paul] Lowe run flares in different directions to get isolated on a linebacker they could outrun. We practiced so much repetition and watched so much film that I can still remember the plays we called."

Hadl threw the ball just 204 times in three seasons at Kansas as a running back and quarterback, so it was a bit like going straight from high school to a post-graduate education. Gillman taught Hadl that if a defender was looking at the running back, it was man-to-man coverage. And if the defender was looking at the quarterback, it was zone coverage. What Hadl called "adjustment routes" based on coverage were embryonic option routes—years ahead of their time. "If [Lance] Alworth went to the line and saw a certain formation or a player in a certain spot, we'd look at each other and knew we both saw the same thing and make an adjustment to the play at the line," Hadl said. "Gillman also taught us to design our play calls on particular downs and their distance tendencies that Sid would prepare for from all the film he studied. He had a high percentage of correctness, too."

Billy Joe, who played running back for the Denver Broncos, Buffalo Bills, Miami Dolphins, and New York Jets from 1963 through 1969 and thus saw Gillman's offenses through multiple lenses, later coached at Cheyney State College in Pennsylvania and worked his way up the ladder to a position with the Eagles at the same time Gillman was there. "Sid was the passing consultant for [Eagles head coach] Dick Vermeil and he'd come and talk to us about his theories of the passing game," Joe said. "He was still selling the same passing principles in the late '70s and early '80s that he'd developed in the early '60s with the Chargers, and they still proved to be the best and most sound ideas about how to throw the football. It just shows his genius in the passing game and how far ahead of the pack he was back in the early '60s."

That said, the most important game of Gillman's life was the one in which he completely reversed course and presented his opponent with a set of schemes they couldn't stop: the 1963 AFL championship.

1963 AFL Championship: San Diego Chargers 51, Boston Patriots 10

Considering how aggressive Sid Gillman professed his offenses to be, the 1963 AFL Championship win was a master's class in how to react to a defense's tendencies. Gillman knew full well that the Boston Patriots were going to blitz like crazy. It was a major construct of their defense under head coach Mike Holovak, and in two regular season games against the San Diego Chargers, Boston had limited Gillman's offense to a total of 511 yards and gone after John Hadl and fellow quarterback Tobin Rote mercilessly. Keith Lincoln's 71-yard halfback pass in the game at San Diego was the biggest play in either game. Lance Alworth caught 13 passes for 210 yards and a touchdown in the game at Boston, but Gillman's Chargers were no sure thing against Holovak's Patriots and their aggressive defense. San Diego won both regular-season games but scored a total of 24 points.

Counter to the common canard that defense wasn't an AFL priority, Boston allowed 79 rushing yards per game and 265 yards of total offense per contest. Paul Lowe had run for 1,010 yards and a 5.7 yards-per-carry average in 1963, but in two regular-season games against Boston, he gained a grand total of six yards on 12 carries. By some accounts the Patriots blitzed on up to 70 percent of their defensive downs, an astonishing number for the time. "I don't think that I ever saw a team that could blitz as much as they did and get away with it," Gillman said in *The American Football League: A Year-by-Year History, 1960–1969.* "They used a combination of different linebackers and were one of the first teams to use safety blitzes effectively."

With that in mind, Gillman turned to a different plan—the "feast or famine" strategy, in which the Chargers would use Boston's blitzes against them. Now instead of running his receivers ragged and relying on the occasional option pass, Gillman devised a new set of schemes based on a number of concepts: pre-snap motion, play-action as a deceptive practice, the inside trap, and the outside toss. Gillman sent Lincoln and Lowe in motion quite often to force Boston's linebackers to cover; this forced the Patriots to choose between pressure and coverage. He put Alworth and split end Don Norton on the same side of the field and splayed tight end Dave Kocourek to the other side, creating disadvantageous matchups for Boston's safeties.

The Patriots still blitzed, but the results were often disastrous. Gillman seemed to know when and from where the pressure was coming. He would call tosses to the outside against inside blitzes and flush multi-gap pressures with trap plays in which the Patriots' aggressiveness was used against them. According to Greg Cosell's game charting in *The Games That Changed the Game,* the Patriots blitzed on 28 of San Diego's 60 offensive plays, and the Chargers gained 352 yards and scored four touchdowns on those blitzes. "We studied their game films. We knew when we could go out into patterns and when we had to block," Lowe said. "We knew what they were going to do. They were a blitzing team, and we decided to trap them. It was a super gameplan."

Rote and Hadl combined for 17-of-26 passes for 305 yards and three touchdowns, but it was the rushing totals that were extraordinary. The Chargers ran the ball 32 times for 318 yards and four touchdowns in the 51–10 win, and the further behind the Patriots got, the more they dug their own hole by sticking to the blitz—even as it was apparent that Gillman had figured that out.

Marion Campbell, Boston's defensive line coach in 1962 and 1963, would go on to coach with four NFL teams, finishing his coaching career with the Georgia Bulldogs in 1994. The 1963 AFL Championship forever changed his views on how to array his defenders to create pressure. "It's easy to let 'er rip with the blitz, but we got hurt badly with that." Campbell said in *The Games That Changed the Game*. "If it fails, like it did against the Chargers, you've got nothing to fall back on. From then on I only coached a controlled system where the other team was going to have to earn every score on its own."

Fate—and Gillman's own shortcomings—kept him to that one AFL title despite his clear innovative brilliance. The Buffalo Bills beat his Chargers in the 1964 and 1965 AFL Championships with a defense that presented multiple fronts and a discipline that had San Diego's best players stopped short again and again—not to mention with Jack Kemp, the quarterback Gillman thought he could hide through the league's waiver system and subsequently lost for $100. Gillman's refusal to pay his players what other teams would resulted in the loss of defensive talent; a defensive line that Kansas City Chiefs quarterback Len Dawson called the AFL's best in 1963 started to hemorrhage talent, including players like Earl Faison and Ernie Ladd in the mid-1960s. Transfer of team ownership from Barron Hilton to Gene Klein magnified a lack of understanding of the concept of player worth. This led to a series of four straight third-place finishes in the AFL's Western Division to finish off Gillman's time with the team.

Gillman's time with the Houston Oilers in 1973 and 1974 was marked by a remarkable turnaround from 1–8 in his first season to 7–7 in his second. He then lost a power struggle to Bum Phillips, who had been Gillman's defensive coordinator in San Diego from 1967 through 1970 and had tried to implement the 3-4 as a base defense during that time, a move that would have predated the eventual installation of the 3-4 by a number of years. But Gillman insisted that Phillips revert back to the 4-3 after a couple of nerve-racking showings.

After leaving Houston in 1974, Gillman spent the rest of his professional life as an offensive consultant for everyone from the

Philadelphia Eagles to the United States International University.
Until the end of his life, he watched tape from his extensive library
and looked for ways to destroy defenses. "The real treasure I got
from Sid was learning how to be a winner, what it took: commitment, love of football, excellence, work ethic," Al Davis told *Sports
Illustrated* in 1991. "No one could ever outwork Sid. He taught
me how an organization should be run. There are just so many
intangibles that came from Sid, the foundation of how we practice,
for instance. See it, write it, learn it, do it."

His lone championship neither diminishes Gillman's radical
genius nor the debt every modern NFL team owes to it. As much as
any coach in the history of professional football, Gillman created a
new structure in which teams could win—through all generations.
After Gillman's Chargers won the 1963 AFL title, he reached out
to NFL commissioner Pete Rozelle, asking for a matchup between
the champions of the two leagues. No NFL team had played an
AFL team before. But given San Diego's balance on offense and
defense, it was thought by many that if the Chargers couldn't beat
the NFL champion Chicago Bears, they could have at least given
Chicago a more competitive game than the Kansas City Chiefs
and Oakland Raiders offered a few years later against the Green
Bay Packers in the first two Super Bowls.

Apparently, the specter of a possible AFL upset wasn't appealing to Rozelle. Gillman sent a letter to the NFL commissioner,
who had worked with him in the Rams' front office, using the
recent Second Ecumenical Council. Pope John Paul XXIII hoped
to eliminate longstanding bitterness between Catholicism and
Judaism. The Pope had stated: "The Jews should not be presented
as rejected or accursed by God."

"Pope John was a great man because he recognized 'the other
league,'" Gillman wrote.

"Yes, but it took a thousand years," Rozelle responded.

The frustration wasn't just that the NFL would not entertain Gillman's request for an interleague championship; it was also that the NFL kept taking shots at the AFL's methodology. "I don't think too much of the AFL yet," Johnny Unitas told writer Ed Fitzgerald in 1964. "It seems to me they play strictly offensive football and almost all passing. They have no defense at all. I know it has been said that some of their clubs could beat some of our clubs. But I can't see it. I don't think they would stand a chance principally because they don't have any defense. They aren't really complete football teams yet."

That was the perception of the AFL in the first half of the decade, and in some AFL cities, it was true. But in Buffalo Lou Saban and Joe Collier had created a team that would buck those trends with a decidedly old-school approach and a defense that was among the most innovative and effective of its era.

War Memorial: The Bills Bring the NFL to the AFL

The Buffalo Bills of the mid-1960s had an NFL mentality. While the rest of the AFL seemed to be throwing the ball in higher-rent stadiums in line with the new TV contract, Buffalo played in old War Memorial Stadium and had two equal power factors: the running of Cookie Gilchrist and a defense that may have been the best the AFL ever saw.

Gilchrist was the man who kept the power running going, gaining 3,056 yards and scoring 31 rushing touchdowns on 676 carries from 1962 through 1964 before he was traded to the Denver Broncos in February of 1965 after wearing out his welcome with management. But the real heart of the team that won the AFL title in 1964 and 1965 wasn't the run game or even quarterback Jack Kemp. It was a defense that employed advanced principles that would take most of the rest of pro football a decade to employ and implement. The brains behind that outfit was defensive coordinator Joe Collier, who was hired as the team's linebackers and defensive backs coach by head coach Lou Saban in 1962.

Collier, who came from Western Illinois and the Boston Patriots, was much more than that. Given the freedom to merge his schematic concepts with his personnel, Collier started running three-man fronts long before Bum Phillips and Chuck Fairbanks were doing that in the 1970s. Instead of the traditional four-man front with the occasional linebacker blitz, Collier saw the landscape of his defensive front as a more complicated architecture, in which players had varied assignments based on the situation. "We had a fine group of people and we played together," linebacker Mike Stratton said in *Going Long*. "We had it all—good defensive backs, linebackers, and a line strong enough to put the rush on and agile enough to play the run. By playing defense like we did, we put a lot of pressure on the quarterback. That was the key. If we had pressure, we could play game with blitzers and change coverage responsibilities."

Stratton was one of those fine players; he was named to six straight AFL Pro Bowls from 1963 through 1968 and was a first-team All-Pro every year from 1964 through 1966. Defensive tackle Tom Sestak joined the Bills as a 245-pound linebacker/tight end prospect but bulked up to 270 pounds and became one of the strongest interior defenders in professional football.

The 1964 Bills defense led the league with 50 sacks, a team record that wouldn't be broken until 2013. Through the 1964 and 1965 seasons, they put together a 17-game streak, in which they didn't allow a single rushing touchdown. They had 28 interceptions for 470 return yards and two touchdowns in 1964 and 32 interceptions for 393 return yards and a touchdown in 1965. Safety George Saimes was a bibliophile and was nicknamed "Camus in Shoulder Pads" and "the Existentialist Pass Defender."

He was a smaller, quicker range safety who read offenses well and could surprise with the blitz. Cornerbacks Butch Byrd and Booker Edgerson limited receiver releases at the line of scrimmage with the trademark AFL bump-and-run style and they were athletic and agile enough to cover any receiver downfield through any route.

The team Saban and Collier put together for the 1964 season finished their regular season with a league-best 12–2 record. Their two losses were by a total of 11 points. They led the AFL in both points scored (400) and points allowed (242). The only thing that stood between the Bills and the franchise's first championship was the San Diego Chargers team that had so confused the Patriots in the 1963 Championship Game.

The 1964 AFL Championship: Buffalo Bills 20, San Diego Chargers 7

The 1964 Chargers couldn't quite match the 1963 Chargers. The '64 team went 8–5–1 and ranked fourth in the AFL in points scored as opposed to first the year before. Quarterback Tobin Rote started the season, but John Hadl took over after the team went 1–2–1 in Rote's early games. San Diego rattled off a five-game winning streak with the smart, mobile Hadl under center. However, they lost both of their regular-season contests against the Buffalo Bills, so the potential result of the championship game against the Bills on December 26 should have been on Sid Gillman's radar.

The plan Joe Collier put together, though, was the real story of this game. To checkmate Gillman's varied and multiple formations, he set his defenders up in equally diverse ways and completely confused the smartest coach in football. The Chargers started off hot, though. The first drive started with a draw handoff from Rote to Keith Lincoln, in which Lincoln rumbled upfield for

38 yards. Three plays later Rote hit tight end Dave Kocourek for a 26-yard touchdown pass off play-action, in which Rote did a fine job of moving backward out of the pocket and hitting Kocourek over the middle.

On San Diego's next drive, everything changed when Bills linebacker Mike Stratton absolutely poleaxed Lincoln on a half-back flare pass, causing Lincoln to suffer broken ribs.

It was later called "the Hit Heard 'Round the World," and hyperbole aside, it completely changed the complexion of the game and established the Bills as the bullies on the block. The play itself was based on defensive intelligence, though: Stratton adjusted to a halfback pattern he'd seen the Chargers run before. Stratton had noticed that on one particular curl/flat pattern if the linebacker to the quarterback's front side was playing off, the halfback would be the quarterback's primary read. Stratton baited Rote into throwing the ball to Lincoln by playing off and then drove toward Lincoln after he caught the ball. "I started back to Lincoln and I saw that they were throwing to him," Stratton said in *Going Long*. "It was just: put your head down and try to dig the dirt because, golly, if Lincoln caught the ball in time to give me a juke, hell, he could have been gone. I was trying to get there just as he caught it or after he caught it, where I could get a hand on him. But it worked out a little differently."

According to Lincoln, the play happened that way in part because of Rote's late read. Paul Lowe ran a deep wheel pattern up the left seam from a split-back set, while Lincoln faked a block and wound up in the left flat area, waiting for the ball. "The first time [Rote] looked at me, Stratton was about 20 yards downfield," Lincoln said. "He saw me out there, knew I was his man. So, he started coming. In the meantime Rote decided he was coming to me. The rush was in on him; he threw the goddamned ball to me like you'd throw a snowball down the chimney. And just as the ball got to me, Stratton hit me. He separated my sternum, rib cage. It was a good hit, a clean hit."

Taking Lincoln out of the game hurt the Chargers, and the Bills had more coming for Gillman. They alternated between heavy over fronts, in which the line was slanted to the strong side with three-man fronts, and the linebackers dropped into coverage. This negated Gillman's Field Balance Theory because Collier placed his defenders in every area just as Gillman intended to do with his offensive players.

The Bills came out of the game with three interceptions— two from Rote and one from Hadl—and at least two more from Rote that could have been intercepted if they weren't dropped. Buffalo did a fantastic job of limiting San Diego's sideline passes, created pressure without blitzing, and when the Bills did blitz, they showed some different looks such as having an inside linebacker cheat up over the center at a 45-degree angle, predating Joe Greene's stunt 4-3 angle rush by a decade.

San Diego got a bit of traction in the run game by attacking three-man fronts with draws and delays, but its defense couldn't match the power of Cookie Gilchrist, who gained 122 yards on 16 carries. Add in the 70 yards on 18 carries from Wray Carlton and the 16 yards and one touchdown on five carries from Jack Kemp, and Buffalo's two-sided strategy paid the ultimate dividend—the team's first championship.

The Bills won the rematch in the 1965 AFL title game in a 23–0 blowout, but Lou Saban left Buffalo after the 1965 season and was replaced by Collier. As often happens, Collier, who went on to design the "Orange Crush" defenses of the 1970s for the Denver Broncos and brought hybrid concepts and three-man base fronts to the NFL at a time when Bum Phillips and Chuck Fairbanks were also doing so, proved to be a better defensive coordinator than he was a head coach.

Collier should ultimately be remembered as one of the NFL's greatest defensive minds. His key to the kingdom is that he was able to outsmart Gillman more than once. Collier wasn't the only AFL coach coming forward with defensive innovations. In Kansas City Hank Stram rewrote his playbook in multiple ways, and this would lead to the most wins of any coach in the league's history, as well as the league's most dominant victory over the NFL. Before that could happen, though, he would have to go through a blow-torch of perfect execution that had already confounded every NFL team more than once.

Matriculation: Hank Stram's Constant Innovation

Hank Stram was one of the more unconventional coaches in professional football history and certainly one of the most innovative. A cocky rooster with mile-a-minute sarcasm and a penchant for tailored suits, Stram was so obsessed with football formations that restaurateurs in the Kansas City area would rush to his table when he was seated to give him paper napkins so he wouldn't draw X's and O's on the cloth ones. "He was a piece of work," Kansas City Chiefs defensive tackle Ed Lothamer said in *When It Was Just a Game*. Stram spent time as an assistant coach in college from 1948 through 1959 at Purdue, SMU, Notre Dame, and Miami, and the first head coaching job he had in football was with the Dallas Texans of the AFL, starting in 1960. He was hired by Texans owner/AFL founder Lamar Hunt, who had played for Stram at SMU, after Bud Wilkinson and Tom Landry turned the job down.

The Texans became the Kansas City Chiefs in 1963, and by then Stram had taken his team to an AFL title in 1962. Two more AFL titles followed in 1966 and 1969, and so did two Super Bowls—a crushing 35–10 loss to the Green Bay Packers in Super Bowl I and an equally convincing 23–7 victory against the Minnesota Vikings in Super Bowl IV—the last game in AFL history.

Stram was one of the few people involved in the AFL throughout its history and he's the winningest coach in the league's annals with a regular-season record of 87–48–5 and a postseason mark of 4–2 from 1960 through 1969. From the start he proved to be an outstanding talent scout, helping to bring aboard multiple Hall of Fame and working with scout Lloyd C.A. Wells to find players at smaller African American schools in the south.

Stram spent the first few seasons in Kansas City building that team around a young base of talent, leading to an 11–2–1 record in 1966. After thrashing the two-time defending league champion Buffalo Bills 31–7 in the 1966 AFL title game, Stram thought he and his team were ready for the ultimate challenge—taking on Vince Lombardi and the Packers in the first Super Bowl on January 15, 1967. Stram was right—for about one half of football.

Super Bowl I

The common narrative of the first four Super Bowls is of an NFL that had already established its supremacy and an AFL that caught up quickly. The Green Bay Packers' decisive wins against Hank Stram's Kansas City Chiefs and Al Davis' Oakland Raiders in Super Bowls I and II suggest the Packers were simply an unbeatable force in championship situations, winning the final three NFL titles under Vince Lombardi's watch. The AFL was the more schematically diverse league, but neither the Chiefs nor the Raiders could match Green Bay's experience and discipline.

The 1966 Chiefs had an average age of 26.4 per player; the 1966 Packers averaged 27.6 years of age. But the Packers had 12 starters over the age of 30, while the Chiefs had just two. Stram's inventions would eventually overcome the NFL's stodgier and less flexible teams. The Packers were a different brand of beast when they had to be, though their philosophy stemmed far more from ensuring that every player did his job perfectly. Stram believed in execution, but he also believed that the errors of youth could be masked to a degree by sleight of hand when necessary.

Len Dawson was Stram's quarterback from 1962 through 1974, and his story is perhaps the most prominent example of an NFL misfit finding historic success in the new league. Dawson was selected fifth overall in the 1957 draft by the Pittsburgh Steelers, but he sat on the bench behind Bobby Layne for three seasons and then two more behind Milt Plum with the Cleveland Browns after the Steelers traded him on December 31, 1959. Dawson completed 21-of-45 passes for 204 yards, two touchdowns, and five interceptions in his first five seasons. When the Browns released him, that put him in the sights of Stram, Dawson's coach at Purdue. The Chiefs signed Dawson on June 30, 1962, and the rest was history.

Well, almost history. In Dawson's first three passing attempts for the Chiefs, he threw an interception, fumbled the ball, and missed an open receiver. Still, Stram was patient. "I was shocked at how bad he was at first," Stram said. "But I couldn't help but realize that five years of sitting on the bench or manning telephones didn't make a man sharp. I stuck with him, and he quickly smoothed out the rough spots."

By 1966 Dawson was running one of the most dynamic and diverse offenses in the game, regardless of the league. The Chiefs that season went 11–2–1, the best record in franchise history to that point, and beat the two-time AFL champion Buffalo Bills in the league title game. They were as ready as they could be for any opponent in the first Super Bowl, but these were the Lombardi Packers, winners of five NFL titles in the decade. That they were not as schematically diverse as the Chiefs did not matter. "Green Bay was power and execution," Michael MacCambridge wrote in *America's Game*. "The Packers playbook was not a thick one. It was not as if the Packers were tricking anybody. Bart Starr could have called the plays at the line of scrimmage. From the Packers' mind-set, shifting, men in motion, the moving pocket, the Tight I formation, some of those things were looked at by the NFL as smoke and mirrors. Gimmickry. And to a certain NFL mind-set, it was dishonest. It was a refutation of what pro football was all about."

When, in fact, if you take a longer view, it was part of the game and always had been. And some of the elements of what the Chiefs employed went back into parts of the package of football in the '30s and '40s. The old Lombardi playbook worked when Lombardi was running it, but history would quickly pass it by. Lombardi's view of the football world in 1967 was the NFL's conventional wisdom—out-execute your opponent, and things will go well. But if you look at both styles of play and their play-books, there is a lot more in pro football today that is similar to what the Chiefs did in Super Bowl I than what the Packers did. The success of Lombardi's simplicity was based entirely on belief and execution. Stram and many of his AFL cohorts had a different view—that the multiplicity of a playbook was its own inherent advantage.

This played out pretty well for the Chiefs in the first half of Super Bowl I. They went into halftime with just a 14–10 deficit and had to feel that they had at least half a chance of pulling off a major upset. Running back Curtis McClinton's first-half touchdown—the only touchdown the Chiefs scored on the day—had elements of the modern principle of bringing multiple play options from a single look. The touchdown came from a play called *54 Mike Backs O*. "I felt like a champion to be crowned,"

McClinton said. "It was a matter of straightening up the tie and straightening the hat. The first part of that comes from the 54, which is a mountain because that's where we made most of our rushing touchdowns. We'd kick out the ends, bring down the tackle, and run through the hole, making the linebacker come up. And if they came up, we would fake that we were running and send the back out into the backfield and the end down the field. It was a very tough play for linebackers, middle linebackers, and cornerbacks because we would run that play successfully as a run, successfully as a pass in the flat, and successfully as a pass to the other side. It was the meat and butter of our game because [any] one of those plays could hurt you. And we had the personnel to do it."

The Packers didn't argue that point. "The Chiefs were more talented than any other team we on the Packers had ever faced," defensive end Willie Davis said in *The Ultimate Super Bowl Book*. "Bigger, stronger, faster. We knew the game could have gone the other way. But they were not experienced."

On defense, the Chiefs came out with their Triple Stack front with the linebackers directly behind the ends and other varied fronts, which caused further confusion for the Packers, the experienced champions who thought they'd seen everything. "You didn't really know what you were going up against," Packers offensive lineman Forrest Gregg said. "We were used to going up against a basic four-man line. We went to the line of scrimmage, and Kansas City showed a defensive front we had not seen before. It was puzzling, out of our realm of experience on a football field. Jerry Kramer was playing right guard. I looked over at Jerry. He looked over at me and threw his hands up and shrugged his shoulders like, 'I don't know.'"

The Chiefs also ran a lot of five-man receiving formations early in the game, thinking they could get away with that because the Packers blitzed so infrequently. This left Dawson relatively unprotected as the backs flared out of the backfield, but that's where the moving pocket came in—Dawson could read the pressure, move away from it, and make the throw against base defenses. That's common in today's NFL, of course, but back then it presented a problem. Green Bay linebacker Dave Robinson said that Dawson told him later that he and Stram had analyzed the Packers' 1966 defense, discovering that they blitzed the opposing quarterback about three times per game. "Lenny told me that if that happened to them, they would either throw the ball away or take a sack for those three downs and really tax our defense as far as coverage was concerned," Robinson said.

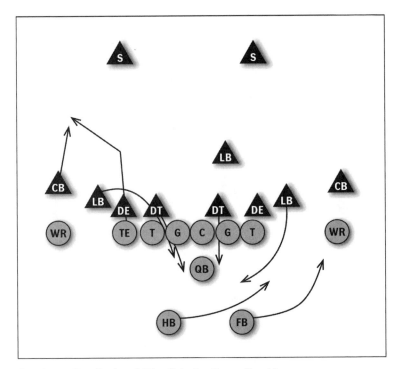

The Green Bay Packers' *Blitz-3* during Super Bowl I

Lombardi's adjustment to a more aggressive defensive approach in the second half paid obvious dividends. Davis later said that the Packers played conservatively in the first half because Lombardi was worried about the Chiefs getting a few big plays off, and as Davis put it, "then, we'd have a tiger by the tail."

That changed early in the second half, when the Packers called *Blitz-3*, which sent Robinson and linebacker Lee Roy Caffey with tackle Henry Jordan leading the way. Robinson held up tight end Fred Arbanas and then blew through to the backfield. Jordan arrived as Caffey did, and Dawson, who wasn't expecting the blitz, threw the ball up to get rid of it. The ball landed easily in the hands of Packers cornerback Willie Wood, who returned the interception to the Kansas City 5-yard line. Running back Elijah Pitts ran the ball in for Green Bay's third touchdown on the next play, and the game was effectively over. The Chiefs were a great young team, but the Packers had been in championship situations at a different level.

Now, the Chiefs couldn't run their five-man patterns because they needed to keep backs and tight ends in to block against the blitz. And the Packers were able to play ball control, forcing even more of a sense of desperation from Stram's team. "The key to winning that game was our blitz on third and 8," Robinson said. "That was the key because after that we had complete control of them. Once we neutralized their five-man patterns in the third quarter, they didn't score a point."

The Packers came back to the Super Bowl at the end of the 1967 season and beat the Raiders 33–14. But with the Packers' core players aging and Lombardi stepping down as head coach, the balance of power would shift very quickly in the NFL—and the AFL was more than ready to take advantage against teams that may have been even better but didn't have the same standard of execution and were more vulnerable to advanced schematic concepts.

Super Bowl III

The 1968 Baltimore Colts were supposed to go down as the greatest team in pro football's history. Don Shula's team built their success on a vicious, ravenous defense and the MVP season of quarterback Earl Morrall. They finished the regular season with a 13–1 record and crushed the Cleveland Browns, the one team that had previously beaten them, 34–0 in the NFL Championship Game. They allowed just 144 points in the regular season while scoring 402. They went into the third Super Bowl favored by anywhere from 17 to 21 points, and the New York Jets, the AFL's entrant, seemed like cannon fodder on the way to the Colts' coronation.

NFL commissioner Pete Rozelle was concerned about the level of competition before the game. Given the Green Bay Packers' wins in the first two games and a specter of a Colts' blowout, Rozelle was considering making future Super Bowls contests between the two best teams regardless of league or conference. That would have complicated matters, but as it turned out, the Jets were about to take that matter out of Rozelle's hands with one of the most stunning upsets in sports history.

This was not the Jets team many AFL observers expected. Joe Namath had become the first professional quarterback to throw for more than 4,000 yards in a season in 1967, but he was not nearly as productive in 1968—he threw for 3,147 yards, completed just 49.2 percent of his passes, and failed to throw a touchdown pass in six consecutive games from October 5 through November 10. Defensive end Gerry Philbin is fond of intimating that Namath's off-field pursuits had caught up with and surpassed his on-field dedication. Still, speed end Don Maynard and wily possession receiver George Sauer each exceeded 1,000 yards on the season.

But the two reasons the Jets made and won the Super Bowl for the first and only time in franchise history were their rushing attack led by Matt Snell and Emerson Boozer and an outstanding defense that went very much under the radar. Philbin was the team's primary sackmaster. Film study has shown that he amassed 19 sacks in the 1968 regular season. And the secondary—led by cornerbacks Johnny Sample and Randy Beverly—was exceptional. The Jets ranked second in the AFL behind the Kansas City Chiefs with 28 interceptions, second behind the Houston Oilers in passing yards allowed with 2,168, and allowed a league low 3.2 yards per rushing attempt.

The game was more of a tough guy slog than an aerial battle. The Colts stopped the Jets out of the gate with their own stellar defense, but when the decision was made to focus more on the ground game than Namath's arm, the Jets established their dominance by throwing the advanced version of the playbook out. Namath's 39-yard pass to Sauer with a minute left in the third quarter was the last pass he threw in the game. Up 16–0 the Jets wanted to control the ball and they were moving very well against Baltimore's defensive line. On New York's second-quarter touchdown drive, the Jets kept calling the same run play over and over because Baltimore couldn't stop it—and no matter the era, that's one of the most convincing ways to dominate your opponent. "It was the same play we had called for the whole series—up and down the field," Snell said. "Weeb called it *19 straight*, which meant that I had the option to break the play any way I saw it. I would look at Boozer's block through [left tackle] Winston Hill. If Winston blocked his man out, Boozer would lead through the inside on the linebacker. If Winston hooked his man, Boozer would lead outside. George Sauer ran [cornerback] Lenny Lyles off. By the time [linebacker] Mike Curtis got over there, I was in the end zone."

If there was one game that perfectly personified the perception that the NFL was the inflexible league while the AFL was the league of adaptability, it was Super Bowl III. Shula believed in execution as opposed to adjustment, so as the game dragged on for the Colts, the adjustments that should have been made weren't. "They ran at me about three times," Colts Hall of Fame end Bubba Smith said. "At halftime I said, 'Let me go over center. I can stop Snell there.' Shula said, 'Just play your fucking position.'"

As for Morrall, he was experiencing his own disasters. The Colts actually outrushed the Jets 143–142, but it didn't matter because Morrall completed just 6-of-17 passes for 71 yards, no touchdowns, and three back-breaking interceptions. These picks, and the option pass that should have worked in Baltimore's favor, made the difference in the game. Morrall was so atypically bad that conspiracy theorists, who believe that Super Bowl III was fixed to give the AFL the appearance of equality, point to his game as the primary evidence.

In truth Morrall's nightmare of a day came down to excellent preparation by defensive coordinator Walt Michaels and New York's defensive backs. Morrall's first pick happened in the red zone, when a six-yard pass to tight end Tom Mitchell went off Mitchell's hands and into the awaiting arms of Beverly. The second pick came when Sample read a slant to receiver Willie Richardson in the end zone based on a circle route run in the backfield by fullback Jerry Hill. Sample had seen that route combination on film and jumped the route at the Jets' 1-yard line.

Morrall's third pick and the weirdest play of the game came when the Colts tried a flea flicker near the end of the first half. Morrall handed the ball to halfback Tom Matte, who threw the ball back to Morrall behind the line of scrimmage. Earlier in the season against the Atlanta Falcons, this had worked for a long touchdown to split end Jimmy Orr, who worked his way downfield uncovered as the Falcons tried to suss out Baltimore's backfield trickery, and Morrall threw for the easy score.

This time Orr was wide open downfield again, but for whatever reason, Morrall turned and threw over the middle to Hill, who ran a slant. Safety Jim Hudson was all over Hill and came away with Morrall's final mistake. Even as Morrall released the ball, you could hear broadcaster Curt Gowdy saying, "They've got Orr wide open…nobody within 15 yards of him!"

Matte later said that Morrall didn't see Orr open because the Colts' marching band was behind Orr and ready to come onto the field for halftime. Orr had a blue and white uniform, the band had blue and white uniforms, and that was that. "People say Jimmy Orr was wide open," Michaels later said. "I'll take you into plays in every professional football game where a defender will slough off his coverage, and a receiver will be wide open. That's fine. Let the quarterback see him every time. This became obvious when the cameras were on the play. There were about five ifs. If Earl was smart enough. If he would have seen it. If he had that much time. Nobody wants to give my cornerback, Randy Beverly, credit for the fact that he could run 4.3 and probably would have been back in time."

Sample agreed, pointing to a general lack of velocity in Morrall's passes. "I told all the other defensive backs—he's not going to throw the ball deep because he doesn't have that kind of arm," Sample said. "And even if he does try to throw the ball deep, there's going to be a hump in the ball; it won't be on a line. And you'll have a chance to react and go and catch the football. That's the advantage we had on him—we knew what he could do and what he could not do."

Whatever the reason, the Colts became the personification of the NFL's greatest fear in that 16–7 loss—the first NFL team to lose to the younger and supposedly inferior league. Namath countered Baltimore's blitzes with short passes, turned to other targets when the Colts double-teamed deep receiver Don

Maynard, and blew apart the right side of Baltimore's defense over and over with old-school fullback lead runs. This was no fluke—this was an AFL team showing its superiority over one of the best NFL teams ever. Now, with one season left in the AFL's future, a man who had been in the league all along would have his ultimate vindication.

Super Bowl IV and Hank Stram's Multiplicity

Hank Stram didn't just have to suffer the indignity of losing the first Super Bowl and hearing Vince Lombardi's remarks about the inferiority of his league. He also had to wait a while to get back to the big game. The Kansas City Chiefs missed the playoffs entirely in 1967 with a 9–5 record and then were demolished 41–6 by the Oakland Raiders in the divisional round of the 1968 post-season. Seeing the Raiders lose to the New York Jets in the AFL championship and the Jets winning Super Bowl III did give the next (and final) AFL entrant hope for the 1969 season. The Chiefs would be that entrant, though they faced more than enough challenges to get there.

Len Dawson started just seven games in the regular season due to a knee injury, but with decent quarterback play from backups Mike Livingston and Jacky Lee and a tremendous defense, Kansas City finished with an 11–3 record. Then it had to wade through the previous two AFL champions to even get to Super Bowl IV. The Chiefs beat the Jets 13–6 in the divisional playoff and overcame the Raiders 17–7 in the league championship. Then they had to face a Minnesota Vikings team built much like the 1968 Baltimore Colts with a veteran quarterback (Joe Kapp), a defense that was strong in all facets, and a risk-free approach that focused more on execution (and Kapp's occasional improvisation) than schematic trickery. The 1969 Vikings led the NFL in both points scored and points allowed, so if the Chiefs were to pull this off, they'd have to bring their best.

And if Stram was going to lose another Super Bowl, he certainly wasn't going to do it without a ton of play-calling diversity. The Chiefs went into Super Bowl IV with 18 basic plays and a set of 66 formations they'd used in the regular season. To the execution-based Vikings, this was some kind of sorcerery—stuff they didn't see from their NFL opponents. In the first Super Bowl, Stram had no real answers after the Packers' blitzes blew apart his five-receiver schemes. Now, he would bring to the field at Tulane Stadium all kinds of stuff the Vikings couldn't counter, including the moving pocket, the Tight End I, and an improved stack defense that would give him a perfect plan to foil Minnesota's efforts.

The moving pocket was something that Stram and Dawson had perfected by the end of the decade. Again, this wasn't just Dawson scrambling. He was moving to specific locations between the tackles to get different throwing lanes, to cut the field in half, to make reads under pressure easier, and to force the defense to play a wider pocket when bringing that pressure.

The Tight End I was a big deal in Super Bowl IV. Stram would line one of two tight ends up behind Dawson with the fullback and halfback behind the tight end. Pre-snap the tight end could stay put to block, run his route from the backfield, or motion to the edge of the line while the backs stayed in an I formation (directly behind the quarterback). The Chiefs also could switch to a pro-set formation, in which the tight ends aligned to either side of Dawson and a few yards back. The whole idea here was to present a dizzying array of pre-snap formations to set the defense on its heels. This is a common construct in the modern NFL, but in early 1970, not so much. "When we reduce the other team's read-and-react time, we feel we have an edge," Stram said in *Pass Receiving in Early Pro Football: A History to the 1960s*. "We also feel we will force them to play a normal defense. They can't overshift because they don't know what the formation will be; they can't locate the tight end. We, in effect, freeze them—and pick up another edge."

AFL defenses were used to Stram's Wild West Show, but the Vikings proved early in the game that they either hadn't studied Kansas City's pre-snap tendencies or they figured it was high school stuff that could be easily sussed out by the pure talent of their defense. More tellingly, Bud Grant's team went into Super Bowl IV without a single man in motion or pre-snap shift. Minnesota's philosophy was to line up and go at 'em, but they didn't have the gap discipline of the Lombardi Packers, and Stram's Chiefs had ascended to a different level in both talent and schematic multiplicity, which was necessitated by the ever-expanding defensive concepts common in the AFL. "We feel that if we can complicate the recognition responsibility for the other teams, then we have created doubt and indecision, and the opponent is more apt to make mistakes," Stram said of his general philosophy. The Vikings certainly felt the pain of this in Super Bowl IV—over and over, as Stram's schematic brilliance was the dominant story.

Or it would have been the dominant story had NFL Films founder Ed Sabol not gone to Stram's hotel room the night before the game and asked him to be the first head coach miked up for a Super Bowl. After some back and forth and the nebulous promise of a $1,000 "honorarium" for Stram, the coach agreed to do it. The result was one of the best bits in NFL Films history and a fascinating look into Stram's sideline manner. Dawson, who was used to calling the plays in the huddle after discussing a series on the sideline, was a bit curious as to why Stram kept feeding him the plays. He didn't know for sure until the official Super Bowl IV highlight film came out months later. Stram used a malapropism to exhort his players to "keep matriculating the ball down the field," opined that Vikings linebacker Karl Kassulke was "running around there like it was a Chinese fire drill," and espoused the virtues of the play that would lead to Kansas City's first touchdown of the afternoon: the now legendary *65 Toss Power Trap*.

It was a relatively simple play designed to use the aggression of Minnesota's "Purple People Eaters" front four against it. Left tackle Jim Tyrer kicked out to the edge, influencing the right defensive end Jim Marshall to think that a sweep was coming. On this play, though, it was tackle Alan Page who took the bait, leaving a huge gap for Garrett as tight end Fred Arbanas moved up

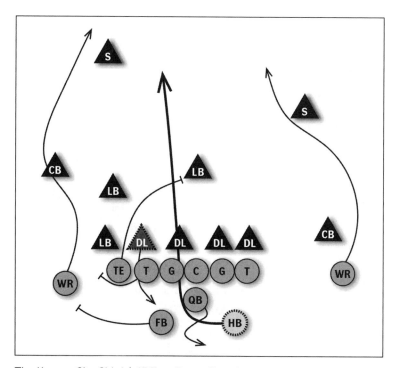

The Kansas City Chiefs' *65 Toss Power Trap* during Super Bowl IV

to block middle linebacker Lonnie Warwick. "I've never been hit any harder than Arbanas hit me," Warwick told *The* (Wilmington, Delaware) *News Journal*.

Stram said that it was the only time the Chiefs had used the play all season long, and taking Page out of the equation was the focus. "Page was a great player. Quick. Sharp. Alert," Stram said via goldenrankings.com. "In a short-yardage situation, they would put him between the center and the left guard. If the backs were split, it looked like there might be an outside play to Page's right. Then, he'd have to get in the gap between the guard and the tackle. If he saw the tackle pull, he was going to run like hell. It worked just like you draw it up on paper." Stram also called reverses to receiver Frank Pitts, and the misdirection plays further exposed the quickness of Minnesota's defense.

Kansas City's second touchdown came in the third quarter, when Dawson threw to receiver Otis Taylor underneath, and Taylor sprinted 46 yards to the end zone. Stram had instructed Dawson to throw short under Minnesota's zones; such passes would be "like stealing," the coach exhorted. Dawson threw underneath to Taylor on this particular play against a Vikings blitz much like the one that caused the interception to Willie Wood in Super Bowl 1. This time Dawson and the Chiefs had all the answers.

At no time in the AFL's history did one of its teams present such an object lesson in scheme and execution to an NFL team. It was an entirely fitting way to conclude the AFL's 10-year span and it was even more appropriate that Stram was the point man in that final game. He was as responsible for the AFL's innovative growth as anyone. "I don't know if there is anything ever new in football, but we were doing things in the '60s that teams are doing now," Dawson told *The Kansas City Star*. "Hank came up with so many new twists and doesn't get the credit he deserves. He wasn't afraid to try things. Back in those days, guys didn't try anything. They pretty much stayed with what the Green Bay Packers or New York Giants were doing. Well, Hank decided: let's do some things different. We were playing the West Coast Offense before it was the West Coast Offense."

CHAPTER 4

RESPONDING WITH A ROAR
The NFL in the 1960s

> *"Individual commitment to a group effort—*
> *that is what makes a team work, a company work,*
> *a society work, a civilization work."*
> —Vince Lombardi

A s the 1960s began, the NFL was still on a high of public awareness from the 1958 Championship Game and working fervently toward its current status as the country's most popular sport. Before that would truly take effect, however, the old league would have to endure by far the toughest set of challenges it ever faced from a rival league, as the American Football League set its own course that effectively ended in a merger between the two leagues in 1966. At first, the NFL seemed blind to the AFL's innovations, but by the middle of the decade, that was no longer the case. Buoyed by brilliant innovators and a far more progressive attitude toward race, the AFL caught up quickly and took the NFL to task when it didn't adapt.

The common myth is that the NFL was a staid, earthbound league in the 1960s in comparison to the AFL, but that wasn't always the case. The AFL's Sid Gillman and Hank Stram were two of the most impressive minds in the history of the game, but the old league had its own share of geniuses and was led by the two coaches who would define the decade for the NFL.

Tom Landry brought the Flex Defense and the shotgun formation to Dallas, and Vince Lombardi's allegedly simple system in Green Bay was actually a fervently detailed and practiced set of ideas that included the application of option routes for receivers, different splits for linemen, and zone blocking concepts implemented decades before their supposed invention. The Dallas Cowboys also used the first computers to aid in their scouting process and brought different kinds of athletes to the game—and new schemes to the table as a result.

Both Lombardi and Landry got their NFL start with the New York Giants of the 1950s. Lombardi, the offensive coordinator, was emotional, profane, and took time for his schematic concepts to bear fruit. Landry, the cool tactician, generally was more comfortable with schemes than players and proved to have a legendary gift for innovation. In the 1960s these two men would define the NFL and lay the groundwork for its future.

Vince Lombardi

Vince Lombardi remains for many the example of discipline and sacrifice among all NFL coaches. It's his name on the trophy given to every Super Bowl winner, and with five NFL championships and the first two Super Bowl wins on his resume after just nine years as the Green Bay Packers' head coach, that's a fitting tribute. Lombardi was an ideal distillation of the coach as teacher and was one of the most effective motivators of his era—regardless of profession.

Regarding his schematic influence, however, Lombardi was not an innovator the way Tom Landry was—or the most effective coaches of the AFL were. Instead, Lombardi had a great sense of how to teach the preferred schemes and methods he derived from others. His beloved power sweep was something he ran at Fordham University as one of the "Seven Blocks of Granite" from 1933 through 1936. His rule blocking schemes, an early precursor to today's zone blocking concepts, was something he picked up as Army's offensive line coach from 1949 through 1953 and were derived from meetings he had with Gillman at West Point in the late 1940s back when Lombardi was the head coach at St. Cecelia High School in New Jersey. Gillman preceded Lombardi as Red Blaik's offensive line coach and recommended that Lombardi replace him when he left to become the head coach at Cincinnati.

The pass patterns the Packers ran were more advanced than many people remember in retrospect, but there was nothing about them that put defenses out of sorts from a schematic perspective as Gillman's and Stram's did. He wasn't the innovator that Landry was—very few men in NFL history were—but few if any coaches have been better at taking an entire methodology and making it his own through repetition and education. Lombardi would run a play over and over if he believed it was important and he was a firm believer in the idea that his players should be so well-schooled on everything they did that instinct would take over. For Lombardi the power sweep defined his coaching method more than anything else.

The Packer Sweep

The power sweep wasn't just Vince Lombardi's bread-and-butter play—it was a larger personification of his entire belief system about football and about life, that the ability to bend one's will to the collective good was part of the paradigm of sacrifice that led to success. Decades after his time with the Seven Blocks of

Granite, Lombardi still saw himself—and the game—through the prism of the offensive line. "It takes a special kind of man to play on the offensive line," Lombardi wrote in *Vince Lombardi on Football*. "He must have the determination and the mental discipline to practice the various blocks constantly. He must be dedicated to perfection and recognize that perfection can be achieved only by the drudgery of practice. There are no shortcuts to success in football. The individual who tries to find them will lose his way. Each day, each player, All-Pro or rookie, must discipline himself mentally and devote himself physically to fundamentals. Only then will his actions become automatic, and his excellence instinctive, as it must be for the offensive linemen called upon in the split point of a second to initiate those blocks that make the offense go. A lineman seldom finds his name in headlines. I know, for I was one myself. The band seldom plays for him, but when he does his job, he knows it."

Lombardi called his sweep: "The play that the team must make go and the one the opponents know they must stop." He first came upon the sweep concept when he played for Fordham, playing against the Pitt teams of the Jock Sutherland era. He later dove into the single-wing while attending coaching clinics, and, as he advanced in the coaching ranks, he saw the logic in centering his entire offense around various concepts of choreographed, intelligent blocking schemes. But the sweep was his baby. Lombardi had versions of the sweep that would work against 4-3 defenses, 4-4 stacks, or 6-2 defenses in which the middle linebacker was more of a middle guard. This was not a one-dimensional concept that the Green Bay Packers would have to move away from against this or that defense. Lombardi worked the sweep before and after Landry turned Sam Huff into the first real middle linebacker, and the Detroit Lions were doing the same with Joe Schmidt.

When John Madden attended a Lombardi coaching clinic in the early 1960s, he was amazed to discover that Lombardi, who Madden idolized, was able to talk about one play—that power sweep—all day long. It was an education for Madden, the relative neophyte, into just how deep strategic thought in professional football had to be. "I saved up everything I had to go up to a coaching clinic, and Vince Lombardi was the speaker," Madden said in *A Football Life: Vince Lombardi*. "At this time I was a young coach—I was coaching in junior college—and to be honest with you, I thought I knew it all. I go in and I sit in the back, and this is how stupid I was. And Vince Lombardi talks for eight hours on one play—the Green Bay sweep—talked for four hours, took a break, and talked for four hours more. I left after that, and I said, 'I don't know a damned thing.'"

The chestnut NFL Films footage of Lombardi saying he wanted: "A seal here [at the center's right shoulder] and a seal here [outside the left tackle] and run it…into the alley" was just the tip of the iceberg. Lombardi was able to talk about the sweep in such detail and drill his players and coaches on the fundamentals and macro details of it for hours because it was at the root of his philosophy. "It's a kind of complex play that looks very simple," Jerry Kramer said. "There's a lot of things that have to happen for the play to work well. If they do this, we do that. If they do that, we do this. And we adjust to where the defense goes, so that the defense is almost always wrong, and the back will run to daylight. We ran it to perfection."

Lombardi wanted his tight end—what he called the "Y End"—to open his position between six and nine feet from his tackle. Once set, the tight end was directed to "set as on a pass" or to use precisely the same techniques his linemen used to protect the quarterback. The tight end put his weight on his inside foot, keeping his eyes right on the numbers on the defender's jersey, so that if the lineman or linebacker moves to the inside quickly, he could move his defender down the line. Using momentum—carrying the defender where he was already going—was a big part of the tight end's job.

Lombardi said that the ideal way to run the sweep was to have the defender over the tight end move to the inside. If the defender moved to the outside to avoid getting caught up in the sweep, the tight end was to open with his outside foot, focus his eyes on the defender's numbers, and block to the outside so that the running back could cut to the inside. If the defender over the tight end got outside penetration, that didn't bother Lombardi as much because he knew that the pulling guard and the running back's read to cut back to the inside would take care of that. But allowing penetration to the inside was not acceptable under any circumstances. "Everyone was important in the sweep. It's really all of life. We have to do things together to make this thing we call America great," Packers tight end Ron Kramer said in *When Pride Still Mattered*. "If we don't, we're fucked."

In Lombardi's system the sweep could be called either even or odd based on the alignment of the defensive front and linebackers and it was up to the center as to how to call it pre-snap. Depending on the alignment and skill level of the nose tackle, the center could make the even call, which had him blocking the nose tackle directly. An odd call would have the center making the cut-off block on the middle linebacker and the right tackle taking the nose tackle in a reach block. The fullback would take the defensive end instead of the linebacker on that call.

The guards were the keys in the Lombardi Sweep; they were the pullers and the ones who led the run to daylight. The price to pay for that visibility was a complex assignment for both the left and right guard. While the right guard had a more complex physical assignment in working his way up the outside of the formation, the left guard was instructed to pull flat or on a direct line just behind the line of scrimmage. Clearly, the left guard's first responsibility was to avoid any clashes with the quarterback as the quarterback dropped back; so there was a hurry-up-and-wait aspect to this. Once the left guard cleared the quarterback, he became a gap hunter, looking for the first seam in the defensive line and turning up into that hole for all he was worth.

The right guard's responsibility was to pull to the right side of the formation and take the first defender outside the tight end's block. He was to pull to the right at a 45-degree angle, and his lead leg was supposed to be at a 45-degree angle as he left the line of scrimmage. In addition to that test of strength and athleticism, he also had to be aware of the timing of the fullback's block upfield. If he wasn't, the right guard and fullback could collide, leading to a string of Lombardi invectives. So the timing of this play had the right guard moving after the fullback went up to take his defender. Lombardi would sometimes allow his right guard to move inside the tight end's block or to go further outside to block on the cornerback, but it was always fundamentals before freedom.

The left tackle had what Lombardi called a very difficult assignment—he had to pull deep and move to his right to avoid any possible penetration from the defensive tackle to the left side of the center. The right tackle had to deliver a blow to drive the defensive lineman right in front of him. If there was no defender straight in front of him, the left tackle slammed the defensive end and moved on to the inside of his gap to seal for the middle linebacker.

The fullback was a major player in the sweep; Lombardi had a lot of coaching notes for him. The fullback delivered a drive block to the first defender outside the right tackle. Generally, this was the defensive end, but if the end crashed inside for the right tackle to deal with, the fullback charged upfield to deal with the linebacker to that side. Lombardi directed his fullbacks to align their blocks to the outside leg of the tackle and drive right at the first defender that became visible—whether it's the defensive end or the linebacker. On an odd call, the fullback would replace the right tackle as the man to take the left defensive end.

Lombardi also told his fullbacks to avoid any circular approach to his blocking target and he denoted this as a common mistake in the NFL of that era. Instead, he taught his fullbacks to go as quickly as possible to their blocks, even cheating up to the line if necessary to get that block and avoid any leakage to that side. As he often said, "Penetration is the one thing we do not want on this play."

Lombardi wasn't necessarily interested in speed when it came to the halfbacks who were the primary ballcarriers on the sweep. When he talked about Frank Gifford and Paul Hornung, he spoke of their quickness and intelligence that allowed them to control their styles and use their blockers to their greatest effect. The Lombardi sweep was choreography, and the halfback had to mind his dance steps just like everybody else.

The halfback was directed to lead step to his right and move as quickly as he possibly could in a straight line parallel to the line of scrimmage. He dipped slightly and keyed whether to go inside or outside based on the tight end block. From there it got pretty simple. If the defensive end or linebacker was driven inside, the halfback ran outside and vice versa. As Lombardi wrote, "That's one of the great advantages to this play. It really has two holes. We are looking for an isolation between the Y end [tight end] and the linebacker and we also want to create an alley between the linebacker and the defensive end. That's what we're looking for—the block out by the Y end on the linebacker, the block by the guard on the [defensive back], and the block by the wingback on the safety man. The seal by the tackle and fullback, cutting off pursuit, and the isolation of the Y end and linebacker give the ball carrier two alleys in which to run."

The weak-side sweep relied on the tight end to block the safety to that side, as the safety might be cheating up to get a quick pursuit to the halfback. The left tackle—the play-side tackle in this case—influenced the defensive end to that side by crashing into the end and then helped seal the weak-side linebacker. The guards reversed their strong-side protections.

When teams adjusted to the sweep by directing their defensive tackles to crash through the line as the guards pulled, Lombardi would turn to the sucker play—in which the defensive linemen would be given a free gap to run through on a fake sweep, and the ball carrier ran through the vacated gap. The Miami Dolphins of the early 1970s ran a very successful version of this concept. Lombardi pointed to the eight-yard gain late in the Ice Bowl 1967 NFL championship against the Dallas Cowboys. The sucker sweep was a response to Bob Lilly, the Cowboys' Hall of Fame defensive tackle, and his quickness through gaps. "We lined up in the sweep formation. The ball was snapped," Lombardi wrote. "Gale Gillingham, the offside guard, pulled hard, the halfback came across hard, and Lilly charged hard. Starr opened up just like the sweep handoff but instead gave the ball to the fullback, Chuck Mercein, who blew into the hole vacated by the defensive tackle, and he got to the 3-yard line of Dallas before he was tackled. It was superb football."

It was indeed superb and predicated on Lombardi's intelligence and commitment to his blocking schemes. The common picture of Lombardi as a schematically inflexible coach who had just a handful of plays and didn't adjust to circumstances is one of the most unfortunate canards in NFL history. Lombardi believed in the fundamental execution of his concepts through repetition, to be sure, but he had wrinkles in his playbooks that are used today. His blocking concepts are very similar to the zone blocking principles of the modern era, and he did at times want his receivers to adjust their routes to the coverage—yet another precursor to modern option routes.

Yes, Lombardi wanted his offense predicated on the running game, but he also got a ton of deep passes off that rushing attack. From 1959 through 1967, the years Lombardi coached the Packers, no quarterback in either the NFL or the AFL with at least 100 starts could match Bart Starr's yards per attempt total of 8.19. Starr completed 2,119 passes in that era—10th most in either league. He threw for the seventh most yards with 17,320 and he had the highest completion percentage at 57.9.

Lombardi and defensive coordinator Phil Bengston, to whom he gave more latitude than anyone else on his staff, had a highly intriguing combination of blitzes when needed, including the all-out blitz on Len Dawson that forced pressure and caused Willie Wood's game-changing interception early in the second half of Super Bowl I. The Packers were not known for blitzing through the regular season, but when the Kansas City Chiefs were keeping pace with empty backfields and quick passes, Lombardi deployed them.

He also believed that the New York Jets would beat the Baltimore Colts in Super Bowl III primarily because of the talents and quick release of Joe Namath—a player who on the surface would seem to be the antithesis of the Lombardi prototype with his white low-cut shoes, Fu Manchu mustache, and well-known proclivity for late-night activity. Far from a mindless dictator, Lombardi eased up on his players when needed and often sent his assistant coaches into Green Bay-area bars to inform his players that the coach was coming and that they'd better skedaddle.

Though Lombardi used zone coverages as did every coach to a greater or lesser degree in the 1960s, he was well aware of the coverage's limitations. When speaking of the prevent defense, Lombardi presaged today's offenses with their advanced use of no-huddle snaps. "I've often felt, watching my team in the two-minute drill, that it could play a whole game without ever needing a huddle," Lombardi said. "I know it's never been done, but I know it could. That would really shake up that defense."

Lombardi had halfback-option passes and fake sweeps in his playbook and was quite happy to use them as much as possible with halfbacks who could throw the ball. Hornung attempted 49 passes in the Lombardi era, completing 23 for 384 yards…and five touchdowns.

In the 1966 NFL championship against the Dallas Cowboys, end Boyd Dowler scored a touchdown on a passing play called *Flood Left X Delay*. This play had the fullback and halfback aligned in an offset I formation to execute a flat/seam combination route, and the halfback carried his fly route upfield while the fullback hung in the flat. Meanwhile, the tight end blocked the strong-side linebacker before releasing into an outside drag route. The split end blocked the weakside linebacker aggressively for two counts and then ran a crossing route to the area vacated by the middle linebacker, who would be keying on the fullback, if everything went as planned. If the middle linebacker stayed put and obstructed the split end, the quarterback could throw to the tight end in the flat. On this play the middle linebacker was held by the movement of the fullback, and Starr threw to Dowler, who scored a touchdown despite the fact that he was flipped in the air by safety Mike Gaechter and suffered a dislocated shoulder when he landed.

You might not think of Lombardi as the kind of coach who had flood concepts in his playbook, but the volume of his play-calling concepts was greater than is often perceived. "The passing game is practice and it is precision," Lombardi wrote. "That is obvious. What isn't obvious is the persistence: the persistence of the practice field, the persistence of the playbook, the persistence of the quarterback and receivers who must read those defenses and read them correctly, the persistence of those unsung linemen up front who must put on those pass blocks and make them stick, the persistence of the end and flanker and back who must run a route precisely to move their defender to clear an area for the receiver to get clear and catch that ball. That's the passing game and that is why, from original concept to final execution, every phase of the passing game must be perfected to the utmost."

Lombardi was not about schematic diversity as the base of his philosophy. His philosophy centered around the need for schematic diversity to adjust when opponents countered his perfected plans, and those adjustments were part of the perfection. But mostly, his philosophy centered around the idea that with discipline, toughness, and repetition, a group of men could come together as one to set an entire league on its ear. Lombardi was perhaps the greatest teacher the game has ever known, and that's why his relative biographical truth as a non-innovator was rendered irrelevant by his ability to command and win.

Tom Landry

Tom Landry was all about schematic invention and diversity—to the point that he is rightfully thought to be one of the NFL's greatest innovators. He was also a complicated man who, at times, seemed to think of his players as chess pieces that frustrated him by failing to live up to the plan, a phenomenon that is somewhat common. While Vince Lombardi led with a compelling mixture of psychology and intimidation, Landry brought a bit colder touch to the visceral game of football. "Tom is a warm person, but not so much with his players. Sometimes he gets impatient with them, doesn't pat them on the back. He expects them to do their jobs," New York Giants head coach Jim Lee Howell said in *Landry: The Legend and The Legacy*. "He's so much smarter than most of them. Maybe he should be more of a dope like me. He's like Paul Brown, a perfectionist. But he's smarter than anybody."

Landry's regular-season record of 250–162–6 combined with his 20–16 postseason record as the head coach of the Dallas Cowboys from the franchise's inception in 1960 through 1988 puts him fourth all time in victories for NFL head coaches. He won two Super Bowls, and his teams appeared in 12 NFL and NFC title games from 1966 through 1982. The Cowboys were in 10 NFC Championship Games from 1970 through 1982, and Landry's teams appeared in five Super Bowls in the 1970s—with all three losses coming in agonizing fashion.

The Cowboys lost the 1966 NFL title game to Lombardi's Packers when quarterback Don Meredith threw a last-second red-zone interception. That put the Green Bay Packers in Super Bowl I. At the end of the 1967 NFL season, Dallas lost to the Packers again in the legendary Ice Bowl game. Landry was known for a very long time as the coach who couldn't win the big one, and even when his teams beat the Miami Dolphins in Super Bowl VI and the Denver Broncos in Super Bowl XII, the postseason losses remained a ding in his overall legacy that prevented him from climbing to the same mythological heights as Lombardi, who won five NFL titles; Bill Walsh, who won all four of his Super Bowls; or Bill Belichick, who performed perhaps the most impressive feat of winning five Super Bowls in the free-agency era.

Landry left a legacy that isn't easy to summarize in bite-size pieces. Clearer is his status as one of the most influential innovators in NFL history. In the 1950s he created a defense that is still one of the two base standards for the league decades later. He was partially responsible for the reinvigoration of what has become the league's most popular offensive formation and he did that in the early 1960s.

More impressively, Landry may have been the most well-rounded coach in league annals because of his ability to see the offensive and defensive structures of his teams equally. He would create, advance, or perfect a concept on one side of the ball, and that would spur him on to an innovation on the other. As a player in the AAFC (All-America Football Conference) and NFL, he was increasingly tasked to relay plays and concepts to his teammates. By the time he became the Giants' defensive coordinator in 1954, continuing his career as a defensive back as well through 1955, Landry had been a coach in effect for years.

One prime example of his acumen was the establishment of the 4-3 defense in the 1950s. Detroit Lions head coach Joe Schmidt had experimented with the formation around the same time that Giants head coach Steve Owen was looking to expand on the old Eagle, Stack, and Umbrella Defenses. When Paul Brown came to the NFL out of the AAFC in 1950, it gave the rest of the league a serious need for a more expansive defense. Owen would come up with his own 4-3 variants and, more often than not, direct Landry to detail the new schemes to the players.

The 4-3 as it's known today really came of age when the Giants selected West Virginia linebacker Sam Huff in the third round of the 1956 draft. Landry quickly surmised that Huff had the athleticism, temperament, and intelligence to be the ideal rover as the middle linebacker in a 4-3 set—assets in that scheme that are required to this day. With that Landry took team defense into a new era. He expanded on the zone defenses of the day, ensuring that his cornerbacks and safeties covered their receivers and handed them off to each other with impressive efficiency. He tinkered with pre-snap formation as much as Sid Gillman did, and both coaches were decades ahead of their time in that department.

The Flex Defense, which Landry started using in 1964 and put into effect full time in 1965, was a variant of the four-man front, in which the defensive linemen alternately aligned on the line of scrimmage and a bit behind. Landry came up with it in part to counter Lombardi's power sweep. "The Flex Defense was a gap defense," Hall of Fame defensive tackle Bob Lilly said in *Cowboys Have Always Been My Heroes: The Definitive Oral History of America's Team.* "A lot of teams back in those days played a gap defense where the men were actually *in* the gaps. They had a defender between center and guard and another one between guard and tackle. The defensive end was out wide, and the linebackers were in the gaps that weren't covered. Therefore, the guy in front of you knew exactly what you were going to do. But with the Flex, what we tried to do was to disguise it, to keep our strategy from the offensive linemen."

Lilly's short-area quickness was the key to the Flex's success against the sweep. Lilly could run past the pulling guard and keep pace with the halfback, preventing the center from blocking him out of the play. When the Cowboys started alternating Flex looks with more standard 4-3 fronts, Lilly found an additional outlet for his rare talents, and Dallas' defense started to become great.

Landry also augmented his offensive pre-snap motions with an offensive line move he called "the hitch." Before the snap Landry's offensive linemen were directed to stand up out of their stances and then return their hands to the field. The idea here was to give defenses pause because they couldn't see the total pre-snap shift. He revived the shotgun formation and made it a working part of his offense when nearly every other coach in the NFL thought it to be a weird notion. He toyed with slot receivers and slot defenders a full generation before both concepts became *de rigueur.*

Still, Landry had complications to deal with. When he became the Cowboys' head coach in 1960, he spent the first few years of his tenure trying to assemble the kind of team on offense and defense that could execute his schemes. Lombardi had inherited a team with a ton of future Hall of Fame talent in need of direction, primarily thanks to super scout Jack Vainisi, who had stocked the personnel cupboard before Lombardi's entrance with names like Bart Starr, Paul Hornung, Jim Taylor, Boyd Dowler, Max McGee, Henry Jordan, Ray Nitschke, Emlen Tunnell, Jerry Kramer, Forrest Gregg, and Jim Ringo. Landry, on the other hand, had castoffs from the other NFL teams and a talent pool further diminished by the arrival of the American Football League in 1960.

So, the early years were a bit rough. Landry's Cowboys didn't have a winning record until 1966, the first season the Cowboys tried to upset the Packers in the NFL Championship Game. Landry had the advantage of his own personnel acumen, as well as the Cowboys' revolutionary use of computers to help them scour the country for ideal talent, but it took a while.

The Packers were Landry's first *bete noire*. The Pittsburgh Steelers of the 1970s were his second—the other team that stole the idea of a dynasty away from him and took it as their own. Pittsburgh beat Dallas in two Super Bowls—21–17 in Super Bowl X and 35–31 in Super Bowl XIII. Landry's teams lost two of the most thrilling championship games in any sport to one of the greatest series of teams of all time. No shame in that, but players on both teams pointed to Landry's adherence to complexity as an unintentional weakness. "Shoot, there was no big mystery about how to beat the Flex," Steelers quarterback Terry Bradshaw said in *The Last Cowboy*. "You throw on first down. The corners were almost always man-to-man on first down because the Flex was geared to stop the run. I almost felt sorry for their cornerbacks. I had Lynn Swann and John Stallworth out there and all I had to do was throw the ball, and they'd go get it."

Cowboys safety Cliff Harris had his own issues in retrospect. "We overprepared for the Steelers," he said in *The Super '70s: Memories from Pro Football's Greatest Era.* "We overanalyzed them. The Steelers had a very basic, fundamental offensive attack. Smart, but fundamental and basic, and that's a real tribute to their coaching staff. On the other hand, we had very complex offensive and defensive schemes. There were a lot of reads and shifts. We out-thought ourselves and, as a result, we weren't as physically aggressive as we needed to be to beat that team. If we'd played the defenses that worked for us the best, we would've had better success against them. You had to match the Steelers blow-for-blow, man-for-man. You couldn't stand there all day and take their roundhouses all day and expect to knock them out with a sucker punch."

Harris pointed to the preparation for Super Bowl XIII, in particular, as an instance in which the Steelers were able to execute their way through Dallas' defensive labyrinth. "I was very discouraged by the complexity of the schemes our coaches were preparing for us," he said. "They overloaded us. Jack Lambert once said, 'When you play the Cowboys, you feel like they're trying to trick you.' There may have been some truth to that statement. Preparation can be a good thing, and it was definitely one of the strengths of the Cowboys of the 1970s. We prepared well and knew teams' tendencies and went out and demolished them. Three years earlier, in Super Bowl X, our scheme wasn't nearly as complex, and we played Pittsburgh much closer and could have won the ballgame."

In the Cowboys' 1969 divisional playoff loss to the Cleveland Browns, Landry changed the defensive gameplan before the game, alternating Otto Brown and Mel Renfro between safety and cornerback to cover receiver Paul Warfield. The Browns went after Otto Brown, and Warfield caught eight passes for 99 yards. "That just confused everybody, and everybody had a lack of confidence in what we were doing because we hadn't had the time to get any repetitions on the field with it," said linebacker Lee Roy Jordan, who played for Landry from 1963 through 1976. "Once you work on something for two or three days and feel like, 'This is our best plan, let's go with it, it's going to work for us,' then you have to let football players take care of the little things that happen during the course of the game—those one-play deals or an occasional play."

After that 38–14 loss, the Cowboys headed down to the Playoff Bowl—a game between playoff losing teams for third place in the NFL, which was played in the 1960s—to face the Rams in Los Angeles, and his players begged him to let them run a less complicated defense. Throw out the Flex, they said, and let us use our instincts. Dallas lost 31–0, and that was the end of that.

There were times when Landry's complexities got in the way of the visceral nature of the game, but more often he was able to maximize the potential of his players due to an uncanny instinct for opponent tendencies brought about by a lifetime of obsessive film study. Dick Nolan, who played in the Giants' secondary from 1954 through 1957 and again from 1959 through 1961, also played his final season in Dallas in 1962. Nolan then coached the San Francisco 49ers from 1968 through 1975 and the New Orleans Saints from 1978 through 1980. He knew Landry very well as both coach and player and once recalled Landry's absolute certainty when it came to what an opponent would do. When Landry was the Giants' defensive coordinator, there was a "what if" slogan for which he was known. Nolan and his teammates would test Landry on that hypothetical all the time. "One time, he drove me crazy," Nolan recalled. "He said a certain thing would happen, and I said, 'But what if the guy does this instead of that?'"

"He won't," was the inevitable response.

"Okay, but let's say he does. Then what?"

"He won't."

"But what if he did?"

Landry looked at Nolan with his usual calm demeanor and insisted, "He won't."

Nolan laughed at the memory and said, "He was right most of the time. And if he wasn't, he wouldn't admit it."

Landry was right more often than not because, like Paul Brown and Gillman, he elevated the art of tape study to decipher what an opponent would do. He filled his defensive playbooks with keys or tendencies the opponent would give away in a repetitive fashion. He drilled his players on these keys over and over, though he wasn't always aware of the ones he was giving away. The most famous example came in the Ice Bowl. Speed receiver Bob Hayes, trying in vain to protect himself from the subzero temperatures in Green Bay, put his hands in his pants before every run play.

What caused Landry's demise, and the subsequent regression of the Cowboys in the 1980s, was that Landry stopped innovating, and the rest of the league caught up to him. Advanced from Gillman, Don Coryell had his expansive three-digit passing game and the Roving Y tight end. Walsh had his West Coast Offense, which was to become the new standard in the NFL for the next number of decades. Buddy Ryan brought a new aggression to defensive football with the 46 Defense and the Bear Front, sending seemingly endless linemen and linebackers after the quarterback. The Cincinnati Bengals and Buffalo Bills toyed with hurry-up offenses in different ways. Landry brought mostly the same old songs, and while that worked for a time, it was only because he was so far ahead of the league for so many years.

Perhaps the most glaring example of the unfortunate fact that the game had passed Landry by came on November 17, 1985, when Mike Ditka's Bears employed Ryan's defense to beat the daylights out of Landry's team in a 44–0 shellacking. It was the worst defeat in franchise history at that time and the first time the Cowboys had been shut out since 1970. Ditka, who served under Landry for 13 years as a player and coach, was not happy about the win because it came at the expense of a man he truly admired. The Cowboys were 7–3 before the Bears debacle; they finished the 1985 season with a 10–6 record and lost to the Rams in the divisional round of the playoffs.

The Cowboys never had another winning season under Landry. The franchise finished 7–9 in 1986 and 7–8 in 1987, bottoming out in 1988 with a 3–13 mark. Then, Jerry Jones bought the Cowboys and unceremoniously fired Landry in favor of Jimmy Johnson. Like Landry a generation ago, Johnson was a young, brilliant, aggressive coach whose schematic acumen and knack for personnel moves would lead to impressive success.

It was a sad end to Landry's career and it can be argued that in the years since Landry hasn't received the credit he deserves for the concepts he either brought to the NFL, revived, or perfected over time. He wasn't one to trumpet his genius. More interested in the perfection of the game than the forwarding of his own legacy, Landry was a stoic engineer to the end. But Landry's influence upon the NFL's current concepts were as great or perhaps greater than about any coach in the history of pro football.

CHAPTER 5

MERGED
The NFL in the 1970s

"There's a philosopher who says:
'As you live your life, it appears to be anarchy and chaos
and random events—non-related events—smashing into
each other and causing this situation. And then this
happens, and it's overwhelming, and it looks like what in
the world is going on? Later, when you look back at it, it
looks like a finely-crafted novel. But at the time? It don't."'
—musician Joe Walsh

With the American Football League folding into the
NFL in time for the 1970 season, the number of NFL
teams grew from 16 to 26, and the sheer volume of
coaching and player talent saw a spike heretofore unparalleled
in the game's evolution. Unsurprisingly, the decade was rife with
innovation, though the long-term effects of those innovations
were more subtle than in later times. The game was still about
ground and pound and defense to a great degree, but the 1970s
saw some of the all-time great iterations of those philosophies. By
the end of the 1970s, the NFL shape-shifted into the precursors
of the pass-heavy schemes we see today, but there were a ton of

hammer and tong games to get the league to that point. At the start of the decade, the game was still about pure power and who wielded it.

Don Shula

Don Shula was a winner for a long time before he was recognized as such. He was a defensive back for the Cleveland Browns, Baltimore Colts, and Washington Redskins from 1951 through 1957, racking up 21 interceptions in 73 games before starting his coaching career at the University of Virginia and University of Kentucky in the late 1950s and moving up to the NFL as the Detroit Lions' defensive coordinator in 1962. The Colts hired him as their head man in 1963, and Shula built one of the best defenses of all time in Baltimore. The 1968 Colts defense was the lead dog on a team that went 13–1 in the regular season and destroyed the Browns, the only team to beat the Colts in the regular season, in the 1968 NFL Championship Game. Shula's Colts were double-digit favorites to take apart the New York Jets in Super Bowl III, but everyone remotely familiar with NFL history knows how that turned out: the Jets earned the first win for the American Football League by a 16–7 margin, and the Colts were on the wrong side of what was then the biggest upset in sports history.

The following year showed the cracks that loss caused. Baltimore managed just eight wins and missed the playoffs; moreover, Shula found it tougher and tougher to get his message across. Before the 1970 season, Miami Dolphins owner Joe Robbie contacted the Colts about acquiring Shula, a process that ended with Shula moving to Miami, and the Dolphins being penalized their 1970 first-round pick for violating the NFL's tampering rules. The Colts took running back Don McCauley with that extra first rounder in 1971. McCauley ran for 2,627 yards and scored 40 touchdowns during his 11-year career; Shula won 257 regular-season games and 17 postseason games for the Dolphins over 26 years. It's safe to say the Dolphins got the better end of that deal.

Shula inherited a fine Miami team in many respects, especially for a young franchise that did not benefit from the league's later adjustments to help expansion franchises. Shula, through the auspices of Joe Thomas, the general manager from 1965 through 1971, walked in the door for that 1970 season with quarterback Bob Griese; running backs Larry Csonka, Jim Kiick and Eugene "Mercury" Morris; offensive linemen Larry Little and Norm Evans; defensive tackle Manny Fernandez; linebacker Nick Buoniconti; and safety Dick Anderson as starters. The 1970 draft brought defensive backs Jake Scott, Curtis Johnson, and tight end Jim Mandich. Through management of the existing roster and a real knack for picking up otherwise jettisoned players from around the league—the 1970 trade with the Browns for receiver Paul Warfield was particularly lopsided in Miami's favor—Shula's Dolphins went 10–4 and lost to the Oakland Raiders in the first AFC divisional playoffs, a huge improvement from 1969's 3–10–1 mark. In 1971 Miami went 10–3–1 and lost Super Bowl VI to the Dallas Cowboys 24–3. It was a second Super Bowl humiliation for Shula, who told his team after the game that they never wanted to feel like that again. He started the 1972 season, according to Csonka and several other players, by predicting a perfect 17–0 season, which, of course, actually happened.

Shula's developmental teams, and the perfect team that followed, were typical of early 1970s teams in that Griese only threw when he had to, the run game was the fulcrum of the offense, and the defense, run by Bill Arnsparger, was a combination of man and zone coverage that was more mistake-proof than flashy at any time. Shula was a football fundamentalist above all else and he drilled that into his new charges from Day One. Shula claimed to be about as subtle as a punch in the mouth, and that's how he ran things. Former Dolphins head coach George Wilson let things go easy, but Shula had his guys practicing four times a day—a move that would cause open player revolt in the modern era. He created a culture of accountability and toughness the Dolphins hadn't known before, and that combined with the talent on board created the first great dynasty of the 1970s.

Arnsparger's "No-Name Defense" was recognized as the key to Miami's success, but the true base of the offense in Shula's early Miami years was an offensive line that ranked among the best in NFL history and the influence blocking that set things up for Csonka, Kiick, and Morris. Perhaps the finest distillation of that strategy came in Miami's 24–7 win against the Minnesota Vikings in Super Bowl VIII—Shula's second straight Super Bowl win, following the 14–7 victory in Super Bowl VII against the Washington Redskins. Many believe that '73 team was actually better than the '72 undefeated version despite the fact that the former lost two games that year. The Vikings' Purple People Eaters defense was historically great, especially along a defensive line that featured ends Jim Marshall and Carl Eller and tackle Alan Page. It was a ruthlessly fast and powerful front that forced opposing lines into a seemingly unsolvable problem—how can you deal with demon speed and elite leverage at the same time?

Armed with a terrifically schooled bunch of blockers, Shula decided to use the Vikings' aggressiveness against them—much like the Kansas City Chiefs had done in Super Bowl IV. Shula had faced more than enough of that in his last Super Bowl loss, when the Cowboys riddled a younger and less disciplined Dolphins defense for 252 yards on the ground, using traps and counters and draws in Super Bowl VI. Against the Redskins the next year, Miami's defense exhibited correct gap control and angular assignments to crush Washington's cut-back run game, and Larry Brown gained just 72 yards on 22 carries. Now, it was the offense's turn to take a great defense to the woodshed with complex blocking concepts that represented a sea change forward from the old Packers power sweep.

Shula had implemented these run schemes before—but never to this level of effectiveness. "Going into Super Bowl VIII against the Vikings, we felt that one of the critical areas of the ballgame would be the ability of our offensive line to handle Minnesota's great defensive line," Shula told NFL Films in the game's highlight reel. "They predicate everything on coming off the ball as fast as they possibly can. We felt that we were going to be able to take advantage of this tremendous quickness by cross-blocking. On our cross-block, our left tackle, Wayne Moore, comes down

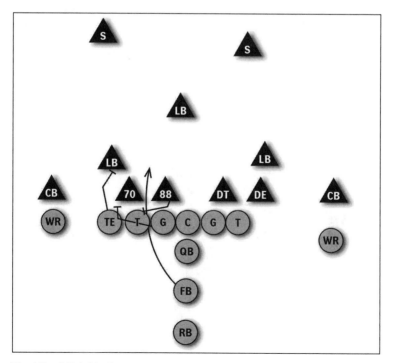

The Miami Dolphins' cross-block during Super Bowl XIII

hard on Alan Page [No. 88]. If [Page] is sliding to the inside, he takes himself out of the play. If he's sliding to the outside, he's coming right into the area that [left tackle] Wayne Moore is blocking down, and this nullifies his outside slant. [Left guard Bob] Kuechenberg on this play lets Wayne Moore go first, and then he pulls outside and blocks out on their defensive end [No. 70 Jim Marshall]. The play was very effective, and it's only because the cross-block was the type of blocking that should be used against these hard-charging defensive linemen."

Throughout all these plays, the theory was not only that Minnesota's defensive line could be negated by using its speed against itself, though that was one more common constraint. Shula and his staff also devised ways in which the veteran acumen of

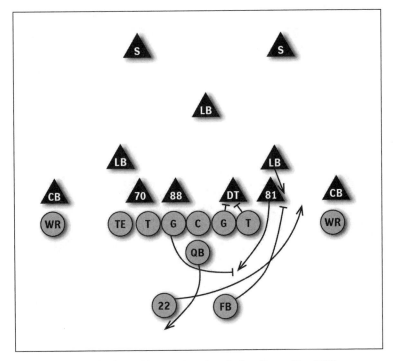

The Miami Dolphins' outside running play during Super Bowl XIII

the Purple People Eaters could be used to their advantage. "There were two plays we had in the game to take advantage of the experience of Carl Eller and Jim Marshall," Shula said. "Eller [No. 81] and Marshall have been playing so long. Every time they read the blocking pattern of the offensive line, they react instinctively to this blocking pattern. The play starts out as a trap on the defensive end [Eller], and when the defensive end reads and reacts tough to the inside, the ball carrier, instead of cutting inside, continues to the outside. We made everything look like it was the inside trap play and, when Eller closed to the inside, we still were able to get the ball outside to Mercury Morris, and it was a very effective play. Another way we were able to make the defensive line hesitate was misdirection. The offensive linemen would pull in one direction, and the backs start out like they're going in that direction, and then Larry Csonka comes back with the football against the flow."

Misdirection was a more common thing—Csonka running against the tide of the line when holes opened up with the flow—but it worked just as well, as did most concepts with a Miami offensive line that should not have been as great as it was. Moore was an undrafted player out of Furman. Kuechenberg was a castoff from the Philadelphia Eagles, who had to find his way with the Chicago Owls of the Continental Football League before Shula came calling. Center Jim Langer was another undrafted player (from another smaller school, South Dakota State). Right guard Larry Little was a free agent who was signed by the San Diego Chargers and then traded to Miami. And right tackle Norm Evans was a 14th round pick of the Houston Oilers in 1965, who was taken by Miami in the 1966 expansion draft. Little became a Hall of Famer, and Langer and Kuechenberg made six Pro Bowls. As Little said years later, it was about working together, fundamentals, and domination. Line coach Monte Clark was Shula's voice among the front five.

And in the second half of Super Bowl VIII, when the Vikings looked for all manner of misdirection, the Dolphins reverted to a brutal man-on-man blocking strategy. Minnesota never knew what hit it—figuratively or literally—and the Dolphins won 24–7. It was as decisive a signature win as the Cowboys had been against the Dolphins two years before. "I have never seen a more dominating team than the Miami Dolphins," Eller told NFL Films. "All afternoon I had the feeling that the outcome had already been decreed on high before we even took the field. It seemed I could hear Scottish bagpipes in the distance, keeping time as they came after us, wave after wave, gaining ground so easily. They seemed to be floating in suspended animation."

Reality was a bit tougher for the Dolphins as the decade wore on. Thomas was fired by Robbie after the 1971 season. Shula displayed a great deal of personnel acumen while coaching Miami through the 1995 season and becoming the winningest coach in NFL history, but he never won another Super Bowl.

There were other offenses with great blockers and schemes during this era, of course. The Pittsburgh Steelers of the 1970s, for example, had a trap play that was a thing of beauty. But the Steelers in this decade would become the first NFL dynasty in which the entire defense was the star of the show.

The Steel Curtain

The two men who started the Pittsburgh Steelers' evolution from 40-year losers to the greatest team of the 1970s arrived in the Steel City within 24 hours of each other, and it took each of them a while to be valued for who they would become. New head coach Chuck Noll, a former guard for the Cleveland Browns in the 1950s and assistant coach for the Los Angeles/San Diego Chargers and the Baltimore Colts in the 1960s, was officially hired on January 27, 1969, two weeks and a day after the Colts, who had Noll on their staff throughout the 1968 season, were shocked by the New York Jets in Super Bowl III. "I worked with three great men—Paul Brown, Sid Gillman, and Don Shula," Noll said at his introductory press conference. "I hope something from those three has rubbed off on me."

It had. Noll was not a motivator; he was a taskmaster. He famously told his players that if he had to motivate them, he would simply get rid of them and get people who did not need that kind of push. Like Shula, Noll played for the Browns in the 1950s; he was one of Paul Brown's messenger guards, who rotated in the lineup and brought Brown's plays to the quarterback. And like Shula, Noll had experienced historical disappointment at the hands of the Jets in Super Bowl III. He was Shula's defensive assistant in 1968, and that Super Bowl loss eclipsed the fact that the 1968 Colts tied the NFL record for fewest points allowed at 144. "Chuck was just a natural teacher," Shula said of Noll in 2008. "He explained how to do things and wrote up the techniques. He was one of the first coaches I was around that wrote up in great detail all of the techniques used by players—for example, the backpedal and the defensive back's position on the receiver. He was like a classroom teacher. He used a lot of those techniques as a football coach."

It was an outgrowth of the Paul Brown approach, and Noll took it with him to Pittsburgh. Linebacker Andy Russell, who had made the Pro Bowl in 1968 as one of the few bright spots on a mordantly bad team, expected more positive praise than he got from Noll. But his new coach dressed Russell down individually for his aggressively undisciplined play and then ripped the existing Steelers team a collective new one in his first training camp speech. "He said, 'I've been watching game films since I got the job,'" Russell told NFL Films. "'And I can tell you the reason you've been losing is not because of your attitude or any of that stuff. The problem is you're not good enough. You can't run fast enough, you can't jump high enough, you're not quick enough. Your techniques are abysmal, and I'm probably going to have to get rid of most of you. We're going to move on.'"

Noll wasn't kidding. Russell was one of five players to make it from that speech to the Steelers' first Super Bowl at the end of the 1974 season. Joe Greene was obviously one of those players, but as an early holdout, he had raised the ire of the veterans on the team, who couldn't wait to get hold of the rookie during training camp. Center Ray Mansfield, another veteran and a third member of that five-man survivor crew, was the first to take on Greene in the Oklahoma drill. It was *mano a mano*. Greene completely demolished Mansfield and put the rest of the offensive line on notice. As fellow defensive lineman L.C. Greenwood, a 10th round pick in 1969 later recalled, you could see those blockers moving as far away from Greene as possible.

Greene grew up in Texas and he was angry for all kinds of reasons. He was angry at the racism he experienced. He was angry because opponents, going back to his high school days, couldn't beat him fair and square, so they'd hold him and play mind games. And he was especially angry about the Steelers' early losing years. It was unsettling at times, but in that anger, Greene showed his teammates that winning was the point of the whole exercise. A less talented man wouldn't get away with it, but Greene backed up everything he said.

He brought that unique rage to the field, and it took a while for Noll to get him under control. In Greene's rookie year, Dick Butkus had poleaxed Greenwood on a special teams play and stood over his man in triumph. Greene walked over to Butkus, screamed a few well-chosen words, and spit right in Butkus' face. Butkus walked off the field without complaint, and with that, the title of the Toughest Man in Football changed hands. During a loss to the

Philadelphia Eagles in 1970, Greene became so frustrated with his own team's performance—and the fact that the officials weren't calling enough holding penalties to his liking—that he picked up the ball and threw it into the stands. But he was already a great player, who would soon carve his name in the pantheon of all-time greats. And he was just the first of many such greats to come down the pike in Noll's first five seasons. "When Noll arrived we became great drafters," Art Rooney II said in *The Super '70s*. "Before that we weren't. Our methodology was in place, but he was the balance that made the difference. He was very difficult to work with because he was so exacting." Noll engaged in extensive debriefing sessions with the team's scouts after practices and had his hand in every aspect of the team's development.

The Steelers' mode of construction wasn't unique, but it was ridiculously successful. Most teams in the pre-free agency days were homegrown for the simple reason that it was far easier to retain one's own talent from year to year. And several teams, most notably the 1960s Kansas City Chiefs with scout Lloyd Wells, had started to mine smaller black colleges for talent. This—and the pragmatic sense of equality espoused by head coach Hank Stram— allowed the Chiefs to develop a far more racially diverse roster to highly positive ends. But the combination of Noll, super scout Bill Nunn, and the team's scouting staff led by then-director of player personnel and now president and co-owner Rooney II put together a list of amazing talent from 1969 through 1974. That final year was unquestionably the best single draft class in NFL history.

Greene, Greenwood, and offensive tackle Jon Kolb came aboard in 1969. The 1970 class added two Hall of Famers— quarterback Terry Bradshaw and cornerback Mel Blount. In 1971 linebacker Jack Ham and the other two fundamental members of the Steel Curtain front four—Ernie Holmes and Dwight White—came aboard. Running back Franco Harris, key reserve defensive tackle Steve Furness (who came in frequently when the Steelers went to their passing-down sub-packages sometimes featuring three down linemen) were drafted in 1972. Cornerback J.T. Thomas made the roster out of the 1973 draft, which was otherwise unimpressive in comparison, but Pittsburgh made up for that with authority in 1974. Four Hall of Famers—receivers Lynn Swann, John Stallworth, linebacker Jack Lambert, and center Mike Webster—came out of the same draft class. No team before or since can brag of such a haul. The Steelers also found success with undrafted players like unheralded safety Donnie Shell, who came to the team from South Carolina State and made five Pro Bowls and three first-team All-Pro teams while intercepting 51 passes during his career.

Nunn, a former sportswriter and editor for the *Pittsburgh Courier*, was a big part of the paper's "Black College All-American" team, which started in 1950. A friend of Art Rooney Sr. talked him into hiring Nunn as a part-time scout, which made Rooney II "pissed purple," as he put it, because he wanted to hire the scouts. But Nunn proved his specific worth immediately. Not only did he have a fine eye for talent, but he also had contacts at smaller black colleges and opened that pipeline for the Steelers. Eventually, Nunn was responsible for scouting or signing seven Super Bowl starters: Stallworth, Holmes, Blount, Greenwood, Shell, Frank Lewis, and Sam Davis. "Nunn quickly became very important to me," the younger Rooney recalled later. "At first, it was just his contacts, then it was his insight, then his dry humor. Before long he became a fine scout of all players. His agenda matured. He had to win, no matter if the prospect was black, white, blue, or green."

So by the time defensive coordinator Bud Carson arrived in 1972, the Steelers had the perfect personnel to run the Cover-2 as a base concept. The base idea of the zone defense wasn't original; it had spread over multiple teams in the previous decade in the

NFL. But for the most part, the root coverage concepts before the Cover-2 were either three-deep zone with a box safety or straight man-to-man coverage. Carson had put together his own defense while he was the head coach at Georgia Tech from 1967 through 1971. He amassed a 27–27 record there and found it tough to replace the legendary Bobby Dodd. But he impressed the exacting Noll during an eight-hour interview. After the talk Carson became the only assistant coach Noll ever hired the same day of an interview. It proved to be a perfect match.

The Cover-2

Bud Carson shared Chuck Noll's passion for discipline on the field. His defense only would work through understanding and discipline; this was not a system for freelancers. Noll foresaw an NFL, in which receiver formations and routes would become more complex and he wanted a defensive coordinator who could match this ideology. Back in his college days, Carson had implemented the Cover-2 as a run defense against various option offenses because his cornerbacks were pressing at the line of scrimmage and reading run, and it created what was essentially a nine-man front. When Carson brought the Cover-2 to Pittsburgh, things changed a bit—and became much more advanced. Now, Carson's cornerbacks would aggressively jam receivers at the line of scrimmage, both forcing those receivers to alter the angles and timing of their routes and creating mismatches in the run game when those receivers were tasked to block bigger cornerbacks. This worked because J.T. Thomas (6'1" and 196 pounds) and Mel Blount (6'3" and 205 pounds) combined game intelligence, athleticism, and intimidation in perfect doses.

Cornerbacks in Carson's Cover-2 were far more than hitmen, though, and Blount took the brunt of Carson's famous invective early in his career when he freelanced more than he stuck with the plan. Early on, Blount and Thomas wanted to play aggressive man-to-man more than they should have and occasionally found themselves schooled by the game's better receivers. More specifically, Carson required that his cornerbacks use their physical style of play and athletic talent to re-route the receivers to the safeties.

Meanwhile, Jack Lambert, who was the key to the Cover-2's intermediate defensive concepts, proved equally adept at covering a tight end up the seam or attacking a running back through the gaps provided by Pittsburgh's astonishingly great front four. From his rookie year on, Lambert was asked to do things that players at his position would generally find unusual. "Bud had me do things that middle linebackers had never done before, especially in pass coverage," Lambert said in *The Games That*

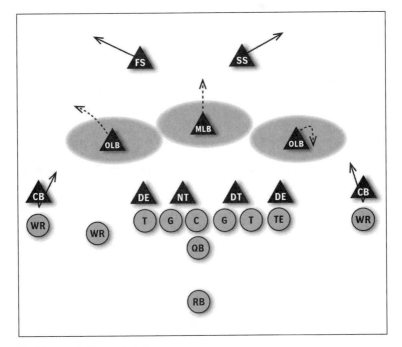

Bud Carson's Cover-2 defense

Changed the Game. "He had me covering tight ends man-to-man, covering halfbacks in a spread formation. He had us doubling wide receivers."

As Lambert noted, such things were not done by his Hall of Fame predecessors like Ray Nitschke, Dick Butkus, and Willie Lanier. And Lambert was a different breed of cat, playing at 6'4" and 215 pounds—soaking wet. Not only did Lambert scrape the seam and take tight end and running backs out in coverage, he also read blocking fronts expertly and used an innate understanding of the game bolstered by obsessive film study to blast through and attack ball carriers in the backfield. Perhaps the best example of this came in Pittsburgh's 21–17 win against the Dallas Cowboys in Super Bowl X, when Joe Greene was dealing with injuries, and Lambert had to be the one to supply constant heat up the middle. He finished the game with 14 tackles.

Were it not for Lynn Swann's all-time acrobatic catches, Lambert might have been named the game's Most Valuable Player. And linebacker Jack Ham could do anything Lambert could do— possibly to an even higher degree. Pittsburgh's linebackers and safeties rarely had to blitz because the foursome of Greene, Ernie Holmes, L.C. Greenwood, and Dwight White simply overpowered opposing offensive lines. "It was not so much what we did. It was the way we did it," White said in *Their Life's Work: The Brotherhood of the 1970s Pittsburgh Steelers, Then and Now.* "We kicked their asses very thoroughly."

And in any great Cover-2 or Tampa-2 defense since then (like the Tampa Bay Buccaneers or the Chicago Bears of the early 2000s), the ability of the front four to disrupt without help from the back seven was of primary importance. It allowed everyone from the intermediate to deep pass defense to stay with their assignments and avoid freelancing. It allowed Andy Russell to develop what he called the "hug-em-up" move, where he pretended to blitz, freezing a releasing back from heading into his designed route. And it allowed Ham (who may have been the best linebacker on the team) to use his incredible field vision and athleticism to shut down even more potential pass plays.

Members of Pittsburgh's front four have argued with the guys in the back seven for decades as to whether the Steel Curtain refers to the four guys on the line or the entire defense. Certainly, no other part of the defense would have worked without the efforts of what was probably the finest defensive line the NFL has ever seen. Greene was obviously the rock star, and his unearthly combination of strength, burst, and speed to the ball carrier was something the league hadn't seen before—or perhaps since. Not only was Greene the alpha on the field in a physical sense; he was also in charge of communicating all front adjustments and stunts, and the Steelers of that era stunted a ton. It was hard enough to deal with Greene, White, Greenwood, and Holmes when they stayed put in their usual positions. Trying to keep them at bay when they were moving to different gaps in concert was just about impossible.

The real Steel Curtain was also hard to attack because they worked so well together, but each member of that front four was different. Greenwood at left end moved like a tight end and was so big (6'6", 245 pounds) that White used to say that when you wanted to block him that you had to decide which half of him to start with. But White at right end was an even bigger, more riotous player. He came to the field with a tank-sized chip on his shoulder. It was White who would dispense *bon mots* such as: "You can take this ass-whooping any way you like, but you're gonna take it!" And right tackle Holmes at 6'3" and 260 pounds may have been the most frightening of them all. With his thousand-yard stare and forward-facing arrowhead shaved into his hair, he looked like a Bond villain. He was not as fast and flexible as Greene, though he

was every bit as strong and perhaps even stronger. At the start of
the peak of the Steel Curtain's efforts, Greene came up with a tactic
that raised the stakes even higher.

The Stunt 4-3

At some point in 1974, Joe Greene proposed to defensive line
coach George Perles that he should position himself at the shoulder of the center at a 45-degree angle in order to blow through any
blocks and devour any ball carriers in his path. Bud Carson and
Chuck Noll obviously had to sign off on it and they did so after
seeing how Greene was able to saw through centers and guards in
practice. Greene became an even more unblockable force than he

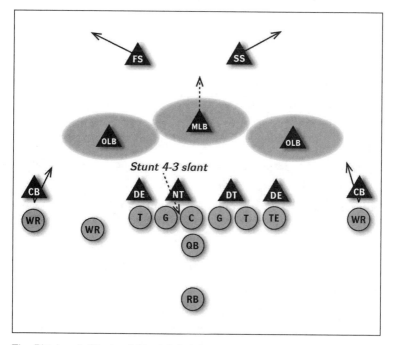

The Pittsburgh Steelers' Stunt 4-3 defense

had been before, and what became known as the "Stunt 4-3" was born. "This offset alignment was something Joe developed himself out of frustration," Andy Russell said in *The Games That Changed the Game*. "He hated to get blocked and wanted to make plays. So it occurred to him that because he was so quick, he should just line up inside between the center and the guard, tip his shoulder sideways, and when the ball was snapped, he'd dart through the hole. He was supposed to line up on the guard. [But] he jumped in the gap between the guard and center, tilted his body, and just blew through that gap, and it was devastating. It was beautiful to see."

Perles further explained the strategy in the book, *Defensive Football Strategies*. "We take our strong-side tackle and put him in the gap between the center and the guard," he said. "He gets into a stance that allows him to hug the ball. He keeps his inside leg back to a point where we don't worry about lining up offside. Normally, we can hug the ball [in formation space] as much as we want. Since the center can't back off the ball, he can't do much about it."

The Pittsburgh Steelers utilized Greene in the Stunt 4-3 more and more through the 1974 season but really unleashed him against the Oakland Raiders in the 1974 AFC Championship Game. It would become the entry into Pittsburgh's first of four Super Bowl titles in a six-year stretch, but it wasn't going to be easy. Oakland led the league in points scored and point differential in 1974 and had derailed the two-time Super Bowl champion Miami Dolphins the week before in the divisional round.

It didn't take long for the new scheme to provide dividends. On the third play of the game, Raiders quarterback Ken Stabler took a standard seven-step drop and found Greene all over him before he could scan the field and go through his reads. Greene had beaten the double team of center Jim Otto, a Hall of Famer in his own right, and right guard George Buehler, of whom teammate John Matuszak said in *Cruisin' with The Tooz*, "We felt that he blocked Joe Greene better than anyone in the league." Not in this case. Otto and Buehler rose from the snap to double-team Greene, but Greene not only came off the ball in the stunt angle, he also turned his shoulders to make himself smaller and therefore even harder to block. He threw Otto to the ground, karate-kicked his way past Buehler, and came away with a sack of Stabler as his reward. "One moment, Greene and Otto were head to head and then they formed a blur together, and then Otto was more or less where he had been, only lying down," Roy Blount Jr. wrote. "And Greene was entangled with the Oakland backfield in a pile."

The Raiders tried different strategies—cut blocks and traps were the order of the day—throughout the game to deal with a Stunt 4-3 they really hadn't seen before, but Greene was simply too fast and too strong for enemy blockers to deal with. That was true before, but the Stunt 4-3 turned Greene into a next-level force. One advantage the Stunt 4-3 presented (and still presents to this day) is that it forces offensive lines into geometric equations they aren't equipped to handle. "It's really been around more than you noticed," Seattle Seahawks head coach Pete Carroll told me in 2013. "It's just a style of play. Some guys are better playing square-shouldered, and some guys can play cocked like that. Brandon [Mebane] has a good feel for that and he utilizes it really well. It's really a style of player, and our coaching is looking for what guys do well. Brandon does a really good job when he's offset like that."

That alignment was part of the Seahawks' defense even before Carroll showed up. Mebane said that he learned it years before from teammates Rocky Bernard and Chuck Darby before taking it to a new level when Dan Quinn and Carroll got hold of him. "It just provides a good view," Mebane said simply of the technique.

However, it's a misnomer to say that the Steelers' Cover-2 exactly resembled the Cover-2 concepts implemented in the 1990s through today. Befitting the run heavy offenses of the time, Pittsburgh's base formation on run downs looked more like a six-man front pre-snap with Russell and Jack Ham at the line, allowing the two linebackers to respond accordingly to backs either moving out of the backfield to catch screens and swing passes or help with run support. Now, you'll see far more of the 4-3-4 setup Pittsburgh used as a passing defense.

Safety Mike Wagner said that the two teams that gave the Steelers of the 1970s the most trouble on defense were the Cincinnati Bengals of Paul Brown and Bill Walsh—because of the timing-based passing game that presaged the West Coast Offense—and Tom Landry's Dallas Cowboys because of their combination of raw talent and endless motions and shifts. These days, most offenses present a truly kaleidoscopic series of pre-snap problems for opposing defenses to solve, but such things were far less common back then. "They always tried to shake us up, but our coaches insisted we wouldn't let any offense dictate what our defense did," Wagner said in *The Super '70s: Memories from Pro Football's Greatest Era*.

Landry was one of the first NFL coaches to use pre-snap motion specifically to discern whether defenses were playing man or zone, and it was a brilliant response to the increase in zone-based defenses throughout the 1970s. The Bengals did the same, and Walsh began to build that same offensive mind-set with the San Francisco 49ers that would allow him to dominate the next decade.

It was generally a tough play for opposing defenses to read because of the formation and conceptual diversity. As exemplified in Super Bowl X, the play design was meant to fool the defense in multiple ways. Both Cowboys guards pulled after the snap. Left guard Burton Lawless did a little bucket step move to get in front of Roger Staubach and keep him protected, while right guard Blaine Nye pulled out to the right edge to stay in front of running back Preston Pearson, who motioned pre-snap from the left slot to the backfield in a pro-set, split-back formation. Fullback Robert Newhouse power blocked his way up the line. Preston Pearson was in a position to take a screen pass, which forced safety J.T. Thomas to keep one eye on him, and Drew Pearson exacerbated Thomas' assignment by running an inside over route from his initial position outside. With Thomas on a string and Pittsburgh's safeties playing back, Pearson had a wide berth to the end zone. It was the first touchdown the Steelers had allowed in the first quarter all season.

Based on their pregame examinations of the Dallas offense, the Steelers knew what was coming. They just couldn't stop it in this case due to a specific miscommunication. "The Cowboys

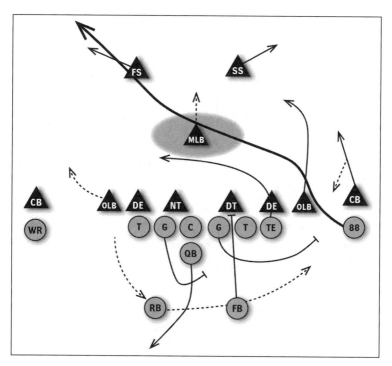

Dallas Cowboys wide receiver Drew Pearson's first-quarter touchdown in Super Bowl X

scored on a play, which we had studied, and I said, 'Gee, I think this play's going to happen with this formation,'" Wagner later recalled. "I'm trying to check out of the formation, and it was very noisy, so I wasn't comfortable that everybody was getting the checks. So as a safety, I decided to play it safe and I just backed up." Wagner then espoused a simple belief from then on: "If they run this play again, I'm not going to hesitate. I'm going to go."

That proved to be true, and Wagner's fourth-quarter interception of a Staubach pass from the same formation proved his ability to read the play, Carson's ability to adjust, and the Steelers' ability to bring their best in the biggest moments. With 8:32 left in the game and the Steelers up 12–10, Dallas tried to go back to the well with the same idea. This time Wagner cut into the zone void exploited by Pearson in the first quarter and came away with a vital interception that led to a Roy Gerela field goal and a 15–10 lead. "It was our bread-and-butter play all season," Staubach later said. "It was the first time it didn't work."

The Cowboys mounted their own furious comeback effort in the final moments, but Pittsburgh won the game 21–17 and had their second straight Super Bowl victory in check.

In the end that was the greatness of Carson's Cover-2—the capacity for adjustments in a highly disciplined structure. This was no vanilla zone defense with a handful of checks. Lambert told *Sports Illustrated* in 1974 that the Steelers had 30 different defensive situations in which the linebackers provided coverage, and Carson was legendary with his checks—pre-snap adjustments based on offensive formations and tendencies.

In that era most defenses would check to a basic zone in certain instances, but Carson's modus operandi was far more complex. The base defenses were numbered: "Defense No. 1," "Defense No. 2," and so on, but what Carson did not want was for his defenses to respond to pre-snap motion. He wanted his defenses to dictate the action at all times. Russell told of an instance in which the Steelers were facing the Bengals in the '70s, and Carson decided in the pregame tunnel to change all the checks he had given to the team on Friday. Then Carson told Russell that he believed Bengals offensive coordinator Bill Walsh was getting too much of a feel for what the Steelers were doing on defense. (Given Walsh's obvious football genius, that's entirely possible.) So for the rest of the game, Carson had his defense alternating the Friday checks and the Sunday checks on every series. "I'm not saying we were a bunch of rocket scientists, but if you didn't have some relatively smart guys on defense, we couldn't have done this," Russell said. He once told Walsh what had happened during that game, and Walsh was incredulous. "Now I understand why I couldn't figure out what you guys were doing," the great coach replied.

The apex of the Steel Curtain defense came in 1976, ironically a year in which the Steelers did not play in one of their four 1970s Super Bowls. In that season Pittsburgh pitched five shutouts in a 14-game season and allowed just 28 total points in its last nine games. However, Terry Bradshaw missed time in the first month of the season, the Steelers had to overcome a 1–4 start as a result, and both Franco Harris and Rocky Bleier were unavailable for the 1976 AFC Championship Game against the eventual Super Bowl champion Oakland Raiders.

From 1978 through the end of their reign, the Steelers would be as much or more about offense as defense, as rules changes allowed a new focus on the passing game, and the Steel Curtain aged without proper reinforcements. The early 1980s saw Noll move to a 3-4 defense to try and adjust to changing personnel in the college game, which was certainly a different philosophy than the one espoused back in the day when the Steelers had a decided advantage as a result of their awareness that small black colleges were teeming with NFL talent.

Tony Dungy, a reserve defensive back for the Steelers in 1977 and 1978, later took Carson's and Chuck Noll's philosophies about the Cover-2 defense and modernized them into the Tampa-2 system that took the league by storm in the late 1990s and early part of the new millennium. But in the moment, the 3-4 defense was about to have its way as a base defense for the first time in league history.

The 3-4 Defense

They say that history only remembers the winners, and that's certainly true in an unfortunate sense for two of the most interesting and successful teams of the 1970s—Chuck Fairbanks' New England Patriots and Bum Phillips' Houston Oilers. Neither team made the Super Bowl in the decade, but regardless of the vagaries of fate, each team brought different strains of the 3-4 base defense to the NFL and opened up the future of defensive play in truly groundbreaking ways.

From its invention by Tom Landry in the 1950s through the early 1970s, the 4-3 defense was the preferred base attack for most, if not all, professional teams. It was one thing the two leagues had in common in the 1960s. There, though, were a few schematic stragglers in the AFL. The Kansas City Chiefs of the late 1960s liked to use Junious "Buck" Buchanan, their 6'7", 270-pound tackle, in different gap concepts (especially the over stack or Triple Stack front that hung a variable lineman/linebacker on the edge, depending on the play), and the Oakland Raiders occasionally dropped end Dan Birdwell from the line to a linebacker position. Nobody in the NFL was using the 3-4 as a primary down-to-down defense until two men in the AFC—Fairbanks for the Patriots and Phillips for the Oilers changed that—in 1974. And Miami Dolphins defensive coordinator Bill Arnsparger had a huge impact as well.

The 53 Defense

Bill Arnsparger is best known for his time as the Miami Dolphins' defensive coordinator under Don Shula from 1970 through 1973 and again from 1976 through 1983. He was a great coach in other places at the high school, college, and pro levels, but it's his time with the Dolphins that bore the sweetest fruit from a historical perspective. Arnsparger and Shula first met on Blanton Collier's Kentucky staff in 1959, and when Shula became the Baltimore Colts' head coach in 1964, he tabbed Arnsparger as his defensive line coach. A promotion to defensive coordinator came soon after, when Charley Winner was asked to coach the St. Louis Cardinals before the 1966 season, and Arnsparger took his place. It was Arnsparger who helped Shula construct the 1968 Colts defense that tied the NFL mark with 144 points allowed in a 14-game season, a feat long forgotten after Baltimore's loss in Super Bowl III, and it was Arnsparger who followed Shula to Miami, when he took the Dolphins job in 1970. The 1972 Dolphins defense, the epicenter of the only undefeated team in NFL history, is thus credited equally to Arnsparger and Shula. The 1973 defense may have been even better—it allowed an unbelievable 15 touchdowns all season. But for our purposes, Arnsparger's primary achievement was the installation and execution of the 53 defense—a precursor to the 3-4 base defenses that would follow in the NFL.

In 1971 Arnsparger was the leader of a defensive squad that was coming together very nicely and had most of the root personnel that would help create the NFL's only perfect season. But before the '71 season, the coach had a problem—injuries had depleted his personnel and he had to adapt quickly. Defensive end James Riley was out of the picture, and Arnsparger saw something in linebacker Bob Matheson. A first-round pick of the Cleveland Browns in 1967, Matheson was betwixt and between with his first team, but Arnsparger told Shula to pick him up for very specific purposes. "The Browns played Bob at middle linebacker, and he was one of the best players in the league at that position," Arnsparger wrote in *Arnsparger's Coaching Defensive Football.* "Later, he added weight to the point that they virtually gave up on him as a linebacker and tried to use him as a defensive end. It was at this point that he became available to us. Bob joined us, and I immediately began meeting with him to catch up. Because of his background and intense desire to succeed, he was a success almost immediately."

Arnsparger named his new defense the "53" because it was Matheson's number. This meant that the Dolphins used a front

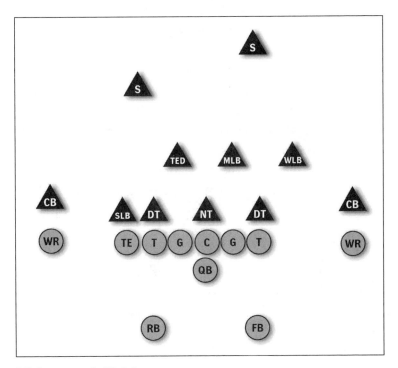

Bill Arnsparger's 53 defense

that looked like a 4-3 but with Matheson as a blitzer from the line in a three-man front. Matheson was a linebacker at the line with his hand off the ground but could bring additional end-style pressure from the strong or weak side. Eventually, as Arnsparger began to realize the value of the moveable chess piece he had, Matheson also blitzed from the inside.

It was a 30 Front defense with a nose tackle and two ends and Matheson in a strong-side linebacker/end designation. The TED and MIKE linebackers—the inside guys—flowed to the action and kept the middle of the field patrolled. The weak-side linebacker disguised his alignment depending on the call, stayed alert for the crack-back run concepts, and each linebacker was directed to play pass coverage in certain instances. It was a tremendously flexible system made great by the personnel Shula and Joe Thomas had put together.

There were other iterations of the 53. There was a 39 Over defense, in which Matheson, the right end, and the nose tackle either played their gaps against the run or blitzed against the pass. The 37 Over defense called for the TED linebacker to blitz. The 38 Under front was a variant of the 39 Over except that it was the nose tackle and the weakside linebacker who either played their gaps or blitzed, depending on the situation. The 36 Under call had the nose tackle and the MIKE linebacker blitzing if it was a pass. *Roger* and *Lou* calls were implemented against run heavy offenses or in predominant run situations. These were the even fronts, in which defenders would flow to the ball. It was a great advancement of previous instances, in which coaches directed their linemen and linebackers to force more diverse blocking schemes with their own multiple gap and attack ideas and it set the pace for the 3-4 base defense.

The Base 3-4

Chuck Fairbanks and Bum Phillips switched their fronts for different reasons, though both got the idea from the same source. Both men coached in Oklahoma before they hit the NFL—Fairbanks was Oklahoma's head coach from 1967 through 1972 before the New England Patriots hired him in 1973, and Phillips was an assistant at Oklahoma State before he was hired as the Houston Oilers' defensive coordinator in 1974 and promoted to head coach in 1975. It's no surprise that the impetus to bring the 3-4 to the pros came from two men who spent time in that state, as Oklahoma coaching legend Bud Wilkinson is the man most often credited with the invention of the 3–4 base defense, and Fairbanks learned it directly from Wilkinson.

As the 1970s began, the 3-4 defense was *de rigueur* in college football and thus it became more and more difficult to find the four down linemen it took to maintain a top-level 4-3 base front. "It was a move we had to make because of the depth on our team," said Phillips, who had actually tried to use the 3-4 with the San Diego Chargers in the late 1960s, much to Sid Gillman's dismay. "We could find four good linebackers—even if we had to use free agents. But you can't find many really good defensive linemen, and we only had two. And if you only have two, you'd better play a 3-4 rather than a 4–3. If you're stubborn and stick with a 4-3, then you're in trouble."

Fairbanks concurred, and a new strategy was born in the NFL. "At the time everyone in professional football thought of the 3-4 as a prevent defense to be used in passing situations," Fairbanks said. "Well, we had a shortage of quality, prototypical defensive linemen. They just weren't around; 85 to 90 percent of all college teams at that time were using a three-man defensive line. There were far more linebackers available than top quality defensive linemen, so I built a defense that required less of them. I felt it was the only way we were going to have a chance to stop teams."

As John Madden told *Sports Illustrated* in 1977, one year after his Oakland Raiders team had switched from the 4-3 to the 3-4: "If your fourth linebacker is better than your fourth lineman, the 3-4 is for you." Madden and Al Davis had decided to make the change after injuries decimated their defensive line in the preseason.

In Fairbanks' first year with the Patriots, he stuck with the standard 4-3 but found that his defense as constructed had no ability to stop the run. New England allowed a league-worst 2,850 yards against the run, and the Patriots finished 5–9. After an off-season of studying game tape comprehensively, Fairbanks decided to make the switch, and his new defense ranked fourth against the run, allowing just 1,587 yards—nearly 1,000 yards fewer in an era

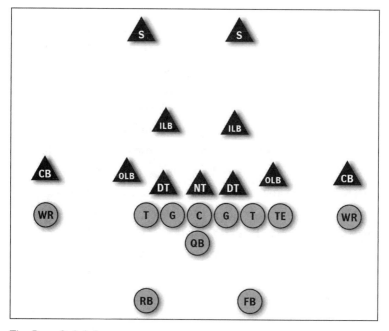

The Base 3-4 defense

when rushing for 1,000 yards in a season was a really big deal.

The difference against the run for every team was immediate for those teams who moved to the 3-4. With four linebackers instead of three, defenses could create new pursuit angles and dictate the action. Each 3-4 defense seemed to have one transformative player who locked the new system in. There was Bob Matheson for the Miami Dolphins. There was Ted Hendricks for the Raiders. Nose tackle Curley Culp, who had played on the Kansas City Chiefs' odd stacked fronts from 1967 through 1974, was traded for end John Matuszak after Matuszak, a noted renegade, ran afoul of Houston head coach Sid Gillman's sense of team discipline. Matuszak made his way to the Raiders in time for the 1976 season and, as a 6'7", 272-pound end, had a similarly transformative effect as Hendricks did with Oakland's 3-4. The Denver Broncos had a number of key players who excelled in new positions when they moved to the 3-4 in 1976 after an injury to defensive end Lyle Alzado, but it was a group of linebackers—Randy Gradishar, Bob Swenson, Joe Rizzo, and Tom Jackson—who made that great defense go.

Generally, the linemen up front did not appreciate the switch. Defensive tackles used to splitting blocks and getting through gaps were charged with holding the point so that a more varied palette of front seven defenders could flow through and disrupt, and ends, who were used to flying off the edge, were now dealing with life between the tackle and the guard. The inside and outside linebackers (like it is now) became the rock stars for the most part—especially before the days in which the base 3-4 became more of a hybrid in the 1980s and beyond. "I don't like the word, 'sacrificial,' but that's what you'd call the 3-4, a sacrificial defense," Culp said in 1977. "We sacrifice our bodies so the linebackers can make tackles. I guess we're the garbage collectors. Personally, I don't particularly care for the three-man front. If you took a consensus of the linemen around the league, I think you'd find that nobody likes the 3-4."

NFL coaches liked it, though. Buoyed by the success of the Dolphins, Patriots, and Oilers, the Raiders, Philadelphia Eagles, and Tampa Bay Buccaneers were using the 3-4 as their base defense by 1977. The number of teams employing it would ebb and flow throughout the corresponding decades, but the 3-4 was now a root concept in the NFL and would be so going forward. The advantages were many. Subbing out one defensive end for a linebacker made the defense faster and more adept. Blitz packages were far more variable with four linebackers instead of three, and as Fairbanks, Phillips, and Chuck Noll all intimated, the switch to a more linebacker-heavy defense mirrored the college game and the pipeline to the top. Those advantages—especially the need to blitz more often and with far more complexity—became clearly necessary as the NFL expanded its passing game in the late 1970s like never before.

Before the 1978 season, the NFL put two transformative changes into effect. First, the regular-season schedule expanded from 14 to 16 games. Second, a series of rules alterations to make the passing game easier and friendlier were implemented. The most famous of those alterations became known as the "Mel Blount Rule" after the Steelers cornerback, who was famous for crowding opposing receivers at the line of scrimmage, never giving them an inch of free space as they ran up the field, and punishing them severely if they actually caught the ball. That level of receiver intimidation was a hallmark of the Steel Curtain defense (and every other great defense of the 1970s and before), but teams would have to find new ways to deal with receivers from that point on.

Now receivers had the first five yards from scrimmage free to develop their routes before defenders could bump and re-direct them. It was a huge difference-maker, especially for teams used to playing against zone defenses and creating openings under those zones. With that one rule change, passing the ball became per-missible—advantageous even—in a way the NFL had never seen before. "If it's enforced, it's going to open up the passing game as far as crossing patterns and hooks," Cincinnati Bengals receiver Isaac Curtis told *The Cincinnati Enquirer* in 1978. "Now, they can't take shots and screw up your timing with the quarterback. I don't have to worry about the linebackers. I don't have to worry about weaving in and out of traffic. But I don't even respect it until I see it enforced."

Oh, it was enforced, and the differences in the NFL's offensive structure were obvious and immediate. In 1977 teams averaged 12.8 completions and 25 passing attempts per game. By 1979 teams were completing 15.7 passes on 29 attempts per game. The Steelers were perhaps the clearest beneficiaries of the differ-ence between the old and new NFL. Terry Bradshaw went from 2,523 passing yards in 1977, to 2,915 in 1978, and to 3,724 in 1979. The Steelers' last two Super Bowls of the 1970s featured a passing offense just as definitive as their historically great defense, and now it was guys like Blount who were playing catch-up to their quarterbacks. Several coaches were ready to take advantage of this new guideline, and the two most celebrated—Bill Walsh and Don Coryell—changed the game forever.

Air Coryell

Don Coryell was many things in his 85 years on this Earth. He was an Army paratrooper during World War II, a defensive back for the Washington Huskies, a longtime high school and college coach, the head coach of the St. Louis Cardinals and San Diego Chargers, and, finally, a retiree living a gentle life in the Pacific Northwest. Most prominently, of course, during his time in the

NFL from 1973 through 1986, he took the Sid Gillman vertical passing game, added his own rushing formation concepts, and spun the NFL's passing offense forward a generation. Coryell can be considered the functional link between the deep passing games of the 1960s and 1970s and the West Coast Offense that followed into the 1980s and 1990s. As much as any coach in the history of football, Coryell preached the gospel of the nuanced passing game wherever he went—and wherever he went he got results. "I don't think there's ever been a coach who was more courageous about creating offense," Chargers quarterback Dan Fouts said.

Coryell created that offense at San Diego State from 1961 through 1972, when he developed an explosive passing game that befuddled opponents, got his players into the NFL in impressive numbers, and set the stage for his own NFL induction. He had run one of the first iterations of the I formation backfield at Whittier College before that and showed it to John McKay when Coryell was one of McKay's assistants in 1960. There, he established the formation that would define USC as the epicenter of collegiate running backs for the next few decades. But when he joined the Aztecs as their head coach, it became about the kind of speed that could open up a vertical passing game that was impossible to consistently defend. "There were a number of reasons why we developed the passing game with the Aztecs," Coryell told *The San Diego Union-Tribune* years later. "We could only recruit a limited number of runners and linemen against schools like USC and UCLA. And there were a lot of kids in Southern California passing and catching the ball. There seemed to be a deeper supply of quarterbacks and receivers. And the passing game was also open to some new ideas."

Coryell inherited a program on the verge of collapse and turned it around decisively. The Aztecs compiled a 104–19–2 record under Coryell, had three undefeated seasons, and winning streaks of 25 and 31 games. Unusual for a smaller school, San Diego State sent several quarterbacks—Dennis Shaw, Don Horn, Rod Dowhower, Brian Sipe—to the NFL in the 1960s and early 1970s. Then there were the receivers: Isaac Curtis, Haven Moses, Gary Garrison, and Tommy Reynolds. And the list of coaches he developed there includes two Hall of Famers in John Madden and Joe Gibbs, along with Ernie Zampese, Tom Bass, and Jim Hanifan. Dowhower also learned to coach under Coryell's auspices. The Aztecs moved from Division II to Division I in 1969, and Coryell moved to the NFL in 1973 after the Cardinals hired him.

The Cardinals were one of the original (American Football Professional Association) AFPA franchises (then in Chicago), but their long run hadn't produced much. Coryell's new team hadn't been in the postseason since 1948 and enjoyed sporadic spurts of winning at best. Coryell's first year there saw the Cardinals match the 4–9–1 mark from the previous season, but the offense improved from 25th to 12th in yards and 23rd to 11th in points. In the next three seasons, St. Louis ranked in the top 10 in most offensive categories and won at least 10 games in each of those campaigns—something the franchise hadn't done since 1948 and wouldn't do again until 2009.

Coryell found no issue in adapting his college schemes to the pros. With all the talk about the passing game, there was also a multi-faceted ground attack and an offensive line led by Dan Dierdorf and the infamous Conrad Dobler that kept quarterback Jim Hart upright as well as any front five in league history. In 1975 that line allowed an unofficial total of eight sacks in the entire season, and Hart was on the field for just six of them. "Don's idea was to pass to set up the run," Hart said in *The Super '70s*. "He wanted to attack the defense and move the chains in an era when teams would establish the run to set up the pass. Don actually wanted to [pass] the ball even more that we did. It was only because of [assistant coach and offensive line mastermind Jim Hanifan] that we ever called running plays."

Despite the innovator at the helm, things started to go downhill for the Coryell Cardinals in 1977. Team owner Bill Bidwill was notoriously cheap and let a large number of the team's best players walk out the door instead of compensating them fairly. Bidwill refused to let Coryell have a serious hand in personnel matters, and things came to a head in January 1978. It was then that Coryell stood Bidwill up when the two men were to have a meeting about the coach's future; Coryell was on a plane to Los Angeles to inquire about the Rams' open head coach position. Bidwill responded by refusing to let Coryell out of the last three years of his contract, blocking his potential moves to Los Angeles and San Diego, and eventually locking him out of his own office. "Don saw the handwriting on the wall that nothing good was going to come of staying in St. Louis," Hart said. "We were very upset that he left. We knew Don was going to be successful wherever he coached and we wanted to be a part of it. His tenure with the Cardinals coincided with my best years, so to say I was sorry to see him go was an understatement."

Bidwill finally and mercifully fired Coryell in February of that year, replacing him with Bud Wilkinson. "I'd be inclined to seek out an offensive-oriented coach," Bidwell told *The News-Palladium*. "I like offense." Well, he had that before. Wilkinson wasn't a stick-in-the-mud as he has sometimes been portrayed—he tried to beef up St. Louis' offense with no-huddle concepts and full-house backfields that were ahead of their time, but Bidwill had already poisoned the water. Coryell, on the other hand, headed back to San Diego. The Chargers hired him to replace Tommy Prothro on September 25, 1978. At that point, the Chargers were 1–3, but under Coryell they finished 9–7 with seven wins in their last eight games. Over the next four seasons, Coryell's Chargers went 39–18 in the regular season and made the playoffs each year—not bad for a franchise that hadn't made the postseason since 1965. With Fouts at quarterback and a battery of talented players just waiting for a coach like him, the Chargers of the early 1980s became one of the greatest offenses the NFL has ever seen. It had become abundantly clear that because of his offensive genius Coryell could turn teams around drastically at any level. "He's a pacemaker, a trend-setter," then-Chiefs head coach Marv Levy told *Sports Illustrated* in 1981. "Don was in low-cuts when the rest of us were in high-tops."

Though his overall offensive structures may have thrown off some of his colleagues at first, that may have had more to do with the fact that in the 1970s the NFL was an earthbound league for the most part, and Coryell, along with Bill Walsh, were bringing different ideas to the field. But painting Coryell as an unbalanced offensive designer solely concerned with his quarterbacks hurling the ball through the air as much as possible would be a complete misrepresentation and a disservice to how balanced his best offenses truly were. In St. Louis, Coryell had fullback Jim Otis and scatback Terry Metcalf, and the Cardinals finished in the top eight in rushing attempts, rushing yards, and rushing touchdowns in both 1975 and 1976. The rushing attempts diminished somewhat in San Diego as the passing offense opened up, but the Chargers ranked first in the league in rushing touchdowns in 1981 and 1982 and fourth in rushing yards per attempt in 1982.

Those numbers were a result of the trade with the New Orleans Saints that brought Chuck Muncie to the backfield during the 1980 season. Then, Muncie was the bellcow, while James Brooks was the Metcalf-style scatback. It was a primary construct of Coryell's offense to employ two backs until the Chargers started doing revolutionary things with tight end Kellen Winslow and veered to the one-back offense. "The beauty of Air Coryell is it works against any defense," Chargers fullback Hank Bauer told NFL Films. "You want to pressure us? Fine. You want to stack to stop the run? Fine. You want to be stupid and try to play man coverage outside? Fine. It's all timing and reads by the receivers and reads by the quarterback. It's very difficult to defend, and nobody had seen that."

The stats prove the theory. The Chargers led the NFL in passing every year from 1978 to 1983, a six-year stretch unrivaled in NFL annals. In 1979 Fouts became the second player in pro football history to throw for more than 4,000 yards (following Joe Namath in 1967) when he amassed 4,082 yards. He then went on to best that mark by quite some measure in the next two seasons with 4,715 yards in 1980 and 4,802 yards in 1981. Only a strike-shortened season prevented him from doing it again in 1982, but in that season, he led the league in passing yards for the fourth straight year with 2,883 yards in just nine games. John Jefferson became the first receiver in NFL history to gain more than 1,000 yards in each of his first three seasons. When the Chargers traded Jefferson away due to a contract dispute, Coryell plugged in Wes Chandler, who led the league with 129 receiving yards per game in 1982. In 1985, the year the San Francisco 49ers' Roger Craig became the first running back to rush and receive for more than 1,000 yards in the same season, it was San Diego back Lionel "Little Train" James who actually set the NFL record for receiving yards by a back with 1,027. Charlie Joiner, Winslow, and Fouts all made the Hall of Fame, and each one of them would tell you that without Coryell, none of that would have been possible.

As San Diego's passing game became more complex, the Chargers faced more nickel and dime defenses than ever—perhaps more than any other offense had to that time in NFL history. With so many defensive backs taking linebackers off the field, San Diego's run game became a force multiplier. Backs were also used as read decoys and pawns in Coryell's offenses. He sent them out on quick screens, so Fouts had that escape hatch if an enemy defense actually did cover all his targets. And it was Coryell's version of the three-digit passing game that welded everything together.

Coryell's Three-Digit System

As with many schematic entities throughout the NFL's history, the origin of the three-digit play-calling system is somewhat nebulous. Don Coryell is recognized as one innovator, though Sid Gillman used it in the AFL. What Coryell did with it made the argument over who was responsible for the "big bang" irrelevant; he took the three-digit system to the point where he

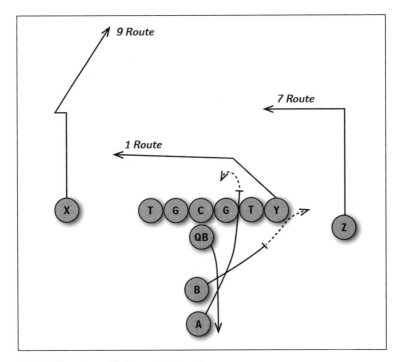

Y 719 in Don Coryell's three-digit system

could've walked into an NFL huddle in the second decade of the new millennium and immediately recognized the calls in many of today's offenses.

The three-digit system Coryell developed at San Diego State was out of necessity. As the coach of a smaller college, he had to acquire his players through less traditional recruiting methods. (As an independent college at the time, San Diego State wasn't under the watch of conferences regarding transfer and eligibility regulations.) As a result he often had a new receiver on the field the same week he joined the team. So as opposed to the wordier calls of the time, Coryell devised his own system that designated the routes for his receivers and made things easier for those new charges. That in itself was a nice idea, but what made Coryell's system special was that the three-digit concept did not decrease the complexity of the route concepts. It was a malleable system that could work with various passing concepts, and that's why it's used by many NFL coaches to this day in different iterations.

In Coryell's system, Gillman's system, and most of the systems since, the numbers in the play call are based on routes for the backs and the inside and outside receivers. The outside receivers have the same route numbers, while the inside receivers and backs have their own numerical catalogue of routes and numbers. If the outside receivers didn't mirror their routes, that would be included in the call.

For example, on an *I Right 54 Y 719* call, I Right is the formation, 54 is the blocking scheme (54 to the weak side, 55 to the strong side), and Y 719 tells the receivers what to do from right to left. The Z receiver runs a deep 7 route and turns in if there's zone coverage. The Y receiver (most likely a tight end) runs a shallow 1 route five to seven yards upfield across the formation. The X receiver runs a deep 9 route. It's a two-back, play-action play. The fullback replaces the Y receiver to front-side pass protect, and the halfback takes the play-fake and heads up between the guard and tackle, whose assignments are covered in the 54 blocking scheme designation. Dan Fouts looked to the Y receiver (let's say Kellen Winslow) as his first read. The X receiver would be the second read, and the halfback outlet up top would be the bailout. Fouts would see all of this and make his call in the time it took to drop back five steps.

A more likely call, as the Chargers started to spread the field with Winslow away from the formation, would be *I Right Flex Roll X 388*. Here, the X receiver runs a long crossing route from a wider split, while the Y tight end and Z receiver run their own individual deep 8 routes. The quarterback rolls right and eyes the flexed X receiver as his first read. If the defense comes down on the

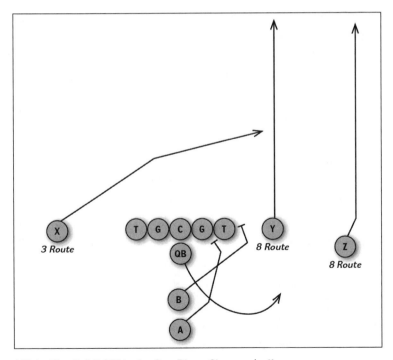

I Right Flex Roll X 388 in the San Diego Chargers' offense

X, the Y and Z receivers are hopefully open. No matter the call, the quarterback and his receivers were easily on the same page.

This stuff was hard enough for defenses to deal with, but it became just about impossible to defend consistently when Coryell added his dizzying motion concepts to the pre-snap phase of the play. In his 1983 playbook, Coryell illustrated the nine objectives of pre-snap movement and why it was a key construct of his offense.

1. To create a personnel advantage by creating coverage mismatches on our receivers or backs

2. To create a personnel advantage by effecting changes in run support and force responsibilities

3. To create secondary movement in an effort to better enable our quarterbacks to recognize coverages

4. To get our personnel in better position to execute their given assignment

5. To create problems for the defense in man under coverages when attempting to hold or bump receivers at the line of scrimmage

6. To create an opportunity for indecision, confusion, and/or misalignment by the secondary

7. To cause movement on the part of the defense in an effort to realign its personnel with the coverage calls and changes and not allow them to set themselves and react to familiar offensive patterns, make the defense play "on the move"

8. To force opponents to spend practice time and effort on adjusting to movement patterns rather than improving defensive skills and schemes

9. To create a visual complexity to the defense yet be able to run the same basic plays from a variety of looks

It's specifically important to deliniate Coryell's reasons for using pre-snap motion as much as he did because when you look through these nine points you see a lot of the NFL's current passing philosophy in there, and before Coryell perfected his structure, that wasn't the case to this degree. Coryell's motions could come in all kinds of forms—halfbacks flexing out wide from the backfield, wide-side receivers moving inside slot receivers in moveable twins looks, and the Roving Y moving all over the place. Anticipation was also a big part of the Coryell passing game. He wanted his receivers to break to the ball as it was thrown and beat the defender to the ball. Coryell also trusted his receivers with leverage reads. They adjusted their breaks based on how the coverage was leaning. From the pre-snap phase to the end of the route, the idea was to have the defense on its heels no matter what it did.

The Roving Y Move Tight End

Don Coryell did move his tight ends out wide from time to time at San Diego State, and J.V. Cain played the role of the hybrid receiver/tight end with the St. Louis Cardinals, but it was really Kellen Winslow who redefined the position with his own special physical abilities and mental acumen, which perfectly complemented Coryell's expansive philosophy. The San Diego Chargers selected Winslow out of Missouri with the 13th overall pick in the 1979 draft, and after a rookie season in which he was limited with a leg injury and caught just 25 passes in seven games, he came back with a flourish the next two years, leading the NFL with 89 catches in 1980 and 88 in 1981. Winslow was the perfect prototype of the modern tight end—he was big enough to overwhelm cornerbacks and safeties, beating even aggressive double coverage easily with his physicality, and quick enough to make life nightmarish for the linebackers of the day. Moreover, he bought in completely to Coryell's system and became an outstanding route runner and catalyst for the entire offense. There were other tight ends of the era who had the ability to do what Winslow did—like Ozzie Newsome of the Cleveland Browns and Todd Christensen of the Oakland Raiders—but Winslow was the one in the right place at the right time.

It didn't hurt that Coryell had some great assistants early on with the Chargers. Joe Gibbs played tight end for Coryell at San Diego State and he later coached the offensive line at San Diego State from 1964 to 1966 and the Cardinals running backs from 1973 to 1977. He was the offensive coordinator with the Chargers in 1979 and 1980 before moving on to a long career as Washington Redskins head coach, in which he won three Super Bowls with three different quarterbacks. But with the Chargers, it was Gibbs, the former tight end, who consulted with Coryell, receivers coach Ernie Zampese, and offensive line coach Jim Hanifan to find the best ways in which to get Winslow more involved.

The solution? Flex him out more often from the formation and make him a moving target on every down. He wasn't a messenger tight end available in a situational role but the crux of a receiver corps that had Charlie Joiner, John Jefferson, Wes Chandler, Chuck Muncie, and James Brooks. When it all was working, it was too much for any defense to stop, and Winslow was the integral figure. He was a force multiplier in San Diego's pre-snap packages. Wherever he went, the defense was going to guess wrong and wind up in a bad spot. If you're an outside left cornerback and you're expecting pre-snap to cover the Z receiver on a go route, and all of a sudden, here comes Winslow outside the Z receiver in motion from the left side of the formation to run an 18-yard skinny post, what are you supposed to do? Winslow, more than anyone in Coryell's offenses, made the math difficult for anyone facing him. And in doing so, he inspired generations of coaches after him to work those schematic advantages. "During the early years of Air Coryell, the strong safety wasn't much more than a glorified linebacker," former Denver Broncos defensive coordinator Joe Collier said in *The Games That Changed the Game*. "Basically, a run defender who could cover an average tight end. You put a guy like Winslow in the slot, and he's going up against coverage that's a lot slower than he is. It's not the matchup on defense we liked. So, we'd try to give that strong safety some help like bringing a linebacker out to him or bringing the other safety over to help."

Of course, when you put that much attention on Winslow, someone else was going to win their inevitable one-on-one matchup, and that's one reason it seemed that on every passing play at least one Chargers receiver was open throughout the down. Winslow ended his career with 541 catches for 6,741 yards and 45 touchdowns and was inducted into the Hall of Fame in 1995. The game he's best remembered for is the 41–38 Chargers win against the Miami Dolphins in the 1981 divisional playoff round. Winslow caught 13 passes for 166 yards and a touchdown and was pawed at by Miami's defense throughout the game to the point where he had to be helped off the field by teammates after the game due to injury, cramps, and dehydration. It was an epic performance, though several bitter former Dolphins swear to this day that Winslow was engaging in a bit of method acting. Still, his place in NFL history is unique and eternal—Winslow was the player who truly made it acceptable for tight ends to be the primary targets in NFL passing offenses on a week-to-week basis.

As much of an innovator as he was, Coryell passed away on July 1, 2010, without seeing his own induction in the Pro Football Hall of Fame—a monumentally silly snub that continues to this day. Coryell's teams were never able to reach a Super Bowl. His distant relationship with his own defenses was a serious cause, and the Chargers were never able to mount a serious defensive threat after defensive end Fred Dean was traded to the San Francisco 49ers in a fit of cheapness from team owner Gene Klein. Dean went on to a different level of greatness and eventually the Hall of Fame under Bill Walsh, and a defense that was once as stout as its offense quickly fell apart. You can point to Coryell's own short-comings when looking at his 3–6 postseason record, and there's merit to that, but there's also truth to the idea that if Coryell had ever worked with an owner as concerned with the product on the field as he was with the checkbook, things would have been different. He retired after the 1986 season and moved back to the state of Washington and his cabin in the island woods.

And in that retirement, he saw his influence bloom. Coryell's place as an all-time NFL innovator is secure not only because his concepts worked so well when he was coaching, but also because the coaches of today will tell you that those same concepts are a major part of their own playbooks. More specifically, if you were to superimpose the most expansive versions of the passing game Coryell unleashed in San Diego over the most challenging passing offenses of the modern age, it would be a fairly easy fit. "We've lost a man who has contributed to the game of pro football in a very lasting way with his innovations and with his style," Dan Fouts said upon his old coach's passing. "They say that imitation is the highest form of flattery. Look around; it's there."

His other proteges agree. "If Don Coryell walked in and looked at our call sheet, he'd recognize about half the plays," then-Redskins head coach Norv Turner told *The Sporting News* in 1999. "It's not about plays; it's about personnel, execution, getting people to believe and doing it right." Mike Martz, who took the three-digit system to the St. Louis Rams and the "Greatest Show on Turf" Rams, perhaps said it best. "Don is the father of the modern passing game. People talk about the West Coast Offense, but Don started the West Coast decades ago and kept updating it," he told the Voice of San Diego. "You look around the NFL now, and so many teams are running a version of the Coryell offense. Coaches have added their own touches, but it's still Coryell's offense. He has disciples all over the league. He changed the game." And as the NFL moved into the 1980s, his concepts would spread far and wide—to the next generation of champions.

CHAPTER 6

HOGS AND GENIUSES
The NFL in the 1980s

---

*"Greed, for lack of a better word, is good. Greed is right.
Greed works. Greed clarifies, cuts through, and captures the
essence of the evolutionary spirit. Greed—in all of its forms—
greed for life, for money, for love, knowledge, has marked
the upward surge of mankind."*
—Michael Douglas as Gordon Gekko in *Wall Street*

T he 1980s were a decade of excess in many ways, and
the NFL followed suit with the flashiest, most complex
versions of the pro game anyone had ever seen. Many
innovators defined the era, but one stood above all the rest, and he
came as close to the perfect version of offensive football as could be
imagined. The rest of the league would be forced to respond to the
trail that Bill Walsh had finally been allowed to blaze.

Bill Walsh: The Genius

Bill Walsh was informed to a great extent by perhaps the
NFL's two greatest offensive geniuses before him and he took the
things he learned from Sid Gillman and Paul Brown to a new

level, building what eventually became known as the West Coast Offense while putting his stamp on the game forever.

Walsh started his professional coaching career as the Oakland Raiders' running backs coach in 1966, and Raiders main man Al Davis was a Gillman acolyte. Davis worked under Gillman as an assistant with the San Diego Chargers from 1960 through 1962. It was under Davis' auspices that Walsh started to see his own versions of the brilliance of Gillman's geometry. The timing of the passing plays and the mathematical precision of passing concepts came to Walsh's mind from Gillman's work in the American Football League. Gillman was fond of saying that a football field is 53 ⅓ yards wide and 100 yards long and he was going to force defenses to cover the entire width and length of it.

Gillman did so with innovative vertical concepts, but he also did so with geometry. In the early 1960s, Gillman spoke with assistant Tom Bass about the triangular nature of the ideal combination of the quarterback's passing and the receiver's route running. If the angles were correct, Gillman hypothesized that the quarterback and receiver could be timed up before the snap of the ball even happened.

Bass met with a mathematics professor from San Diego State in 1964, and the two men deduced that the perfect combination of quarterback, receiver, and route was indeed triangular in nature. In its basic form, the triangle consisted of: the route the receiver ran until he cut to a different angle, the remainder of the route run after the break, and the movement of the ball from quarterback to receiver. No matter the route, Gillman saw consistency in the geometry. "It was a fully dimensional approach, utilizing the backs and tight ends more extensively than other offenses," Walsh said years later in *The Genius*. "A typical NFL team might have three or four pass patterns for the halfback, but the Raiders' system had as many as 20, and even they didn't use anything close to Gillman's whole playbook. To develop an understanding of it took time, but once learned, it was invaluable."

Brown hired Walsh to be an offensive assistant on Gillman's recommendation before the 1968 season for the expansion Cincinnati Bengals, and it wasn't long before Walsh's quick mind—and the things he had learned on the way up—gave Brown the confidence to hand his passing game over. Walsh moved from the position of wide receivers coach to offensive coordinator in 1971. While assistant coach Bill "Tiger" Johnson handled the running game, Walsh called all of Cincinnati's passing plays from the coach's box. Because Brown wanted to maintain the illusion of control, it was a laborious process. Walsh radioed the call down to Johnson's headset, Johnson told Brown the call, and Brown relayed the play to a messenger guard—a player going in for that play who would give the call to the quarterback.

In return, Walsh received a comprehensive education—everything from play-calling to game management to player personnel to dealing with the media—from the man who had formed a large percentage of the league's *modus operandi*.

Complications arose when Walsh started to get too much credit for the design of Cincinnati's offense, but years before that, there was a far more vexing issue on the field when quarterback Greg Cook suffered a severe injury in 1969. Selected in the first round of the 1969 AFL Draft, Cook was, according to Walsh's account in an NFL.com story, "the greatest talent ever to play the position—like Steve Young, but bigger," and the Bengals' original plan was to use Cook's arm and mobility to develop a complex vertical passing game.

It didn't take long for things to unravel dramatically. Cook was tackled on his throwing shoulder in the third game of his NFL career by Kansas City Chiefs linebacker Jim Lynch and tore his rotator cuff in the process. With the knowledge that Cook would be out for the 1970 season, Walsh and Brown had to make do with Virgil Carter, who had completed a total of 91 passes in two seasons with the Chicago Bears before the Bengals acquired him. Carter was a journeyman at best but an important footnote to football history in that his limitations forced Walsh to create entirely new concepts for his team.

Carter's first NFL start came in Week 4 of the 1970 season, as Brown returned to Cleveland for the first time since his firing in January of 1963. Brown and Walsh used Carter's mobility to roll him out of the pocket frequently, and Carter's relatively weak arm didn't matter because Walsh had designed an offense that relied on timing patterns that Carter could easily complete. He completed 20-of-28 passes for 218 yards, one touchdown, and one interception in that first start. Cincinnati lost the game, but the die had been cast for this new offense. The 1970 Bengals won the new AFC Central division with Carter completing 51.4 percent of his passes—a solid number for the era. One season later, Carter led the NFL with a 62.2 percent completion rate. Carter was eventually usurped by Ken Anderson, who was taken in the third round of the 1971 draft and would become Cincinnati's primary quarterback from 1972 through 1984. "It was high-percentage throwing," then-Bengals backup quarterback and eventual Walsh assistant coach Sam Wyche told the NFL Network. "Lay the ball off short and let the receiver make the total yardage with the run after the catch."

That was the basic beginning of an offensive philosophy which would become far, far more complex in time. Walsh's innovations during his time in Cincinnati were voluminous, and sometimes came from random chance. In his autobiography, *Building a Champion,* he described how he started to use the tight end in motion from one side of the formation to the other. "We used the tight end in motion first by mistake," he said. "Cincinnati was playing the Raiders in Oakland. In the third quarter, Bob Trumpy lined up on the wrong side by mistake. He had to shift over quickly to the other side, and all hell broke loose. At that time, the Raiders had very specialized [defenders]. They had a weak-side linebacker, they had a strong-side linebacker, they had a defensive end who only played on the tight-end side, and they would shift their two inside linebackers. They all ran into each other in the middle of the field, trying to adjust."

After the game Johnson suggested that the Bengals put motion in the playbook on purpose. Walsh said that they looked at each other and doubled over laughing, but that's how motion became a seminal part of the Walsh offense. And the motion concept was nightmarish for the more static defenses of the time. Against defenses with specific linebacker designations (weak-side and strong-side), Walsh could direct his tight end to create unfavorable matchups. "If a weak-side linebacker was fast but had trouble handling a big, blocking tight end, we could force him to defend on the strong-side anytime we wanted simply by moving the tight end to his side," Walsh said.

From there, Walsh started to split Trumpy outside of the formation, forcing those linebackers to stray from their preferred places and opening up other alternatives. By the time he was hired in San Francisco, Walsh was using receivers and backs in motion. Everything was about getting the defense off-balance before the snap even happened. Walsh saw the defense as a moveable canvas onto which he would paint exacting structural concepts, and motion was a major part of this. Walsh also discovered that by putting different players in motion, a quarterback could discern whether the defense was playing man or zone. "If a back goes in motion and the linebackers begin to loosen, the quarterback can expect a zone," he said. "If a linebacker immediately moves with the back in motion, the quarterback can see man-to-man coverage."

This worked at a basic level because defenses were relatively rudimentary in the 1970s, and the substitutions and hybrid positions of the current era were rarely seen. Teams use motion to discern coverage concepts to this day, though disguised and split coverage concepts are the norm in the modern age. Back then? Teams didn't know how to adapt.

But the most important aspects of the West Coast Offense were timing and placement. "The basis of our passing game remained the same: timed passes and precise patterns, which we practiced extensively," Walsh wrote. "Each year I was with the Bengals, we isolated the skills we needed and the timing that was necessary until we were very proficient in all phases of offense. Whether the passes were deep downfield or five-yarders designed to control the ball, it was a system that early on made the most of limited personnel and, when we acquired talented men at the skill positions, made full use of their potential."

Walsh's own potential as a head coach was severely affected by the surprise announcement before the 1976 season that Brown was retiring as the Bengals' head coach and would choose Johnson to be his replacement. It was a crushing blow for Walsh, who believed he deserved and had been promised the position. Brown responded by telling Walsh that he was expected to continue as the team's offensive coordinator. Walsh insisted that he would leave the team as soon as his contract was up, which just happened to be a week after their meeting.

Walsh had already cut a deal with head coach Tommy Prothro of the Chargers to be Prothro's offensive coordinator. Brown responded with disdain and allegedly a campaign to blacklist Walsh throughout the league as a head coaching candidate. Walsh spent one year in San Diego, observed that no NFL team was willing to close the deal at that point, and headed to Stanford for a head coaching position that lasted through the 1978 season.

The 49ers broke the NFL logjam in 1979, and the team Walsh inherited was an absolute mess in a personnel sense. With their 2–14 record in 1978, the 49ers would have had the first overall pick in the 1979 draft except that former general manager Joe Thomas had traded that pick to the Buffalo Bills for the broken-down version of O.J. Simpson. The new 49ers would have to make do with very little at the start of Walsh's tenure, and it showed on the field. His team went 2–14 again in 1979 and raised the profile up to 6–10 in 1980. Walsh later referred to the 1981 Super Bowl season, in which the 49ers finished the regular season with a 13–3 record, as "Camelot." He may have regarded that team so highly because from a pure talent perspective it was the one that required the most—and best—coaching. In any regard 1981 was the year it all came together for coach and team, as Walsh's offensive mind-set really took hold.

Walsh's belief was that the passing game could hold the key to efficient possession, and he advanced that concept in an era when the running game was thought to be the key to drive consistency, while the forward pass brought about the explosive play in less frequent bursts. In Super Bowl VIII at the end of the 1973 season, the Miami Dolphins beat the Minnesota Vikings, and Miami quarterback Bob Griese completed seven passes in eight attempts for 73 yards. He didn't have to do any more than that because Miami's rushing attack and defense were so formidable. At the end of the next season, the Pittsburgh Steelers beat the Vikings in Super Bowl IX with Steelers quarterback Terry Bradshaw completing 9-of-14 passes for 96 yards. Again, more wasn't required; Bradshaw was buttressed by a fantastic running game and perhaps the best defense the NFL has ever seen.

In that era completion percentage was an afterthought to many because the passing game wasn't as dimensional. In 1979, Walsh's first year as an NFL head coach, the league's completion rate was 54.1 percent. A decade later, in Walsh's last season in 1988, the league's completion percentage was 54.3. More was expected of Walsh's quarterbacks and the quarterbacks in the system he created. Anderson, Carter's replacement in Cincinnati, led the league in completion percentage in 1974, 1981, and 1982. Joe Montana led the NFL in completion percentage four different times from 1980 through 1987 and had a completion rate under 60 just once in his career as a starter—in 1989 when he "regressed" to a 59.9 rate.

Yes, Walsh helped his quarterbacks in this regard by designing short passes, but Anderson led the league in yards per attempts twice under Walsh's tutelage (1974 and 1975), and Montana did the same in 1989. Timing was a big part of his offense. So was geometry. Flooding coverage areas with more receivers than a defense could handle was a major functional construct. But the primary invention that Walsh brought to the NFL was a passing game that was so complex and artistic, and so exacting in its methodology, that it was beautiful in a symphonic sense and impossible to stop in a physical sense—all at the same time. "You think about Michelangelo and all the phenomenal things that he did," 49ers CEO/president Carmen Policy said while describing Walsh to NFL Films. "And you almost have the sense there might have been some divine intervention there."

Whether it was with help from up above or not, Walsh was at least three steps ahead of his contemporaries. "I remember a time on the practice field. Joe had completed a ball to Jerry Rice," Mike Holmgren, who was Walsh's quarterbacks coach and offensive assistant from 1986 through 1988, told NFL Films. "Beautiful pass, 30 yards downfield. And Jerry just had to move slightly to catch the ball at full stride. And I said, 'Nice play. Good throw.'

Bill was closer to me and he said, 'Mike, that's not good enough. I want the ball delivered one foot in front of the numbers. I don't want it over here; I want it right *here*.'"

Getting it right *here* was the whole point. Walsh didn't want to hear about how this player or that player could have beaten his man deep. He was not impressed with feats of strength or speed. "As Paul Brown would say, we're a precision machine," Walsh said in *A Football Life: Paul Brown*. "We're the San Francisco 49ers, and that was sort of our label—a precision machine, a machine that effectively and precisely destroyed the opponent. Our system of football sustained itself, and we refined it further and further each year until at some point it might have even been an art form."

Walsh knew that physical attributes without a command of the entire structure transformed into useless energy and he set the path accordingly. He was tough and exacting on his players, but the reward for his players was clear: they would be more productive in this system than in any other.

And that's where Montana came in. There was some truth to the notion that Walsh could succeed with any functional quarterback, but it was clear that when Montana got up to speed with the West Coast Offense, he took it to an entirely new level with a specific skillset that seemed divinely tailored to Walsh's preferences. Montana didn't have a cannon arm, but he understood the importance of functional velocity. He knew how and when to take a bit off the throw—and when to turn on the jets. He was incredibly mobile in and out of the pocket, which allowed him to take full advantage of Walsh's option route concepts and highly-developed route systems. Plays could be developed for longer periods of time because Montana would keep the play alive. And together, Walsh and Montana became legends.

The plays and concepts also became legend. There was the *Brown Right Sprint Right Option* play that became "The Catch."

There were an array of option routes, in which Walsh's players could re-determine their passages through a defense based on that defense's structure. There was the slant, which Montana really perfected with Rice. Montana once told Rice that the receiver added five years to the quarterback's career because he could take a five-yard slant to the house. Walsh would flood one side of a defense with multiple receivers. He would send a barrage of targets through short and intermediate areas with precise concepts and nearly inevitable results. "It was easy to believe Bill Walsh because he would say things that would happen: 'We're going to run this play against this defense,'" Dwight Clark said in the 1981 episode of *America's Game*. "'When you catch it, there won't be anybody within 10 yards of you.' You'd catch the ball and turn around and get ready to get hit, and there's nobody there. He would do those kinds of things over and over, and it was his designing of plays. You got to the point where everything he said, you just believed. Sometimes football players have that stigma of the dumb jock. But in Bill's offense, you couldn't be the dumb jock. All I knew was that a 10-yard hook [route] was: run 10 yards and hook. In the West Coast Offense, a 10-yard hook could be a cross versus man-to-man. Against inside coverage, it's sliding back outside. If it's man-to-man under, you're looping out and around. To me, that's what made the West Coast Offense really difficult."

For Ronnie Lott and the rest of San Francisco's defense, trying to counter all this stuff made them better—especially against the teams that weren't presenting such complicated offenses. And in the early 1980s, that included every other team in the NFL. "The ability to change routes, to change the depth of your route given the fact that a defense is running a certain [coverage]…Believe me, it's not fair," Lott told NFL Films. "There were times that George Seifert and I would look at some of these plays and go, 'Man, that's gonna be hard to stop.'"

From a purely schematic standpoint, Walsh really planted his flag in the 1981 postseason, when he utilized multiple concepts—several of them relatively unseen in the NFL—to ensure that the 49ers won their first Super Bowl title. In three games Walsh took his keys to the kingdom and set the path for the NFL's modern offensive structure. The strategic troika began against the New York Giants, whose rookie pass-rushing linebacker Lawrence Taylor was single-handedly altering the ways in which offenses deployed their skill position players.

1981 NFC Divisional Playoff: San Francisco 49ers 38, New York Giants 24

In 1981 Washington Redskins head coach Joe Gibbs had altered his vertical passing game to include an "H-back"—a tight end aligned behind and just outside the tackle—to help deal with Lawrence Taylor's furious pass rushing abilities. And in the week before the New York Giants traveled to Candlestick Park to meet the San Francisco 49ers, Taylor had absolutely demolished Philadelphia Eagles left tackle Stan Walters in New York's 27–21 win. Selected second overall in the 1981 draft, Taylor cut a wide swath through the NFL in his rookie season, which was the last in which the league did not keep official sack totals. But there was no question about the transcendent effect on every offense he faced.

The 49ers' strategy against Taylor was important enough to be documented in several books, including *The Games That Changed the Game* by Ron Jaworski and Greg Cosell and *The Blind Side* by Michael Lewis. Walsh wanted to throw the ball on a high percentage of plays, which left out the option of reducing his number of receivers, leaving extra players in to block. His left tackle, Dan Audick, was 6'3" and 250 pounds and wasn't physically up to the challenge Taylor presented—certainly not on a play-after-play, one-on-one basis. Walsh knew that if a two-time Pro Bowler like Walters wasn't up to the task, his guy wouldn't be either.

After a lot of frustrated film study, Bill Walsh threw out the standard paradigm and directed his left guard John Ayers—a 6'5", 258-pound strongman—to face up to Taylor with a "molly block." Taylor telegraphed when he was coming after the quarterback by swinging his arms before the snap, and Ayers moved out to the perimeter of the pocket to block Taylor when he read a pass rush. The reason for this was simple—Taylor had a combination of strength and speed off the snap that made it nearly impossible for tackles to get in their stances and address him with optimal momentum. So, it was up to Ayers to pull from his guard spot and seal Taylor to the edge.

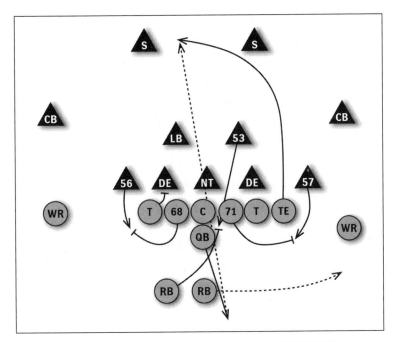

The San Francisco 49ers' crossing route during the 1981 NFC Divisional Playoff Game

The molly block wasn't the only strategy the 49ers used against Taylor. They loaded up their formations to his side and then forced him to cover with specific route concepts. In fact the 49ers employed the molly block on both sides of the line, as right guard Randy Cross used an identical pull block to handle left outside linebacker Byron Hunt. This left tackles Ayers and Keith Fahnhorst to deal with ends George Martin and Gary Jeter one-on-one with quick, decisive blocks. Taylor was effectively negated for the most part; Joe Montana completed 20-of-31 passes, including 17 in the 49ers' first 21 plays; and Walsh's team had passed its first postseason test.

Then-New York defensive coordinator Bill Parcells later said that the Giants' main mistake was that they didn't blitz their inside linebackers when San Francisco's guards pulled out as they did, but the tape shows Walsh's ability to prepare for every possible challenge, including that one.

On a 14-yard pass to tight end Charle Young with 11:46 left in the first half, halfback Ricky Patton blocked left inside linebacker Harry Carson (53), a future Hall of Famer, and it was that block that allowed Montana the time to get the ball out to Young on a crossing route. This play typified Walsh's undersold understanding that power was a key part of his offense. In the NFC Championship Game, the Dallas Cowboys would get a different taste of that on a famous drive.

1981 NFC Championship Game: San Francisco 49ers 28, Dallas Cowboys 27

The San Francisco 49ers and Dallas Cowboys had a very contentious relationship that preceded Bill Walsh's involvement by almost a decade. San Francisco had been eliminated from the playoffs every year from 1970 through 1972 by Dallas, and a 59–14 loss to the Cowboys in 1980 left a bad taste in Walsh's mouth. The 49ers head coach made sure his players knew how he felt about their upcoming opponents running up the score and calling the 1981 team a "fluke." "This goddamn Dallas team," Walsh said during one team meeting that week. "They can't keep their mouths shut. They're doing the same thing again this week. They say, 'This time, the 49ers will be meeting the real Cowboys.' Their press releases are all about how they're going to kick ass…they're so arrogant…Well, I'm fed up with this bullshit…we're going to knock them all over the field."

It didn't quite happen like that. The Cowboys may have been arrogant, but they were also very, very good. The difference in this game was Walsh's ability to discern that his opponent's weakness was not about personnel. It was about a lack of schematic diversity, and he was ready to exploit that for all it was worth.

The Cowboys had an amazing defensive front in Harvey Martin, Randy White, Jethro Pugh, and Ed "Too Tall" Jones, but Walsh felt that he could use Dallas head coach and defensive mastermind Tom Landry's predictability against him. Dallas' defensive coverage was staid, according to Walsh, and he would therefore play against type to gain the advantage. Led by cornerback Everson Walls, Dallas' secondary played heavy man-to-man coverage. Walsh used tight end placement and men in motion to dictate which defender would cover which receiver. "In effect, we would force them to defend with their automatic adjustments rather than to defend with their basic defenses," Walsh said.

This played into the Walsh truism that you always wanted to beat your opponent to the punch, to force him to react from his heels. It didn't always proceed as planned in this game—Joe Montana threw three interceptions and was sacked three times— but on the drive that led up to "The Catch," it worked about as well as Walsh could have possibly imagined.

Danny White's punt and Freddie Solomon's fair catch put the ball on the San Francisco 11-yard line with 4:54 left in the game and the 49ers down 27–21. Because the Cowboys anticipated that Walsh would call passes as long as his team had the ball, they went with a base nickel defense as a result. "Most teams would play a very predictable offense against that defense in this situation," Walsh said. "They would substitute one or two wide receivers and start throwing. The quarterback would be expected to hold the ball until pass patterns developed down the field. The Cowboys would totally disrupt these tactics with their great pass rush, using only an occasional blitz."

Instead, the 49ers went with sweeps and draws, using John Ayers (68) and Randy Cross (51) to move in space and create openings against a Cowboys line that was charging after

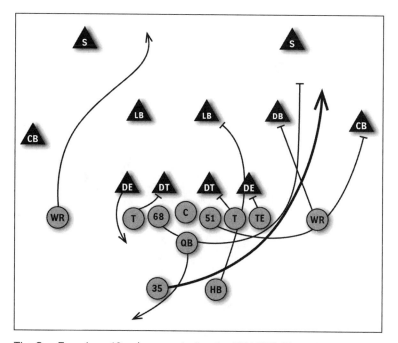

The San Francisco 49ers' sweep during the 1981 NFC Championship Game

Montana. Because Dallas' secondary was focused on coverage and the nickel base defense took a linebacker off the field, that was the sound strategy.

At times Dallas switched to a dime defense, leaving just one linebacker in with six defensive backs on the field. Walsh and offensive line coach Bobb McKittrick reminded each other during that last drive to run the *18–BOB* and *19–BOB* sweeps, in which Ayers and Cross would seal the edges upfield and allow running back Lenvil Elliott to make serious gains on the ground.

Cowboys safety Charlie Waters was pleading with his teammates to key against the run, but as Waters himself said, "We had to keep them to the minimum." Doing so required Dallas to keep the pressure on Montana at the expense of the run defense or at

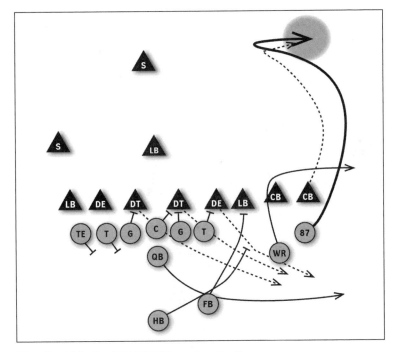

"The Catch" in the 1981 NFC Championship Game

least that's what the Cowboys hypothesized. At this point Walsh was playing chess to Landry's checkers.

Of the drive's first seven plays, four were draws or sweeps to running back Elliott. Then, Walsh called a reverse to Solomon, a play that gained 14 yards from the Dallas 49-yard line to the Dallas 35 as the Cowboys defenders fell for the misdirection because of their aggressive pursuit of the ball. After that Montana threw a sideline pass, a perfect strike, to Dwight Clark at the Dallas 25-yard line that went through two Cowboys defenders.

Sprint Right Option was Walsh's most famous play structure because it worked so well in such an iconic game, but Clark explained that it was also a perfect example of Walsh's precise vision. The coach had pre-planned every part of the play, including the point at which Montana would throw the ball away if things didn't turn out right.

And in this case, it didn't. The play didn't go as diagrammed; Solomon was supposed to clear his man away with a route to the sideline, but he couldn't shake the coverage underneath. The 49ers anticipated that "Too Tall" Jones would rush Montana, but Jones instead waited to see what Montana would do and was one of the many defenders chasing after the quarterback. However, Clark followed Montana as he rolled right—an important part of the option route concept with a mobile quarterback—and Montana threw the ball where only Clark could catch it, which was as high up in the air as Clark could possibly jump. Walsh had specifically told Montana before this play that if he didn't see what he liked, he should simply throw the ball away. The 49ers had one more down if this third-down pass didn't work... but of course, it worked, and San Francisco was on the way to the Super Bowl.

Super Bowl XVI: San Francisco 49ers 26, Cincinnati Bengals 21

"Brother, did 49ers coach Bill Walsh throw some stuff at the Bengals," Paul Zimmerman wrote in his *Sports Illustrated* account of the game. "The triple pass, in which Montana hands to Patton, who hands to Solomon, who pitches back to Montana, who throws downfield to tight end Charle Young, was designed for third and 1. It made its entry on the Niners' first third and 1 situation of the game—in the middle of their long [68 yards], exotic touchdown drive in the first quarter—picked up a neat 14 yards, and then bowed out for the day amid polite applause."

Zimmerman also detailed the plays Walsh had in his quiver that he didn't use—an end-around pass in which Dwight Clark

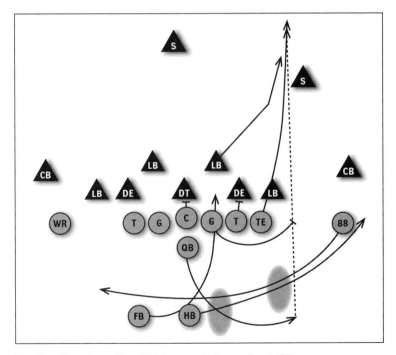

The San Francisco 49ers' triple pass in Super Bowl XVI

throws to receiver Freddie Solomon, Solomon throwing a pass off a reverse, option passes for every one of his running backs, a safety blitz out of the nickel defense. It was a dizzying array of stuff—both seen and unseen—and even the legendary Paul Brown couldn't keep up.

The flashiest play Walsh called was the triple pass in the 49ers' first drive. Joe Montana took the ball from center and handed it to Solomon, who swept in from right to left as if running a reverse. Instead, Solomon handed the ball to running back Ricky Patton, who handed the ball back to Montana. Then, with Montana rolling right and the left side of the Cincinnati Bengals defense in disarray, Montana hit Young on a 14-yard pass for a first down.

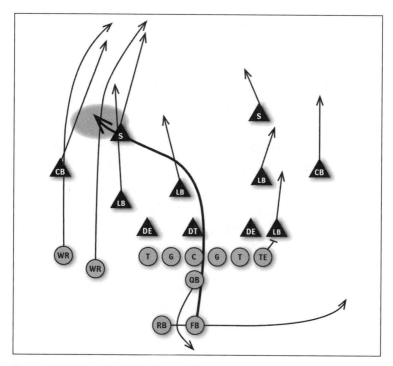

Brown Right Slot—Fox 2 FB Cross in Super Bowl XVI

This was a specific burn strategy. "That was an old Paul Brown play," Walsh said. "Paul in the press box had to watch his old triple pass used successfully against him in the Super Bowl. At that point I remembered his constant admonition to use your own trick plays first. I had done it, but in this instance, Paul probably didn't appreciate it."

Not when his most able lieutenant was now his most gifted opponent. Walsh threw all kinds of things at the Bengals on the way to a 20–0 halftime lead. He added an unbalanced line, in which left tackle John Ayers lined up between Randy Cross and Keith Fahnhorst on the right side. The Bengals didn't see that coming, and it provided the power required for Walsh's running game. The 49ers outran Cincinnati 127 yards to 72 and 40 rushing plays to 24.

San Francisco's second touchdown—at the end of a 92-yard drive—featured another important wrinkle, a variation of the flood concept. Called *Brown Right Slot—Fox 2 FB Cross*, the play had fullback Earl Cooper faking a dive play into the Cincinnati line but then running a route into the left-side seam. Meanwhile, receivers Solomon and Mike Shumann were busy taking the right side of the Bengals' coverage—one linebacker, one cornerback, and one safety—into the end zone. Flooding Cooper into the underside of Cincinnati's zone coverage after Solomon and Shumann ran their clear-out routes meant that Cooper was wide open. In addition, Young ran a quick up route after a quick block of the left outside linebacker, and halfback Patton ran out for a screen. This froze the left side of Cincinnati's coverage, and it was a prime example of Walsh's ability to use the full field in a horizontal sense—just as Sid Gillman used it as a vertical canvas.

In the regular-season opener against the Detroit Lions, Walsh also noticed that the artificial turf at the Pontiac Silverdome reacted oddly to the kicks that scooted along the ground, which occurred because injured kicker Ray Wersching could not boot the ball to his full power. In the Super Bowl, which also took place at the Silverdome, he directed Wersching to boot squib kicks along that turf to make the bounces more unpredictable for Cincinnati's return men. The Bengals fumbled near the end of the first half due to this strategy, and San Francisco recovered. As NFL Films' John Facenda said, Walsh "turned accident into design."

The 49ers weren't out of the woods yet, though. The Bengals fought back like the great team they were, going to a very Walsh-like short passing game and ramping up their defensive efforts. But it was San Francisco's defense that decided the contest, and Cincinnati cooperated by forgetting a key credo of the Walsh philosophy: receivers must run their routes exactly and precisely, and there's a reason for every inch of every route.

The Bengals started a drive at the 50-yard line with 6:52 left in the third quarter and managed to establish third and goal from the 49ers' 3-yard line after a successful fourth-down conversion by fullback Pete Johnson, who then ran for two yards and no yards on the next two plays. On that third and goal, Ken Anderson threw a quick flare to running back Charles Alexander. Linebacker Dan Bunz stopped Alexander a foot short of the goal line, which he was able to do because Alexander cleared his route a yard short of the goal line. Johnson was stopped on fourth and goal by the entire middle of the San Francisco defensive line. Bunz, linebacker Jack "Hacksaw" Reynolds, and defensive back Ronnie Lott served as the primary stoppers. That goal-line stand—perhaps the most famous in Super Bowl history—proved to be the difference. No matter how ferociously Cincinnati tried to recover from their early deficit, it was Walsh who would prove to have the edge. The Bengals could not match Walsh's exactitude, and it cost them dearly.

Walsh's seat-of-the-pants adaptations were not only impressive but necessary. He believed—and remarked several times in the years to come—that his 1981 team didn't quite have the sheer talent to do what it did. "We really did win with 'mirrors' as we were accused of doing all season," Walsh said in *Finding the Winning Edge*. "Physically, the Bengals were bigger and stronger and they ultimately outgained us by a good margin, 356 yards to 275. While preparing for the game, I racked my brain for anything that might work—passes off reverses, anything. Not desperation plays. They were things we had touched on throughout the year. But they were also plays we wouldn't have resorted to in a typical NFL game."

Early on, Walsh's success was seen as gimmicky and fluky in a larger sense. After the divisional win against the New York Giants, various members of that organization intimated that the 49ers would have had a much harder time dealing with Lawrence Taylor if the field at Candlestick Park wasn't slow, wet, and mulchy. After the NFC championship win against Dallas, some Cowboys players said flat-out that the superior team had lost, which they had said before—much to Walsh's consternation. And it took a while for Walsh's atypical philosophies to grab the NFL by the scruff of the neck in a perception sense. The "Finesse-Ass 49ers," as San Francisco linebacker Keena Turner referred to his own team in a sarcastic manner after one key win, were seen as a nickel-and-dime football team unable to maintain the power and intimidation edges common to the game at that time.

It was a canard, and Walsh was able to combine brains and brawn in ways nobody else had ever imagined. In the end it happened as much because Walsh, the personnel man, had a ridiculous eye for talent and stocked his rosters thusly. Montana improved to the point where he became the ultimate agent of distillation of Walsh's genius. He would eventually be replaced by Steve Young, the best left-handed quarterback in NFL history and a fellow Hall of Famer. Roger Craig, selected in the second round of the 1983 draft out of Nebraska, became the first back to gain more than

1,000 yards rushing and 1,000 yards receiving in the same season. Jerry Rice, taken in the first round of the 1985 draft out of tiny Mississippi Valley State, was seen on TV by Walsh in a hotel room while on a scouting trip and would eventually become the greatest receiver in the history of the NFL by an absolutely crushing margin. John Taylor, Rice's second banana in the later years of the Walsh era, would have been a No. 1 receiver on most teams.

And as his teams improved, Walsh really unleashed the far edges of his offensive philosophy. Eventually, he was able to create and implement a system that virtually guaranteed success if his players followed his schemes to the letter. The 1984 team came as close to perfection as any he ever coached, beating the Miami Dolphins in Super Bowl XIX and finishing the season with an 18–1 record that might have ended in a perfect season were it not for a controversial pass interference call in a 20–17 loss to the Pittsburgh Steelers. The 1988 49ers rebounded from a midseason slump to beat the Bengals once again in the Super Bowl in what turned out to be Walsh's last game as an NFL head coach. He went out swinging with Montana engineering a 92-yard, game-winning drive in the closing minutes. And the team he left George Seifert routed the Denver Broncos for another Super Bowl title at the end of the 1989 season.

But no amount of success would satisfy him. "I hate to see bad football," Walsh wrote in his book, *The Score Takes Care of Itself*. "I hate to see a team play bad football, even on a single play—in practice, in a game, anywhere. Bad football makes me ill in the same way, I suppose, a symphony conductor hates to hear an orchestra mangle Bach or Beethoven. There's a reverence for the art. For me, it could be described as a reverence for football the way it could be played, the exquisite beauty of what can occur at its uppermost level. I think top performers in all professions have that same deep respect—even reverence—for their work."

When Walsh compared himself to any other great artist, he wasn't throwing an ego parade—or at least that wasn't the entire function of the message. Walsh implicitly understood the balance between the understanding of human frailties and the deep desire for perfection, as much as that inevitable divide tortured him. He forever regretted leaving the 49ers after the 1988 season. And after all the battles with team owner Eddie DeBartolo, after all the post-season defeats that seemed to crush his soul more than was true for other coaches, and after all the admissions that perfection would never be attained, Walsh eventually had to make an uneasy peace with his own NFL coaching career. But he was also able to look back at a career in which he contributed as much to the NFL as anyone in its history. "I look for the roots of Bill in places that I'm visiting, and they're always there," Young, now an ESPN analyst who travels to each *Monday Night Football* game for the network, said in an NFL Films interview. "The game was coached, played, managed, owned in a very archaic way for a long time. And Bill changed that fundamentally at every level forever."

Two of Walsh's primary rivals during the 1980s—the Chicago Bears and Washington Redskins—had schematic geniuses of their own. Another, the Bengals, would eventually speed up the league with one of Walsh's favorite students at the helm.

Monsters: The 46 Defense

Buddy Ryan is best known as the man who brought the 46 Defense to Chicago in the 1980s, creating perhaps the finest defensive unit the NFL has ever seen. But his entire story is interesting as well. An Army sergeant in the Korean War while he was still in his teens, Ryan worked his way through several small colleges as a coach before getting his big break with the New York Jets in 1968 as their defensive line coach. Ryan saw the extent to which head coach Weeb

Ewbank went out of his way to devise protection schemes for Joe Namath and his wobbly knees, and it occurred to the then-defensive line coach that if there was such a premium put on the protection of quarterbacks, there must be equal value in the disruption of the position. That was the start of Ryan's blitz packages, which helped the Jets upset the Baltimore Colts in Super Bowl III.

Hired as the Chicago Bears' defensive coordinator in 1978 after eight years with the Jets and two more with the Minnesota Vikings, Ryan started to assemble a more traditional defense with iffy talent, but it wasn't the dominant Bears defense it would later become. Chicago finished 10–6 in 1979 with a defense that finished third in points allowed and sixth in yards allowed, but that was the outlier at that time. Inconsistency was the order of the day.

Ryan's point of desperation came in Week 7 of the 1981 season, when the Detroit Lions beat the living hell out of his defense in a 48–17 thrashing. Detroit quarterback Eric Hipple completed just 14-of-25 passes, but those passes traveled 336 yards, and four of them resulted in touchdowns. Rick Kane, a running back who amassed a grand total of 1,486 yards in his entire NFL career, ran for 101 yards. The Bears fell to 1–6 on the season, and Ryan knew something had to change. "Our pass rush wasn't worth a shit," Ryan said in *The Games That Changed the Game*. "We had to find a way to create more pocket pressure because we were getting beaten up by every quarterback in the league."

That would be a challenge because Chicago's next opponent was the San Diego Chargers, who finished the 1981 season ranked first overall in points, yards, passing yards, first downs, passing touchdowns, net yards per passing attempt, and rushing touchdowns. If Ryan was going to unleash a new defense against any opponent, this was the toughest imaginable. The Chargers of Don Coryell, Dan Fouts, and Kellen Winslow were the best vertical passing team in the league.

But nobody ever accused Ryan of lacking guts. Or brains. Ryan debuted an iteration of the 46 Defense against the Chargers—a 5-1-5 formation in which defensive backs blitzed from various areas and linemen were lined up in unexpected places. The 46 Defense (named for the jersey number of safety Doug Plank) had elements of the old Umbrella Defense and Greasy Neale's Stack Defense, but this was a different, far more flexible, animal. "Football is chess," Plank said in *Monsters: The 1985 Chicago Bears and the Wild Heart of Football.* "You can capture all my pawns, but if I tip over that king, I win."

And the Chargers had no earthly clue what to do against this scheme. Fouts had his worst day as an NFL quarterback, completing just 13-of-43 passes for 295 yards with two touchdowns and two interceptions. Ryan countered San Diego's multiple weapons in the passing game by hurrying the count, forcing Fouts to get the ball out more quickly than he would have liked. The Chargers kept their running backs in more often, which took some of Fouts' targets away, and those backs rushed for a total of just 61 yards on 20 carries because it's not easy to run the ball against a talented eight-man front. Otis Wilson, the only true linebacker on the field, was in charge of covering Winslow, who was shredding the rest of the league as the game's best hybrid tight end, and he caught four passes for 78 yards. Receiver Charlie Joiner had a bigger day with five catches for 124 yards and a touchdown, but battery mate Wes Chandler was limited to two catches for 69 yards. Yes, the Bears gave up big plays in the passing game with a scant secondary—as a result of all the action up front—but Ryan had gambled on the idea that an abundance of pressure would overcome that negative effect. He was absolutely right, and the Bears eked out a 20–17 overtime win.

Moreover, since the alignments weren't common, the Chargers didn't know how to block them. "We'd never seen this defense before and weren't prepared to deal with it," running back Hank Bauer said. "When that happens, it's pretty tough to change the game-plan you came in with. And they whacked us around pretty hard."

The Bears defenders knew that their coach was on to something. If this could work against the best offense in the league, how would other offenses adapt to it? Ryan's concepts weren't enough to get the offensively-challenged Bears over the hump in 1981, but the team started putting more talent in place. Wilson had been selected in the first round of the 1980 draft, and line-backer Mike Singletary and safety Jeff Fisher came aboard a year later. The 1983 draft brought end Richard Dent and safety Dave Duerson. Linebacker Wilber Marshall—the most physically gifted player on the defensive side—was taken in the first round in 1984. Cornerback Leslie Frazier was an undrafted free agent from Alcorn State, free safety Gary Fencik was a 10th-round pick of the Miami Dolphins, and tackle Steve McMichael was a castoff from the New England Patriots.

Eventually, the Bears presented Ryan with the right combination of intensity and experience to make the 46 Defense the most formidable in the NFL. The 1985 Bears, the most famous version, gave up the fewest points and yards while leading the league in turnovers and sacks and blazing a trail of pure hell through the season. During one three-game stretch in the regular season, the Bears scored more points on defense than they allowed on offense and they're the only team in history to post back-to-back shutouts in the playoffs.

The Patriots scored 10 points in Super Bowl XX, but the Bears knew the game was theirs from the moment they saw quarterback Tony Eason move under center for New England's first offensive play. "When you looked into [Eason's] eyes, you saw the same eyes the first time we played them this year, a little confused," Singletary said. "We got to him early and rattled him a bit. So I thought, *Let's go get him.*" Added Fencik: "We thought if we put him in a situation where he had to win the game for them, he couldn't do it. They pretty much conceded they couldn't run against us."

The Bears throttled Eason out of the game and made life equally miserable for Steve Grogan, Eason's veteran replacement. New England's quarterbacks were sacked seven times, and the Patriots gained just 123 total yards. Chicago caused six turnovers and allowed seven rushing yards. It was Ryan's last game with the team—he had accepted the Philadelphia Eagles' offer to become their head coach—and Ryan's defenders dedicated their performance to him, carrying him off the field of the Superdome—a very unusual gesture for a defensive coordinator, but fully appropriate in this case.

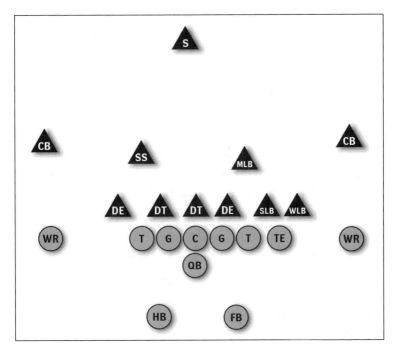

The Chicago Bears' 46 Defense

"The 46 Defense—to make it very plain and to the point— is all about pressure," Singletary said in *America's Game*. "It is all about pressure. We're going to come at you. And we're going to hit your quarterback until you get another one in. It was a nightmare, I know, for the quarterback. First of all, you had Otis [Wilson] and Wilber [Marshall] next to each other, and the quarterback's looking out of his eye. Then, you've got [Richard] Dent on the other side. Then, you've got Dan Hampton in the middle, and the Fridge [William Perry], and Steve McMichael. That's not good."

What made it even less good for opposing offenses was that blocking the base 46 front was a nightmare. Ryan put his nose tackle right over the head of the center and then aligned his two three-technique defenders to the outside shoulders of the guards. These alignments made it very difficult for offensive lines to double-team anyone on the inside because the outside leverage to either guard forced the guards away from the center, who was dealing with the nose tackle one-on-one.

Ryan took his strong-side and weak-side linebackers out of the traditional middle area they'd roam in the standard 4-3 defense. Instead, he aligned them to either side of the tight end. The middle linebacker and strong safety were responsible for second-level run support and blitz assignments, and the corner-backs and free safety were responsible for one-on-one coverage. Ordinarily, putting a three-man secondary on islands over and over would be a recipe for disaster, but Ryan's pressure concepts kept teams from developing the kinds of route concepts that would take advantage.

If you blocked Chicago's six-man 46 base front, you weren't accounting for the middle linebacker, who would blast right up the gut and destroy whatever was going on in the backfield, depending on whether the running backs stayed home to block or not. And if you kept a seventh man in to block the middle linebacker, that didn't take care of the strong safety, who would blitz with alarming alacrity. Basically, however you guessed against the 46 Defense, you guessed wrong. "We're gonna keep coming," Singletary said. "And we're gonna keep you thinking. We're not ducking and dodging. We're gonna have fun out there because the 46 Defense is physical, and it's as nasty as you want to get."

The 46 was also smart. It was an aggressive defense that thought on its feet, and that's because Ryan had the kinds of players who could adjust to various offensive concepts. The Bears adapted to offensive shifts with two pre-snap counters—Automatic Front and Coverage (AFC) and Blitz to Formation (BTF). AFC marked the ways in which the players on the field guided by Singletary would adjust to the offensive formations they saw. The reads they got often were so simple that Singletary could call out the play before it happened.

The Bears could switch from 4-3 to 3-4 looks, bring what looked like extreme blitzes, and drop into multiple coverages. The AFC gave the 46 a level of complexity that took it far beyond a situational blitz package. The Bears never truly used it as their base defense—Ryan preferred a more traditional 4-3 set based on personnel—but the 46 transcended the era because you could build flexibility into it. And it was severely confusing to opposing offenses, who watched as the players in the 46 front moved from strong-side to weak-side, from the inside shoulder to the outside shoulder, and from the line to linebacker depth based on the call.

BTF, as Singletary explained in *The Games That Changed the Game*, was the engine behind Chicago's dizzying array of blitz formations and concepts, and it was more complex than anything else the NFL had going at the time. "When Buddy clapped his hands, there were about 30 or 40 different things that could happen, depending on what our opponent's formation was, where the receivers were lined up, the backfield set, down and distance. We'd factor all that in and make an on-the-spot choice as to where we were going to go with the best blitz for that situation. We're going to run certain fronts. Our corners would do certain things in tandem with our safety. There had to be a lot of communication within that clap Buddy conveyed to our defense."

It also required an agile mind, as Singletary found out the hard way in his first NFL start, which happened to be that over-time win against the Chargers in 1981. Ryan benched Singletary early—and for the rest of the game—after the young linebacker wasted a timeout based on his confusion over a defensive call.

Ryan wasn't always easy to deal with—as a person or as a coach. His three-pronged grading scale while watching film with his players had specific designations: "dumbass," "horseshit," and "asshole." Once in a while, Dent said, you might hear, "Good play." Rex Ryan remembered that "Dad called players only by their numbers until they did something he liked. 'Hey 51, get your ass in gear!' That kind of stuff. If you played hard for him and bled for him, he'd suddenly remember your name just fine." Buddy Ryan's one season as the Houston Oilers' defensive coordinator is remembered most for the time he took a swing at offensive coordinator Kevin Gilbride on the sideline…during a game.

Most of Ryan's players had a love-hate relationship with him. He was hard on them at the best of times, but he also trusted them (when they'd earned that trust) to call things on the field in ways that brought out the best in them. Hired as the Bears' coach before the 1983 season, Mike Ditka had a far more simple relationship with Ryan—barely any at all. Ryan believed he should have been hired when Ditka was, and it was never easy between those two hard-headed men. "I'm not happy he's gone—I'm elated," Ditka said to the *Los Angeles Times* after Ryan accepted the Eagles job. "Never again in history will an assistant coach get as much credit as Buddy did. I handled it well. It will be interesting to see how he handles it, now that he's the head coach…He took a lot of bows, and I let him take them. But he didn't let any of his assistants take any bows. Some people don't give credit to anyone else. Why doesn't [offensive line coach] Dick Stanfel get more credit? We led the league in rushing three years in a row."

Ryan was nonplussed when told of Ditka's happiness at his departure. "I should be so lucky to have a Buddy Ryan around. I'd like to have somebody around to take care of me."

Neither Ryan nor Ditka was as successful without the other. The defense Buddy left behind for the 1986 season was actually statistically better, setting a record for points allowed in a season that stood until 2000, when the Baltimore Ravens broke it. But new defensive coordinator Vince Tobin drew the ire of his players by eliminating elements of the 46 over time. Meanwhile, Ryan's tenures as a head coach in Philadelphia and the Arizona Cardinals were generally marked by great defenses and too little attention paid to the offensive side of the ball. Balance wasn't Buddy's thing. But the 46 Defense was more balanced than it was made out to be.

As the NFL moved to more three and four-receiver sets, the 46 fell out of vogue to a degree; coaches weren't willing to take the coverage risks against more diverse offenses. Jeff Fisher took elements of it with him as a head coach for the Houston Oilers/Tennessee Titans from 1994 through 2010 and with the St. Louis Rams from 2012 to 2016. The real keepers of the 46 flame are Buddy's sons, Rex and Rob, who have called it in different ways since their days as dueling defensive coordinators for Oklahoma and Oklahoma State in the late 1990s. When Rex became the Baltimore Ravens' defensive coordinator in 2005, he was eager to bring 46 aspects to a defense that was already historically great and had the personnel to run it. Ray Lewis took Singletary's old spot as the brains of the outfit, and the Ravens ranked first in the league in both points and yards allowed in 2006—something they didn't even do in their Super Bowl season of 2000. In 2000 they lost the yards allowed title to...Fisher's Titans. "We're going to be aggressive," Rex told *The Washington Post* in the summer of 2005. "We're not just going to play the 46 because my dad is going to kick my [rear] or something. We're going to play it because it makes sense. This defense is hard to block."

Rex used it as the head coach of the New York Jets from 2009 through 2014 and then when he became the Buffalo Bills head coach.

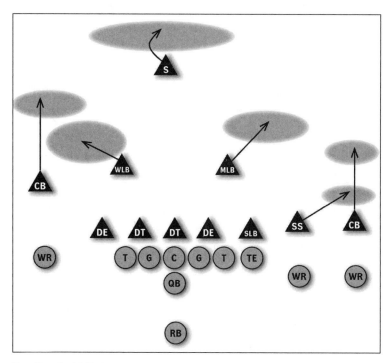

Rex Ryan's 46 Defense

As to the 46's supposed vulnerabilities against spread option attacks and other multiple offensive fronts, Rex was just as defiant as his dad used to be. "We aren't sure where this rumor of a supposed weakness to the option originated, but you can probably guess that it was started by an option coach who didn't want to deal with the 46 on a weekly basis," he wrote in his book, *Coaching Football's 46 Defense.*

To be fair, Rex also added several wrinkles to the base 46—linebackers had more assignments, ends slow played read-option quarterbacks, and deep zone concepts prevented the leaks downfield caused by a more consistently aggressive attack. In the Cover-3 example shown, the weak-side linebacker and strong safety switch positional assignments—the weak-side linebacker drops into coverage, the defensive backs move to zones dependent on the situation, and the linebackers are tasked to adjust to crossing routes in new ways. Although Buddy wanted to dictate an offense's terms on a non-negotiable basis, Rex understood that in a more complicated football world, adaptations would be necessary. As to the debate of the greatest defense in NFL history, Rex was the defensive line coach for one of the universal entrants, the 2000 Ravens, and he deferred to his dad. "Opponents who played Baltimore thought they had a chance to beat us right up until the game began," he said. "Then they'd start playing and realize our speed and size was too much to overcome. Before teams played the Bears, they weren't even thinking about winning. They were just hoping to survive. They didn't want to get the crap kicked out of them. The '85 Bears had teams beat before they even played."

The Counter Trey and Three Quarterbacks: How Joe Gibbs Beat the NFL

Unlike Bill Walsh's San Francisco 49ers and Rex Ryan's Chicago Bears defense, the Washington Redskins weren't totally down in the dumps when they received their schematic injection in the 1980s. When Redskins owner Jack Kent Cooke hired Joe Gibbs to be his new head coach in January of 1981, the team had avoided a losing record in four of the previous five seasons, though there had not been a playoff berth since 1977. But Gibbs, who Hall of Fame general manager Bobby Beathard recommended to Cooke, had a set of innovations and adaptations that became supremely successful.

Gibbs inherited some offensive stars—quarterback Joe Theismann and running back John Riggins in particular—and then eventually tweaked his scheme to fit them. To Riggins' power running style, Gibbs and his staff turned an offensive line full of castoffs and underrated players into the famed Hogs. Both *40* and *50 Gut* power running plays were staples of the Gibbs offense, but Gibbs is best-known for two things—the H-back and the Counter Trey running play.

After starting 0–5 in his first season, Gibbs committed to the players he had instead of the players he wanted—perhaps inspired by a heart-to-heart talk he had with Theismann. The veteran quarterback expressed his commitment to the team, and things proceeded positively from there. "We started to go to the two-tight-end offense," Theismann said in *America's Game*. "We started to change and run the football a little bit more. We became more of a control-the-game-style offense versus a 'Let's try and outscore the world' offense."

Gibbs put the H-back in as a specific response to the pass-rushing outside linebacker in the 3-4 defenses that were popular in the decade. The H-back was a hybrid tight end/fullback blocking in the formation just behind and outside either tackle. Depending on the play call, the H-back could block the outside pass rusher specifically, stem out to block a cornerback on an outside run, address a blitzing safety on a pass, move to the other side of the formation to seal a block on a counter play, or become a big factor in Gibbs' specific receiver formation designs—especially the trips concept. The H-back could also move along the formation pre-snap, depending on the call, to further enhance the overall blocking picture.

The Counter Trey took advantage of Gibbs' belief in the one-back system. Since he'd moved the traditional fullback position out to the tackles, he wanted something that would fool defensive linemen with a power element. Gibbs actually had several counters,

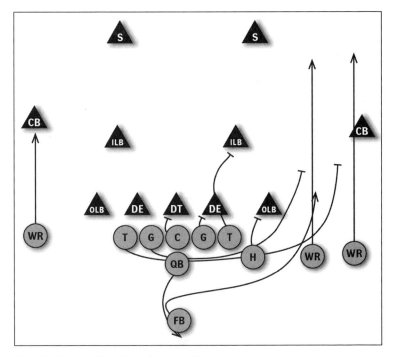

The Washington Redskins' Counter Trey

but the Counter Trey was the most famous version—not that the coach came up with it on his own. "We stole it," Gibbs told *Sports Illustrated* in 2008. "We saw some film on Nebraska, and Tom Osborne was doing some really innovative things with his line up front, and we were watching it and thought, *God, that is good stuff.* So we stole it. We all steal things. You can talk to me all day, and I'll never say I was the first guy to do anything because, sure as heck, there is some coach out there who did it first."

But it was the Redskins that ran it with great success throughout the Gibbs era with backs from Riggins to George Rogers to Timmy Smith to Earnest Byner. It didn't matter who ran the Redskins counters—the line would make them go. "No matter what you have in football, you need something you can do really well and run it over and over again," Gibbs said. "We had the counter game."

It was a brutally intelligent and effective combination of misdirection and power. Gibbs directed the linemen on the strong side to execute standard gap blocks, and the H-back sealed the edge against the outside linebacker. Those gap blocks were taken one step to the weak-side to get the defensive line rolling the wrong way. (That was for a 3-4 defense; against 4-3 over and under fronts and certain kinds of blitzes, the H-back and gap blockers might have different responsibilities.) The weak-side tackle and guard would pull all the way over to the strong side of the formation. Meanwhile, the quarterback sold the counter game by moving to the weak side, and the running back took a step in that direction as well. The optimal result: a defense was one step slow to the ball, and two blockers led the way for Gibbs' power back.

Gibbs was also an advocate of run action. He directed his blockers to fire out on play-action passes, fooling the defensive line and linebackers into aggression when they should have played it differently. And he was very big on draw and delay plays for the same reason; Gibbs had a special talent for putting enemy defenses on a string.

But it wasn't just the Counter Trey that made Washington's offense special. Gibbs coached under Don Coryell in two different locations. He was Coryell's running backs coach for the St. Louis Cardinals from 1973 through 1977 and Coryell's offensive coordinator with the San Diego Chargers in 1979 and 1980. Thus, he was completely conversant in the nuances of the vertical passing game and on the cutting edge when it came to formation diversity. Gibbs knew that there would be openings for the deep pass if he could make the power running game consistently effective.

Gibbs was one of the first NFL coaches to use the bunch formation, where three receivers either line up or align via presnap movement into a triangle on one side of the field. His playbook was also heavy with trips formations, in which three receivers lined up to one side and worked to flood that side of the coverage. "You try to cover them man-to-man, and somebody's going to get picked off right away," Houston Oilers head coach (and Gibbs' predecessor in Washington) Jack Pardee said in 1992. "You zone them, and they kill you that way. They've got such a balanced attack that almost anything they try on you is probably going to work, passing or running. It's a very scary offense. They'll always get five, six yards on first down and then they'll always convert on third and 3, third and 2. It's an offense that can do everything."

By the time the Redskins won their third Super Bowl at the end of the 1991 season, Gibbs' offense was just about impossible to stop. The Redskins finished in the top five in points scored six times in his first tenure there and three straight times from 1989 through 1991. That was after Riggins was long gone and Gibbs was still blowing defenses away with multiple quarterbacks and running backs. His status as the only coach to win three Super Bowls with three different quarterbacks (Joe Theismann, Doug Williams, Mark Rypien) is an amazing record that has a pretty good shot of standing forever.

Sam Wyche and the No-Huddle Offense

Sam Wyche, who had been Bill Walsh's backup to the backup quarterback with the Cincinnati Bengals and his coaching confidant with the San Francisco 49ers, left the Bay Area in 1984 to take the job Walsh had wanted for so long—head coach of the Bengals. Wyche took many aspects of the West Coast Offense with him, but he was also an inveterate tinkerer with formations, concepts, and rules. He would huddle with more than 11 players to confuse defenses, a tactic which has since been outlawed by the NFL.

But the biggest innovation Wyche brought to the league was the use of the no-huddle offense as a primary function. "Originally, we did it to change the tempo," Wyche told TheMMQB.com in 2015. "We would go fast and then slow it down, then we would go fast, fast, fast for a couple—and then slow it down so [the defense] didn't know what was coming. Then we decided we've got to be careful that when we slow it down they don't get fresh people in, so we came up with what we called 'set alerts.' If the defense tries to substitute, we yell, 'Set alert!' That meant we're going to get to the line, the ball is coming up quick, and we're running a play that we had memorized. We would catch them with too many men on the field, which you still see happen."

Not that it was his idea. Teams had been running no-huddle for decades in the two-minute drill—perhaps most famously in the 1958 NFL Championship Game between the Baltimore

Colts and New York Giants—but it was Wyche who codified the idea in more of a full-time sense. "I'm a believer in the coaching tree," Wyche told *Sports Illustrated* in 1989. "It's important to know where ideas started. Once Hank Stram and I were talking, and he said, 'I wonder why teams don't just go ahead and do it?' That kicked me in. You can't go into every game saying, 'We'll just damn well outplay you.' You're looking for the 2 percent edge, the surprise of a safety blitz, the surprise of having fourth and 12 on your own 25 and going for it. These things are sound. They work."

Wyche started running the no-huddle more and more in the late 1980s with great effectiveness. In fact it was so effective that opponents started faking injuries to slow down the tempo. And this brought serious repercussions in the second most important game Wyche ever coached.

Less than two hours before the 1988 AFC Championship Game between the Bengals and Buffalo Bills, Wyche was informed by the league that if his team used a quick count in the no-huddle as determined by the officials, the Bengals would be penalized and the down replayed. "Pete Rozelle cannot change a rule," Wyche said. "That has to be done by 28 owners, and obviously 28 owners haven't congregated overnight. We played for 17 games to get here for this championship game under one set of rules interpreted one way. We have used the no-huddle offense for three-and-a-half years. It has been endorsed by [supervisor of officials] Art McNally and the commissioner. It's the principle."

Wyche didn't stand on principle in the game, which the Bengals won 21–10. His offense led the league in points that year, and his defense coached by Dick LeBeau was good enough to shut the Bills down. That playoff victory brought Wyche head-to-head with Walsh in Super Bowl XXIII. It was, of course, Walsh's last game and it was Joe Montana's last-minute touchdown drive that upended the go-go Bengals 20–16. It was also ironic that the same Bills franchise that had been jawing so much about the no-huddle would use it as a functional construct of the teams that went to four straight Super Bowls in the next decade.

CHAPTER 7

A NEW LEVEL
The NFL in the 1990s

> *"If my answers frighten you, Vincent,*
> *you should cease asking scary questions."*
> —Samuel L. Jackson as Jules Winnfield in *Pulp Fiction*

With its widespread schematic complexity and big personalities, the NFL had become the unquestioned glamour game of America in the 1980s, and that would continue upward into the 1990s, when several constructs built in the previous decade came to full fruition. More than in any other decade, coaches on both sides of the ball furiously sought to outdo each other in what turned out to be the most inventive decade in the league's annals. Most of those inventions carry on today and will do so in the future under altered names and in different guises.

The Mouse that Scored: The Run-and-Shoot Takes Over

While the Sid Gillman-rooted vertical passing game, Bill Walsh's West Coast Offense, and the no-huddle offense all showed the way to more consistently explosive offensive production through the 1980s, the NFL's implementation of the

Run-and-Shoot offense throughout the late 1980s and early 1990s took things to an entirely new level. The Run-and-Shoot had been wildly successful at the collegiate level for years and in the USFL through the mid-1980s, but those in the NFL responsible for such decisions found it difficult to take it seriously as a base concept—until they were dominated by it.

Officially invented by Glenn "Tiger" Ellison in 1958 after the Middletown, Ohio, high school coach watched a bunch of grade school kids play football on a field as he was driving home from a practice, the offense featured four receivers who adjusted their routes based on the defenders, a single running back, no tight end, relatively little in the way of designed play calls, and a quarterback who operated within a moving pocket. Ellison installed the offense for his team the next day, and what was essentially an advanced version of the old double-wing offense got its start. Ellison called it the "Lonesome Polecat" at first because Stan Lewis, Ellison's offensive line coach had said, "Call it the 'Lonesome Polecat' because it stinks!" Eventually, Ellison took an offense with a few reads and plays and developed it into what he called the Run-and-Shoot. "If a man will picture his problem vividly in his mind, brand it on his brain, drive it into his heart, suddenly during a relaxed moment when the situation seems most hopeless, the right answer will pop," Ellison said in his book, *Run and Shoot Football: The Now Attack.* "Put a demand on nature, and she will supply the need. From out of nowhere one bright fall morning popped the 'Lonesome Polecat' bringing us the right answer."

Ellison's other pivotal book, *Run and Shoot Football: Offense of the Future,* was published in 1965 and made its way to the desk of a coach named Darrell "Mouse" Davis, who would take the Run-and-Shoot to entirely new levels through the ensuing decades. From Milwaukie High School in Oregon, to Portland State, to the

Canadian Football League, to the USFL, Davis took his version of the Run-and-Shoot wherever he went and he was always successful with it. At Portland State his teams set 20 NCAA Division I-AA marks and led the nation in scoring three times. In Toronto his offense took the Argonauts from last place to a Grey Cup title. For the Houston Gamblers in 1984, Davis' offense racked up 5,795 passing yards and 45 passing touchdowns in 18 games while being piloted by future NFL Hall of Famer Jim Kelly. The Gamblers' "Mouseketeers" group of receivers boasted the first duo of pass catchers (Richard Johnson and Ricky Sanders) to each amass more than 100 receptions in a single season.

But when Davis entered the NFL, many of the more traditional minds throughout the league derided the Run-and-Shoot as a gimmick that would not last against the best defensive competition. Buddy Ryan famously called it the "chuck-and-duck," and several coaches balked at the idea for different reasons—the running game wasn't variable enough with its traps and draws, the lack of a tight end left quarterbacks too vulnerable, and the overall offense wasn't consistently effective in the end zone. It was going to take a schematic evangelist to escort the Run-and-Shoot into the NFL, and that's exactly what Davis was. "They won't want to look at the facts," Davis told the *Los Angeles Times* of his detractors in 1990. "They just want to bitch about something."

Not surprisingly, the NFL's ultimate acceptance for the Run-and-Shoot began in the city that housed the league's worst offense the year before. In 1988 the Detroit Lions finished dead last in the NFL in total offense (3,405 yards), offensive plays (920), yards per play (3.7), first downs (226), offensive touchdowns (20), and total points (220). There were two head coaches (Darryl Rogers and Wayne Fontes) and two offensive coordinators (Bob Baker and Lew Carpenter), and nobody could figure out how to get the ball in the end zone.

Fontes was the team's interim head coach for the last five games of the 1988 season, and one of the first things he did when the team made it official was to hire Davis as his offensive coordinator. Teams had run plays with four receivers before, of course. The four-vertical concept was a staple of the Gillman offense and ran through the playbooks of everyone from Don Coryell to Joe Gibbs to Mike Martz all the way to Kevin Gilbride with the New York Giants through the 2013 season. But as a base offense? That was just too much, it was assumed. The assumptions were incorrect—at least at first.

In 1989 the Lions improved to 19th in points scored and 18th in yards gained. In 1990 they moved up to fifth in points and 14th in yards. When the Lions' defense matched the high-octane offense in 1991, Detroit made it all the way to the NFC Championship Game before losing to the Washington Redskins. The 12 wins the Lions put up in the 1991 regular season is still the most in franchise history, and that was the last time the franchise came away with a division title. In those first three seasons with Davis as the offensive coordinator, the results were achieved with three different primary quarterbacks—Bob Gagliano in 1989, Rodney Peete in 1990, and Erik Kramer in 1991.

The differences in this offense were obvious and effective. Before the West Coast Offense, receivers primarily got open through their own physical gifts and intellectual guile—feints at the line of scrimmage, covert push-offs, pure downfield speed. Walsh's offense directed its receivers to move in precision as part of a perfectly orchestrated symphony. In the Run-and-Shoot, the receivers were asked to define their routes on the defense's actions. Walsh also called for this, but the Run-and-Shoot directed receivers to do it with more frequency. Quarterbacks would make their first key off the safety closest to the line of scrimmage. If the safeties were deep, there was always a square-in to run underneath the coverage. If the receiver could beat the safety to the near side of the field, that could be the play right there. "The concept of reading the coverage, nobody did it," June Jones, who was Davis' quarterbacks and receivers coach in Detroit and installed his own versions of the Run-and-Shoot with the Houston Oilers and Atlanta Falcons over the years, told Grantland. "Even when I was a player in 1977, every Monday they'd say look at the next team and tell us what you think will work. Well, I'd write a book on reading and how to read the routes and all that stuff. But nobody in the NFL back then allowed their receivers to read coverage. If you're running a curl, you're running a curl. That was it. There was no conversion."

The conversion first happened when Ellison realized that the kids he was watching were simply adjusting their routes to what their defenders were doing. But it's not entirely true that nobody was using option routes until the Run-and-Shoot gurus turned them on full blast. (Coryell implemented routes with different breaking patterns based on coverage with the San Diego Chargers in the 1970s and early 1980s.) Gillman had options for his receivers as well.

But in Davis' offenses, the route conversions were manifold per receiver and they defined the passing offense to a large degree. Each receiver had specific assignments to read against coverages, and the conversions were fairly complex. Against a two-deep nickel defense alone, as Davis detailed in a 1990s coaching clinic, the possibilities were all over the place. "Our first key is the nickel back on the onside slot," he said. "If [the nickel back] doesn't bump over with the motion, we run the motion halfway between the Z and Y receivers and get him uncovered 95 percent of the time. If you think they are going to bounce the coverage to the motion, it doesn't always happen. Sometimes, they want to rush the nickel back off the corner. If they don't bump over, we take the completion the defense gives us. When the nickel bounces to the motion, we go back to our original read against the three-deep pattern. If the split receiver goes deep, the cornerback goes with him. But if you are reading the corner, when he goes back, we throw the ball to the flat. If he rolls to the flat, we throw the ball outside to the split receiver. The quarterback delivers the ball on the third or fifth step. If the cornerback runs off with the split receiver and the nickel back jumps the flat after a bump on the [receiver's] motion, we have to go to the secondary route by the motion man. He is facing a half-field safety; he has to know that. When the motion man doesn't get the ball on the third step, he looks at the safety. If the safety man is right on his face, the receiver runs the post. He beats the safety through the hole in the middle of the field. If the motion man runs his pattern, and the safety man is a damned mile up top, he breaks his pattern off into the middle short."

Phew. That's against one kind of coverage with different specific options and read assignments against other kinds of coverages. The motion of the slot receiver gave the quarterback a clue as to whether the defenses were running man or zone coverages,

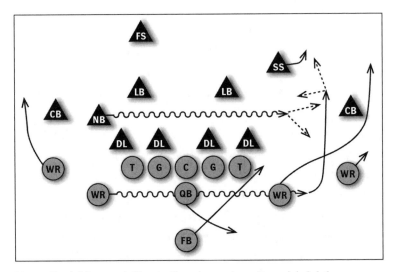

Mouse Davis' Run-and-Shoot offense vs. a two-deep nickel defense

but a lot of this deduction happened on the fly, which is why some mistook the Run-and-Shoot as a simple thing to stop, when in fact the relative simplicity of base calls were just part of a highly nuanced post-snap offense.

Davis busted all the myths of *his* Run-and-Shoot in an interview with Bob Oates of the *Los Angeles Times* in September of 1990. To the insistence that a mobile quarterback was required, he said that the rollouts were generally just a few steps, and that any taller passer with a strong arm—like Kelly with the Houston Gamblers—would do. To the insistence that his quarterbacks were injured more often because of the lack of protection, Davis cited injury data, which told a different story: stationary quarterbacks were actually more vulnerable to getting hurt. Nor was it prone to blitzing. "We don't see many blitzers. Blitzing means single coverage, and our receivers are open right now," he said. "The whole deal [in the Run-and-Shoot] is to get the pass off fast. Blitzers play into our strength. The defense we fear the most is one with four All-Pro pass rushers and seven All-Pro defensive backs. Great talent defeats any offense."

Opponents of the scheme who said that the lack of a second running back and a first tight end led to a sameness that was easily defeated were countered by Davis' assertion that because only one back can run the ball at any time, a fourth receiver puts a defense far more on edge. And Davis believed in the notion that if a tight end was big enough to be a dominant blocker, he wouldn't be fast and agile enough to be an elite receiver. Lastly, he maintained that because the Run-and-Shoot forced defenses to play the pass far more often, running backs had more and better openings in which to gain consistent yardage.

That final philosophy certainly worked for the Lions in the Mouse era. Of course, it helped that Barry Sanders was the Lions' first-round draft pick in 1989. And yes, Sanders was going to be great in any system he was in, but what the Lions called the "Silver Stretch" did give opponents one more reason to pause. How do you counter this fast, mercilessly slippery back when you're already dealing with this weird passing offense that has a higher percentage of your linebackers on the bench? "From the system they're running out of, it makes him very elusive," Chicago Bears middle linebacker Mike Singletary told *Sports Illustrated* in 1990. "You not only have to figure out what's going on, but you have to find him. You have to tackle him with good technique. If you try to blast him, chances are he'll spin out of it, and you'll end up looking a little silly."

But after the 1991 season, which ended when the Lions were decimated 41–10 by the Redskins in the NFC Championship Game, Fontes went to Davis and told him that he wanted to run an offense with the tight end featured more often—that is to say, at all. Davis knew that this was his cue to leave. In the end Fontes wanted a version of the Joe Gibbs offense that had beaten his team and he hired Dan Henning to put it together. "[Fontes] said, 'You can stay if you want to,' but that would be kind of ridiculous," Davis said in 1991. "We did a good job. I don't have any bad feelings. I'm disappointed because we didn't get a chance to finish the job we started out to do."

Still, the Run-and-Shoot had a brief NFL future in different iterations. Jones coached it in Atlanta from 1991 through 1996 as the Falcons' offensive coordinator and eventual head coach, and Jack Pardee ran it as the Oilers' head coach from 1990 through 1994. The Oilers were the most star-crossed of the Run-and-Shoot teams with seemingly all the pieces in place for an NFL title but were never able to put it all together amidst dysfunction and friction among players, coaches, and the front office.

A linebacker for the Los Angeles Rams and Washington Redskins from 1957 through 1973, Pardee compiled an 87–77 record as a head coach for the Bears, Redskins, and Oilers from

1975 through 1994. But his Run-and-Shoot revelation came when he coached with Davis in the USFL with the Houston Gamblers. Before that Pardee, who was at one time as conservative and defensive-oriented a coach as the NFL could field, had another near-revelation when his offensive coordinator for the Bears in 1977, Gillman, raked him over the coals after one landmark game. When Walter Payton set the NFL record with 275 rushing yards in a single game, Gillman told Pardee that it was embarrassing that the Bears could only muster one touchdown out of all that production. The Bears beat the Minnesota Vikings 10–7, and Chicago quarterback Bob Avellini completed four of six passes for 33 yards and an interception.

Eventually, though, the coach changed course. When the USFL folded, Pardee took those Run-and-Shoot principles to the University of Houston. In 1989 the Cougars averaged 53.5 points, 511.3 passing yards, and 624.9 total yards. Each of those marks were the best in the nation. Oilers owner Bud Adams made the call to replace Jerry Glanville with Pardee in January of 1990, saying that Pardee was the only man he wanted for the position.

Gillman, though, did not approve of Pardee's specific way of opening up his passing offense. The father of the modern passing game was not a fan of the Run-and-Shoot. "I just feel that you can't play without a tight end," he said. "At times, when the situation presents itself, I would use four wide receivers and take out the tight end but certainly not on a regular basis. The fact that the quarterback works so close to the line of scrimmage, if he isn't sacked, he's hit. In the Tampa Bay-Detroit game the other night, Rodney Peete almost got killed. I don't know how long a quarterback will last in that system. He had better be able to run."

For the Oilers' version of the Run-and-Shoot, Pardee retained Gilbride, who had been Glanville's offensive coordinator the year before. Glanville had his mercurial moments, to be sure, but neither Pardee nor Gilbride had any idea of the drama they were in for over the next four years. The Oilers made the playoffs all four full seasons that Pardee was their head coach—and between the Run-and-Shoot executed by quarterback Warren Moon and a defense that ranked in the NFL's top 10 in yards and points allowed in 1991 and 1992—Houston appeared to be one of the league's real teams on the move.

Not only did they have Moon, but they also had four perfect receivers for the Run-and-Shoot. There was Haywood Jeffires as the bigger outside receiver with legitimate franchise talent, Drew Hill as the veteran who could drive teams crazy in the slot with his superior route running, Ernest Givins as the do-it-all guy who would hurt you outside and in the slot, and the aggregate speed combination of Curtis Duncan and Tony Jones. "There's no defensive coverage in the world that can stop four good wide receivers," Givins told *Sports Illustrated* in 1991. "The other team can't say, 'We're going to freeze Haywood Jeffires.' You freeze him, Curtis steps up, or Drew, or me. But if we weren't outstanding receivers, we wouldn't have the ability to step up and have great games. We do. We live and die by the pass; they don't. We succeed; they don't. Until you do it, don't knock us. We're happy because of what we've accomplished, don't get us wrong. And we're not trying to be greedy and get all the attention in the NFL. But give us what we deserve. That's all we ask."

The Oilers got a lot of credit for a while. But that all changed on January 3, 1993, in a divisional playoff game against the Buffalo Bills at Buffalo's Rich Stadium. Moon threw four touchdown passes in the first half alone as the Oilers passed their way to a 28–3 halftime lead and a 35–3 third-quarter lead…and then everything fell apart. Jim Kelly was injured, and backup Frank Reich added his name to the pantheon of benchwarmers everywhere when he matched Moon, the future Hall of Famer, with four second-half touchdowns. Meanwhile, Bills head coach Marv Levy made the second-half decision to move from a defense with five and six defensive backs to a more conventional 3-4 front, stymieing the Oilers and their pass-first philosophy. The Bills crowded Houston's smaller receivers with press coverage, splayed their linebackers out in a series of wider zones, and blitzed off the edge with aplomb. The Oilers scored just three more points as the Bills were playing pinball in the fourth quarter and saw the game slip away 41–38 in overtime.

Defensive coordinator Jim Eddy was the man blamed for the collapse and was summarily dismissed. He was replaced by Buddy Ryan on January 30, 1993, and that's when things got really interesting. Ryan was a man with no filter. When he came in to coach a defense, he wanted no other coach telling him how to do it. He was no fan of quarterbacks either. In the 1993 Oilers defensive playbook, he wrote that "QBs are overpaid, overrated pompous bastards, and must be punished." He had no patience at all for the Run-and-Shoot (or, for that matter, any offense that got in the way of the conversation about his defense), and he and Gilbride were on a collision course from the start.

The 1993 Oilers started out 1–4. Moon was benched for a time in favor of Cody Carlson, a hilarious decision in retrospect. Ryan's 46 Defense took time to stick as he matched scheme to personnel, and he would take his defense off the practice field if he didn't like the way things were going. Pardee was more and more of a lame duck—even as the team turned things around and won their last 11 regular-season games. But no amount of winning would solve what was going on behind the scenes—a schism between Gilbride and Ryan that came to a head in the regular-season finale against the New York Jets. Ryan took a swing at Gilbride on the sideline during a game the Oilers won 24–0 to end their regular season with a 12–4 mark. But after the playoff loss to the Kansas

City Chiefs, everything went out the window. Gilbride and Pardee were fired. Ryan went off to coach the Arizona Cardinals. Moon was traded to Minnesota after a decade in Houston, and for all intents and purposes, the Run-and-Shoot was done as a base offensive system. However, there were specific schematic aspects of the system that define the NFL to this day.

Although you won't see any NFL teams running a base offense with four receivers and no tight end anymore, NFL teams use elements of the Run-and-Shoot today. Now, four-verticals passing concepts are much more complex with every receiver basing his route on the actions of a defender to a greater or lesser degree. Speedy slot receivers dominate up the seam and force defenses to pull linebackers off the field in place of defensive backs. Tight ends that barely block and are essentially big receivers frustrate their opponents and become the fourth targets for their quarterbacks. And now, NFL teams use option routes as crucial staples in their playbooks. With the increasing complexity of coverages, teams who don't use option routes would essentially be dooming themselves. The New England Patriots, the most successful team of the new millennium, use more option routes than any other NFL team—and to great effect. "At times, there are four decisions that a receiver needs to make after the snap," wide receivers coach Chad O'Shea told MassLive.com in early 2012. "That's one of the advantages of our offense, that we give players a lot of flexibility within the system to take what the defense gives us. And that's definitely something that's unique about our offense."

Well, it's unique if you're not aware of the Run-and-Shoot, though the Patriots took it to a new level. In their 2004 playbook, there were 25 different single receiver routes, and that doesn't count all the available options. Nor does it cover where those routes are run in a split on the field or how the receivers run routes in tandem. There were 17 different two-man route combos and five different three-man route combos. Once you've mastered all that, there's the matter of the call in any pass play—the name of the route group that a team decides for any pass play. Add in the protection at the line and you have the start of what will be an eventual Patriots play call.

For example, in the *1 Out ZAC Slot* play, the fullback (lined up wide left) runs a 14-yard in, though he should look for an outside release if anyone's cheating up expecting something quick. The halfback reads blitz, hits a run sneak through the A-gap if he's free, and digs sharply to the right. The X or iso receiver does a sight adjustment, reads the coverage, and could either come back outside or loop to the seam, depending again on the coverage. The Z receiver motions from right slot and heads six yards upfield into a four-way option. The Y receiver could turn a chute route or he might hook inside.

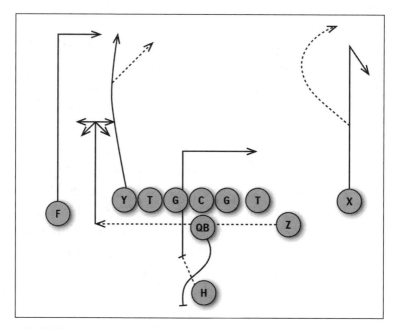

1 Out ZAC Slot in The New England Patriots' offense

That's one pass play—*one variation of a subgroup*—in a playbook that would rival the phone book for any large metropolis in overall ginormosity. "I have to trust in Deion [Branch] and Wes [Welker] and all those guys out there to be in the right spot so I can play fast and anticipate what they're doing," Patriots quarterback Tom Brady told *The Boston Globe* in 2012. "If everyone is not on the same page, it doesn't work. A lot of what these practices are about is everybody getting on the same page. You have a lot of new guys from other teams, rookies. The faster we can get up to speed and get better as a unit, the better we're going to be."

And getting everyone on the same page involved every possible receiver understanding the properties of the team's own individual option routes. That may in the end be the Run-and-Shoot's greatest lasting legacy—the NFL taking Ellison's quick "He go/I stay" mantra and turning it into another dimension in the passing game.

In a West Coast Offense, when timing is the order of the day, you'll see things like "U Take Off" calls (in which an in-line tight end is directed to run up the seam off an in route based on coverage) or a "Deep Over" option where a receiver is tasked to read the safety coverage and head up the seam if it's single-high or the safety to his side is otherwise occupied. On one play an outside receiver may have to discern—and in a big hurry—whether he's running a hot route (close to the quarterback most likely on a blitz read), a 15-yard in-cut or curl, or a 20-yard dash upfield. Obviously, if the quarterback and receiver aren't in sync on this, the quarterback will get pummeled, the ball will fall harmlessly to the ground in a place where the receiver isn't, or someone with the wrong uniform will be catching the pass.

In a three-digit system like the ones employed by the Chargers of Gillman and Coryell and later by Mike Martz with the "Greatest Show on Turf" St. Louis Rams, different issues arise. Receivers are directed to break their routes at times to adjust to a scrambling or pressured quarterback. Martz told his receivers to "break at a friendly angle" to the quarterback. On a simple half-back post, the back could have as many as three different options once he hit the middle of the field based on the coverage. And the receivers? The Rams set up different calls for their routes based on six alternate coverage concepts—retreat zone, retreat man, cloud, trail, bump, and quads. Some adjustments are minimal per those coverages (an up-and-in or chop translates pretty well), while others direct receivers to take different cuts, route tails, or both based on what they see.

With all those inherent complications in all those different systems, the idea with modern option routes is to simplify the process as much as possible without dumbing the offense down and negating the advantage of the option concept. That's where practice comes in. And more practice. After that, a little more practice. Preceded and followed by a long time in meeting rooms, coordinating assignments. "Most everything we do has an option to it," Seattle Seahawks receivers coach Kippy Brown (who directed receivers in a run-based West Coast Offense) told me in 2012. "There are very few routes that are what we call 'run-it' routes. Those are routes that stay on, no matter what. Usually, you have a conversion of some kind. Now, routes I've been associated with that are called options are normally slot routes. Guys in the slot will do certain things depending on how [the defense plays] you. We do our share of those. In the West Coast Offense, an option route could go either way. A lot of people call it a 'jerk' route—where you go in, set the linebacker up, and then go either way. It depends on the terminology and what you want to call an option route, but in our offense, nearly every route has a conversion. If they do this, you do that."

And that's where it becomes complicated for the modern quarterback—or, more accurate to say, where it can't become too complicated. Not only does the quarterback have to read the defense; he also has to know that his receivers are reading the defense the same way he is…and that they're adjusting accordingly. This becomes especially important for teams running more and more no-huddle offenses, as many NFL teams are these days. Your play call may be abbreviated because you have to get up to the line, and while the base routes would be in the name somehow, the options are then implied because there's only so much room in the abbreviated call. "That's why you give them clues and parameters in what they're looking for," Brown said. "You have to make it clear-cut, so there's no confusion and you know that the quarterback and receivers see the same exact thing. You're better off not having a bunch of conversions [if there's confusion], and we have some routes that 'leave home,' no matter what. We run it and, if it's not there, we go somewhere else with the ball. It depends on who you're playing with and what they can handle, whether it's the quarterback or receivers. That's meeting rooms, walk-throughs, pre-practice—it takes a lot of time to get everybody on the same page, especially when you have as many plays as we run. They have to learn the system first. Then they have to learn the conversions."

The Zone Blitz

Mouse Davis' ouster from the NFL and the 1993 Houston Oilers' immolation aside, another thing that killed the Run-and-Shoot as a functional construct in the NFL was the zone blitz. Teams had tried everything from dime coverage to jailbreak blitzes to counter the Run-and-Shoot put forth by the Atlanta Falcons, Detroit Lions, and Houston Oilers in the late 1980s and early

1990s, but it was the zone blitz and its elements of multiple coverage and hidden pressure that forced those Run-and-Shoot teams back to more traditional formations.

Put simply, the zone blitz is a set of schemes in which the quarterback reads certain players as rushers and others as coverage players—only to discover that the defense he's facing has changed after his first read. The zone blitz forced a new level of complexity in pre-snap read and route combinations. Although it wasn't the brainchild of Dick LeBeau, the Hall of Fame defensive back and defensive coordinator made it his own and defined it in the same way that true geniuses have personified key concepts throughout NFL history.

Of course, LeBeau would have had Hall of Fame credentials even if he never coached a down in the NFL. From 1959 through 1972, the Ohio State alum made his bones as one of the NFL's best defensive backs, reaching three Pro Bowls and finishing his career with 62 interceptions (tied for eighth on the all-time list). After his playing career ended, LeBeau took a job as a special teams coach with the Philadelphia Eagles in 1973, working his way up to defensive backs coach of the Green Bay Packers from 1976 through 1979. He took that same job with the Cincinnati Bengals in 1980 and was promoted to defensive coordinator in 1984.

LeBeau had been part of a blitz-happy team in Detroit and, with the advent in the early 1980s of the West Coast Offense and its short, precise passes, he now wanted to devise a way to fool offensive schemes that were far more varied and complex. "My hope was to make [the offense] read [the defense] as one thing and let the attack be something else," he told *The Cincinnati Enquirer* in 1997. "Show pressure and play zone. You have to be willing to take a guy who is usually a point-of-attack player and trust them to drop off the line a little bit. You wouldn't ask them to cover passes for a living, but they hold up in this defense."

LeBeau's first point-of-attack player was David Fulcher, a huge (6'3", 236-pound) safety who was selected in the third round of the 1986 draft and became his coach's first specific weapon in the zone blitz. During his time as the defensive coordinator of the Bengals and Pittsburgh Steelers, LeBeau and the zone blitz became as one in public perception and synonymous with defensive excellence.

Before LeBeau made it work with the Bengals, though, he took a trip to see LSU head coach and former Miami Dolphins defensive coordinator Bill Arnsparger, who had used the zone blitz in different iterations through the 1970s and early 1980s. Like LeBeau, Arnsparger wanted a scheme that combined blitz pressure with a safer coverage concept. "Normal blitzes use man-to-man

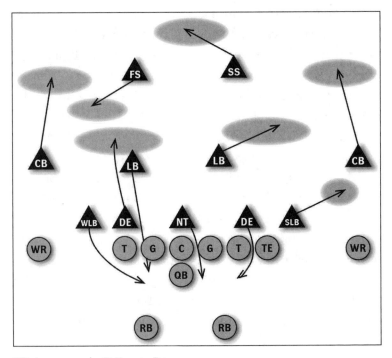

Bill Arnsparger's *31 Zone to Bo*

blitz coverage," Arnsparger wrote in his seminal book, *Coaching Defensive Football.* "The zone blitz uses zone coverage but presents protection problems to the offense. The offensive line and one or two backs are assigned to block the defensive line and linebackers. In the zone blitz, the linebacker blitzes along with a secondary player, but the offensive pick-up is different…because defensive linemen who usually rush are now dropping out to short inside zones to replace the linebacker and secondary player that blitz. Because of the blitzer's path, it is difficult for the offensive lineman to adjust."

Arnsparger detailed one of the zone blitzes he used with the Dolphins in the early 1980s with defensive end Kim Bokamper as the primary instigator. As Arnsparger pointed out, Bokamper had been trained as a linebacker, and the coach used his player's skills to anticipate the timing, spacing, and coverage responsibilities. In a 3-4 base front—and with Bokamper as the weak-side end dropping into coverage—*31 Zone to Bo* created all kinds of problems for opposing offenses. Because for every blitzing linebacker (two on the weak-side in this case), there was an end dropping into coverage, making the usual hot (quick passing) read against the blitz that much more complicated.

When LeBeau came to visit Arnsparger, it was this *31 Zone to Bo* concept the two men discussed, regarding the establishment of defensive pressure without exposing the secondary. LeBeau took that idea back to the NFL and added iterations never seen before. In LeBeau's zone blitzes, virtually anyone could blitz and anyone could cover. There wasn't a set look to which offenses could adjust. LeBeau essentially split the timing of the play in half—he wanted to show the quarterback one pressure package early in the down and then to switch to something else later in the down. And because it's very hard for any quarterback to switch his reads halfway through a play when he's running for his life, the zone blitz worked well from the start. No less an authority than Bill Belichick has said that the zone blitz is the rare concept that needed no correction or adjustment from its inception to the current day.

Now, the challenge for LeBeau was convincing Sam Wyche, Cincinnati's head coach, that the zone blitz was the way to go. "When I looked at it from an offensive standpoint, I saw there were problems that I didn't know how to solve," Wyche said in 1997. "That's when I knew it would be tough for offenses."

It was, especially when it was first unveiled in the 1980s, and nobody had a clue what they were seeing. LeBeau developed the zone blitz into a multi-dimensional idea, blitzing just about everyone from everywhere and throwing the most unexpected players into coverage. This author distinctly remembers Steelers nose tackle Casey Hampton, a 6'1", 320-pound bowling ball-shaped nose tackle, successfully covering running backs on flare passes. LeBeau knew his personnel, knew who could do what, and adjusted accordingly. "It's a circus out there," Jacksonville Jaguars left tackle Tony Boselli told *Sports Illustrated* in 1997. "You've got safeties rushing where defensive ends would be, defensive ends dropping into coverage. I don't know who I'm going to block on any pass play. You get 100 different looks against the zone blitz. That's what it seems like, anyway. Usually I might block two guys, maybe three in a game. Last year against Pittsburgh, I blocked Chad Brown, Kevin Henry, Bill Johnson, Levon Kirkland, Carnell Lake—and I'm probably missing somebody. The whole game's a mental exercise."

Lake, a five-time Pro Bowler who played safety and cornerback for the Steelers from 1989 through 1998 and in zone blitz-heavy schemes devised by LeBeau and Dom Capers from 1992 through 1996, told Ron Jaworski and Greg Cosell in *The Games That Changed the Game* why the zone blitz was so hard for Run-and-Shoot offenses. "The zone blitz stretched the range where offensive linemen had to block," he said. "Instead of just focusing on the front four and linebackers where they could make adjustments fairly easily, now they had to look sideline to sideline when it came to potential blitzers. Before the zone blitz, teams could bring out four wides and multiple routes because they assumed the defense would have to spend extra manpower covering those receivers. They figured they could protect pretty well under those conditions. But with nickel and dime DBs as possible blitzers, that forced offenses to eliminate the four-receiver package. They had to put the tight end in the game and keep a back in to help block. Now they only had three receivers running routes, and the advantage flipped to the defense."

It did until the late 1990s and early 2000s, when offensive coordinators began to realize that when you ran the ball straight into the teeth of the zone blitz, there were vulnerabilities between the ends. Because so many defenders were either blitzing off of— or dropping out of—their gaps, running backs could pick a gap and go. Mobile quarterbacks also caused zone blitz base defenses to break apart because those covering defenders had to peel off to chase the quarterback. If there was enough room and time to get a pass off, a receiver could be wide open. Coaches also started to play to the inherent weakness of the potential coverage matchups. In one famous example, Carolina Panthers nose tackle Greg Kragen had to cover Jerry Rice for two plays. Less than ideal. "If you happen to hit a seam, there's nobody there," Green Bay Packers assistant coach Sherman Lewis said in *The Sporting News*. "And a play-action pass, we thought, would be very effective. Because for those defensive linemen, [they] have to make a decision. If it's a pass, they're going to drop. If it's a run, they're coming. If it's play-action, they don't know which one it is. They play run—they are late dropping, and that leaves a big hole in one of their zones."

Eventually, LeBeau and acolytes like Capers and Ray Horton used the zone blitz as a specialty package, which is often the ultimate destination for concepts that find their schematic counters over time. And LeBeau was able to take it into the new millennium as the Steelers won Super Bowls XL and XLIII while being among the NFL's best defenses. And just as the zone blitz was a factor in those wins (though not as defined as it had been in the previous era), it proved to be very helpful against modern versions of the Run-and-Shoot.

In fact, the most famous zone blitz play in NFL history came at the end of the first half of Super Bowl XLIII between the Steelers and the Arizona Cardinals on February 1, 2009. The Cardinals had the ball at the Pittsburgh 2-yard line with no timeouts and a 10–7 deficit. There were 18 seconds left on the clock as quarterback Kurt Warner strode to his position under center, and the Steelers had something special in mind. Warner took the snap, took a quick drop back against a blitz to his left side, fired a quick pass to receiver Anquan Boldin, and watched in horror

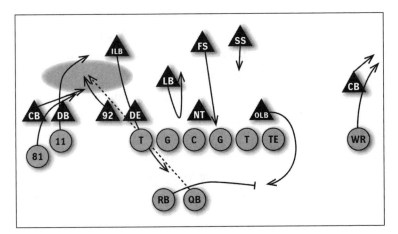

Pittsburgh Steelers LB James Harrison's Pick-6 off a zone blitz in Super Bowl XLIII

as linebacker James Harrison came out of nowhere to not only intercept the pass at the goal line, but also run 100 yards in the other direction.

It was the longest interception in Super Bowl history and perhaps the most atypical. Harrison, an undrafted free agent out of Kent State who had bounced around the league before finding his way as a pass rusher in LeBeau's system in 2007, had dropped into coverage fewer times than any other Steelers linebacker. He had been targeted just 16 times in the regular season; his primary function was to rush the passer, which he did to the tune of 16 sacks in the 2008 season. But the Steelers knew this was the perfect place for a short goal-line pass and therefore a great setup for the zone blitz. Head coach Mike Tomlin could be heard on the sidelines telling his staff that there was no way the Cardinals were going to run on that play.

This played to type. The 2008 Cardinals were about as close to a Run-and-Shoot base offense team as you could find in their era. There was a tight end on the interception in question, but that was a rarity. According to Football Outsiders' charting metrics for the season, the Cardinals dialed up a four-receiver formation on 38 percent—a greater percentage than anyone else in the NFL—of their offensive snaps. They had two tight ends on the field at the same time on 13 percent of their plays, which was next to last in the league. They ran the ball in power situations (goal line and short-yardage) on just 45 percent of their plays. And in Warner they had a quarterback who had learned to run a quick passing offense frequently defined by three and five-step drops. It wasn't quite the Lions' Silver Stretch, but it was pretty close. "We dialed up an all-out blitz with our personnel," Tomlin told NFL Films. "We knew we could bring one more than they could block."

"James was called into that defense as a blitzer," LeBeau recalled.

"I figured they had to do a quick slant in or out," Harrison said. "It seemed like all day we were a step late getting to [Warner]. So I figured that if I stepped at the tackle and got him to step out at me, that would free [Lawrence] Timmons to get inside on his blitz where he was supposed to be, and I'd just drop out and take a gamble."

"In this situation we got exactly what we wanted on the outside," Warner said. "Man-to-man coverage. We had press coverage, so it was just a little inside-out route. My eyes automatically go to the outside, and Anquan Boldin gets free exactly how we thought it was going to play out. [Harrison] takes two steps up like he's blitzing and then he gets [engulfed] by my offensive line, so I can't see him. I'm assuming because of the way he started, that he was blitzing. So, I let the ball go, and that's when I picked up that James Harrison had dropped off and fallen right into the passing lane."

"It was a route that we call 'burst,'" receiver Larry Fitzgerald said. "I'm pushing out wide, trying to touch the numbers, and I'm coming in for a post to the back pylon. Q's [Boldin's] job was to run into the end zone and catch the ball quickly."

"It's one of those things where they can only coach you so much," Harrison concluded. "There comes a point in time where you're on the field, and they're not seeing what you're seeing."

"He was doing such a good job of several things that we encourage," LeBeau said of Harrison. "No. 1, he was thinking. No. 2, he was 100 percent correct. No. 3, he made one hell of a play. That's one of my favorite plays ever. I think it will be one of the most remembered plays in professional football."

Not even Arnsparger would claim to be the inventor of the zone blitz or the zone exchange, in which unexpected players work to the quarterback but are replaced in coverage with an equal number of players. Jaworski noticed Larry Eisenhauer, the 6'5", 250-pound defensive end for the Boston Patriots, drop into coverage in the 1963 AFL Championship Game. Teams would occasionally drop linemen to cover running backs through the 1960s and 1970s, but it was the system devised by Arnsparger—and perfected by LeBeau—that holds up to this day. "On a vacation to Kentucky in 1997, I visited the new Bengals training camp at Georgetown College," Arnsparger recalled in his book, *Arnsparger's Coaching Defensive Football*. "I watched a practice, and afterward Dick and I chatted. I thanked him for his kindness and congratulated him on developing the zone blitz to where it is today. The scheme has grown a great deal since its beginning. Like everything in football, when you see something good, you add your ideas and make it better—and the zone blitz is no exception."

The Buffalo Bills and the K-Gun

When Marv Levy became the Buffalo Bills' head coach in 1986, he already had tons of experience at just about every level of football. The Coe College graduate coached with his alma mater in the early 1950s and then moved on to New Mexico and Cal (where he hired a young assistant named Bill Walsh). After a four-year run as the head coach for William & Mary, Levy got his first NFL gig as a special teams coach for the Philadelphia Eagles and Washington Redskins and became the head coach of the CFL's Montreal Alouettes in 1973. The Kansas City Chiefs came calling in 1978, and he was their head coach through the 1982 season, compiling a 31–42 record. Then, after a two-year hiatus and one season as the head coach of the USFL's Chicago Blitz, Levy got the Buffalo job in November of 1986, replacing Hank Bullough. It was not a prestigious assignment at the time. Levy had been a TV analyst for the Bills' preseason games and he took over a team that hadn't been to the playoffs since 1981 and hadn't won a postseason game since 1965, when they beat the San Diego Chargers for their second straight AFL title.

The Bills had put talent together under general manager Bill Polian but hadn't demonstrated it on the field yet. Polian hired Levy based on their history together in Kansas City and with Chicago, and Levy inherited a team with Jim Kelly at quarterback, Andre Reed at receiver, Bruce Smith at defensive end, and other stars who would be featured in later Super Bowl teams. Levy improved the Bills from 4–12 in that first season to 7–8 in the strike-shortened year of 1987 and lost the AFC Championship Game to the Cincinnati Bengals to end their 1988 season. In that game Levy was quite unhappy about the Bengals' no-huddle tactics, and the NFL famously told Cincinnati head coach Sam Wyche before the game that if he tried to hurry things up too much as decreed by the officials, his team would be repeatedly penalized. But by the beginning of the 1989 season, Levy and the Bills were whistling the same tune.

When the Bills promoted Ted Marchibroda from quarterbacks coach to offensive coordinator before the 1989 season, they adopted the no-huddle offense and improved from 14th and 12th in points and yards in 1988 to third and fifth, respectively, in Marchibroda's first season. From 1989 through 1993, Buffalo never ranked lower than seventh in any offensive category, appeared in four straight Super Bowls, and featured Kelly, Reed, and running back Thurman Thomas, a trio who would earn induction into the Hall of Fame.

Marchibroda had been in the NFL since 1961 as a coach, and his base idea for the no-huddle—what was later called the "K-Gun" in Buffalo's case—happened around that time. "I was driving to work with Bill McPeak and Abe Gibron, and somebody said, 'One day, all the plays will be called at the line of scrimmage; there won't be a huddle,'" Marchibroda told *Newsday* in 1991. "It all came together after 30 years. All the pieces of the puzzle fit. It's a simple, sound, basic offense. It's simple to call at the line of scrimmage. The verbiage is minimal. That's one reason for our success. The defense doesn't have much time to make its calls."

According to Kelly, though, the process was rather complex for the quarterback. And it was better if, as it was for the Bills in that era, there was continuity in personnel from year to year. "Say it was second and 8," Kelly told *Sports Illustrated* in 1992, "I'd hold a finger in the air, like a gun, so the sideline knew I wanted K-Gun personnel if it wasn't already on the field. Then I'd look to see if [the defense] was subbing. If they weren't, I'd yell, 'Eight! Eight!' Tight end right with one wideout and a slot receiver and split end to the left. Then I'd yell, 'Cow! Cow!' My hot read would be to the tight end side. Then I'd yell, 'Ninety-three!' Outside receivers would run 10-yard outs and inside receivers six to eight-yard option routes. Then I'd yell, 'Louisville!' The snap would be on three. Then I'd look over the defense. If I didn't like what I saw, I'd audible at the line. I was so lucky because I had the smartest center in the world, Kent Hull, who could make every line call to account for [defensive] guys moving around, so I'd never have to worry about that. And I knew the tendencies of every one of my guys. I knew what worked. You think I'd have wanted to call my own plays with new guys to break in every year? No way."

Sadly, the K-Gun Bills were lost a bit to the vagaries of history because history remembers the winners. And though Buffalo was the only NFL franchise to appear in four straight Super Bowls (1990–1993), it matters a lot less in the big picture when there are no rings to show for it. The Bills lost Super Bowl XXV to the New York Giants 20–19 after kicker Scott Norwood's late field-goal attempt famously went wide right. Then, they lost 37–24 to the Redskins in Super Bowl XXVI, in which Kelly was sacked five times and threw four interceptions. The Bills' last two Super Bowl losses were to the team that would become the true dynasty of the 1990s led by two coaches with defenses that were built to expose the limitations of every offense it faced.

The Bills' first Super Bowl team may have been its best. In 1990 Buffalo ranked first in points scored and sixth in points allowed, finishing 13–3 in the regular season and thrashing the Los Angeles Raiders 51–3 in the AFC Championship Game. Kelly had Thomas in his backfield and Reed and James Lofton as his primary receiving targets. All four of those players are in the Hall of Fame. The K-Gun offense had the rest of the league on its proverbial heels, and it was up to Giants head coach Bill Parcells and defensive coordinator Bill Belichick to find a way to counter the most dynamic offense in the league.

Belichick's strategy sounded crazy to his players. He theorized that it was perfectly acceptable to have Thomas run for more than 100 yards in the game (which Thomas did, gaining 115 yards and scoring a rushing touchdown on just 15 carries) while the real emphasis had to be on Buffalo's quick passing game. "I thought it was a collective brain fart—like what the hell are you talking about?" linebacker Carl Banks told Giants.com. "We were a team that prided itself defensively on not giving up 100-yard rushers, not even giving up 100-yard games for a total offensive rush stat. But he said it, we are all in an uproar, and we're thinking Bill is just conceding that Thurman is just this good of a football player that we won't be able to stop him. And then he reeled us back in and kinda gave us a method to the madness."

The Giants went with a two-man front for most of the game, alternating between five and six defensive backs years before nickel and dime defenses as base concepts were the norm. The method was clear—Belichick didn't want Buffalo's receivers to catch Kelly's short passes and gain huge swaths of yardage after the catch while lining up in their signature no-huddle and exhausting New York's defense. Instead, allowing Thomas to gain what he gained altered Buffalo's strategy, and Belichick slow-rolled the Bills into doing exactly what the Giants wanted them to do. "I didn't feel like we wanted to get into a game where they threw the ball 45 times," Belichick told Giants.com years later. "I knew if they had some success running the ball, they would stay with it. And I always felt when we needed to stop the run, we could stop it. And the more times they ran it, it was just one less time they could get it to Reed or get it to Lofton or throw it to Thomas, who I thought was more dangerous as a receiver because there's more space than there was when he was a runner."

Super Bowl XXV is mostly known for Norwood's missed field goal late in the game and the Giants' mastery of the time of possession battle. They kept the ball for over 40 minutes in the game—but it's Belichick's defensive playbook that has a place in the Hall of Fame, along with all those Bills offensive players. It was also one of the first national indications that Belichick might have more on the ball than your average coach.

That was merely the first of Buffalo's four Super Bowl nightmares. The Bills were trounced by Joe Gibbs' Redskins at the end of the 1991 season and they then were poleaxed in two straight Super Bowls by a resurgent Dallas Cowboys team that brought new wrinkles to the old Tom Landry defensive line innovations.

Jimmy Johnson and the One-Gap 4-3 Defense

Jimmy Johnson has never lacked confidence in himself. He was confident when he was a hotshot high school football player in Port Arthur, Texas, teasing schoolmate Janis Joplin because she was "the beatnik who wore the black leotards." He was confident when he was an undersized defensive tackle on Arkansas' 1964 national championship team. He was confident when he became

Oklahoma State's head coach in 1979, he was confident when he replaced Howard Schnellenberger at Miami in 1984, and he was most certainly confident in 1989 when he replaced Tom Landry as the only head coach the Dallas Cowboys had ever had.

Put simply, Johnson has always believed in his own greatness. And in a football sense, he has almost always been right. That was true in college, and Johnson's schematic brilliance rooted in simplicity, execution, and controlled aggression transferred very well to the NFL.

The Dallas offense run under Johnson by Norv Turner and Ernie Zampese was very much an offshoot of the principles brought forth by Sid Gillman, Don Coryell, and Joe Gibbs. It was a vertical passing game in a three-digit system buttressed by a power running game and an outstanding offensive line. That was what made Johnson's Cowboys go on that side of the ball. Led by the Triplets (Troy Aikman, Michael Irvin, and Emmitt Smith) and one of the best offensive lines in NFL history, it certainly did go.

But Johnson's defensive mind-set was the real innovation behind his Super Bowl teams.

From the invention of the 4-3 defense in the 1950s, defensive linemen were generally trained to be two-gap defenders or to align head-to-head with blockers and deal with runners as they came to those gaps. Landry's further innovation, the 4-3 Flex Defense, assigned some linemen to specific gaps instead, leaving them with better angles in pursuit. But it was Johnson's insistence that the one-gap 4-3 front could be used to attack in a more prominent fashion. That defined Dallas' defense and changed the way NFL teams used their fronts. "I began to wonder why defensive linemen were always coached to wait and read the offensive blocks before taking action," Johnson wrote in his book, *Turning the Thing Around.* "Why weren't they attacking right from the snap? Why was defense so defensive? Why couldn't defensive be offensive?"

Johnson began to implement his versions of the attack one-gap 4-3 defense through his time as an assistant coach in the 1970s. That path began in 1965, one year after Johnson, a defensive lineman, helped the Arkansas Razorbacks win the 1964 NCAA championship. Instead of opting for the pros, Johnson made his way as an assistant coach through Louisiana Tech, Picayune High School, Wichita State, Iowa State, Oklahoma, Arkansas, and Pitt before he got his first head coaching job with the Oklahoma State Cowboys in 1979. Over the next five years, Johnson turned an inconsistent team into a powerhouse. He won a national championship with the Miami Hurricanes with that same defensive concept and better players in 1987.

His move to the NFL seemed ordained, and he took that defensive philosophy with him when that happened. "I believed, and still do, in creating upfield pressure from a 4-3 stack formation," he wrote. "That is, four down linemen with

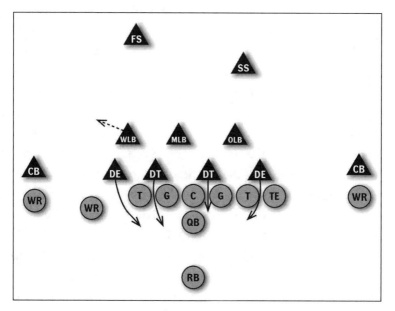

Jimmy Johnson's 4-3 stack formation

three linebackers (true linebackers back off the line of scrimmage rather than hybrid 'up ends'). Let the linebackers do the waiting and reading of blocks. Let the down linemen fire off the snap and charge upfield, creating havoc in the offense. Put simply, *attack* on defense. The traditionalists considered it tantamount to sending the defensive front on kamikaze missions, committing them too soon."

But Johnson had answers for that. He wanted his defensive linemen to be lighter and quicker, more easily able to define pursuit through the gap before it was erased by the blocker. Johnson's ends looked like linebackers, his linebackers looked like big safeties, and it was their job to roam all around the field, catching whatever the line had missed. Beside and behind the linebackers, the secondary was more designed to avoid the big play than to be truly aggressive. It was the inverse principle of many defenses before it, which dictated that aggression would come from the linebackers and secondary, while the line would contain first and pursue second.

More specifically, Johnson developed what we'll call the "Attack 4-3" to ward off two issues: the fact that he wasn't going to get the best high school recruits when coaching an Oklahoma State team that was still dealing with the effects of the sanctions that had been handed down when he took over in 1979 and the specter of the wishbone offense. Option football, like the wishbone, clowned the old head-on-head defenses for years, and Johnson had to find a way to deal with it. Committing his defenders too soon turned out to be the right answer. "We had a match for the wishbone," Miami safety Bennie Blades told *The Oklahoman*. "You need a lot of team speed, but the wishbone was based on teams not protecting their territory. If you weren't disciplined in stopping first the fullback, then the quarterback, and the two options that he had, you were going to get beat 63–0.

We just basically built a line at eight yards and, with the speed we had on defense, took away the first two options. Hey, I was right there. I think one game I had 10 tackles and another I had 16 tackles. We just beat them to the punch most of the time."

The counter for Oklahoma head coach Barry Switzer was simple: when Johnson moved to Miami, his players outranked his Xs and Os. "He couldn't beat us at OSU, and you know why? He didn't have the players," Switzer said. "It's like I always told Jimmy, 'When I had the players, I won. When you had the players, you won.' It didn't matter whether it was college ball or pro ball."

The theory was tested again in 1989. The simplicity and speed that worked so well throughout Johnson's collegiate coaching career would not go so smoothly against more talented and more complex NFL offenses, the story went. "The biggest thing was that when I was in college, I really concentrated on personnel," Johnson told me in 2010. "That was my strength, and I was in essence my own recruiting coordinator. And when I went to the pros, I did the same thing. I handled the draft, I drafted the players, and I was able to get the personnel. The other thing was that when I was at the University of Miami, we ran a pro-style offense and defense. I started each year by going to a pro training camp, I visited with various pro coaches, and I did this for five years. I went to Cowboys camp, Raiders camp, Atlanta Falcons camp, throughout the league. I visited a lot with John Robinson of the Los Angeles Rams at that time. And I think that really helped prepare me and my staff to go into pro football."

As Johnson would say, he didn't want a big slug who knocked people down. He demanded quick playmakers on his front. Johnson's defensive tackles generally weighed around 275 pounds, while his rush ends tipped the scales at 245 or so. His primary front four in Dallas was very light—ends Tony Tolbert and Charles Haley weighed 265 and 245 pounds, respectively, and tackles

Tony Casillas and Russell Maryland topped out at 275 pounds. While Dallas' offensive line featured 300-pound-plus behemoths, Johnson's defensive linemen worked off power and speed, and the back seven cleaned up any mess it missed.

The Cowboys were a complete mess when Jerry Jones bought them and Johnson took over the coaching duties in 1989, and Jones' cavalier dismissal of Landry, the only coach the franchise had ever known, set him up as a villain. Dallas went 1–15 in 1989, but just three years later, the Cowboys' scheme, motivation, and personnel had them facing the K-Gun Buffalo Bills in Super Bowl XXVII at the end of the 1992 season. There they faced a team that ranked third in points in the regular season and had cut a wide swath through the rest of the AFC's best teams in the postseason, including the all-time comeback win that destroyed the Houston Oilers and put a pin in the Run-and-Shoot narrative.

The Super Bowl, though, was a laugher. The Cowboys won 52–17, Buffalo turned the ball over a Super Bowl-record nine times, and quarterback Jim Kelly was knocked out of the game on a blitz. Dallas' defensive adjustments were near perfect after a few early hiccups (especially a switch from base defense to nickel on an early Buffalo goal-line stand), and Johnson's defense was validated as the wave of the now. The 4-3 two-gap wait-and-see defense was officially a thing of the past. Johnson had constructed a perfect marriage of personnel and scheme, and that defense took it to the Bills again in Super Bowl XXVIII the next year, beating the AFC champs 30–13. Dallas might have continued winning Super Bowls under Johnson for years, but Jones insisted on taking credit for moves Johnson made. Johnson left Dallas after the 1993 season, had some success—but far less than he had in Dallas—with the Miami Dolphins from 1996 through 1999, and then turned to television analysis.

Still, his legacy as the man who brought defensive gap schemes—not just pass rush concepts but the entire way of thinking—for a four-man front is well-deserved.

Seattle Seahawks head coach Pete Carroll, designer of a 4-3 base defense responsible for two Super Bowl runs, was asked by the Dallas media in 2014 how his Seahawks teams line up to Johnson's Cowboys era from a schematic and philosophical standpoint. Not surprisingly, Carroll was right in line with that idea. "Both of us come out of a defensive background, and I think we always cherished speed, toughness, and that style, and we built our football team in a mold of defense and special teams and running the football," he said. "That's not much of a difference away from that style that they put forth back in the day. You still need a great quarterback, you need a guy that can do all that, but I think there are some real similarities."

Zone Blocking: Alex Gibbs and the Origin of the Species

Throughout NFL history, blocking schemes changed and advanced as the need flourished due to the increasing complexity of enemy defenses. Through the NFL's first half-century, most blocking was based on aligned and choreographed power. The Packer Sweep was the dominant blocking scheme of the 1960s at least in perception, but Vince Lombardi was also a big believer in what he called 'option' or 'do-dad' blocking, which was the most prominent forerunner to the league's current zone blocking and zone/man blocking hybrid schemes.

The godfather of true zone blocking in the NFL is unquestionably Alex Gibbs, who took the idea of option blocking to an entirely new level, but he definitely had his forbearers. When you hear that Gibbs invented zone blocking in the 1990s (a common canard), keep in mind that while he may have perfected his own (and thus the NFL's) iterations of zone blocking he certainly didn't invent it, and he'd be the first to tell you that. Lombardi's case was different. He based the fundamentals of his offense on fundamentally sound blocking techniques, but it wasn't just the power sweep that kept that offense going. Lombardi called it "area blocking" as opposed to zone blocking, but the principle was similar. And Lombardi used it for the same reasons that his followers used it—to keep the offensive line clean and consistent against changing and more complex defensive schemes. "Do-dad blocking is used against stunting lines or lines that stack one defender behind the other," the coach explained in his seminal book, *Lombardi on Football*. "In the case where the defensive tackle has the inside charge and the middle linebacker is keying the fullback and has the outside responsibility, the middle linebacker will with the snap of the ball move immediately to the hole, making it impossible for the center to cut him down because of the middle linebacker's key on the fullback. In this case, we will use do-dad blocking.

"The center is the lead blocker—the apex. He will lead step, the same technique as for the down block, for the [lower body] of the defensive tackle. The offensive guard, using the same technique

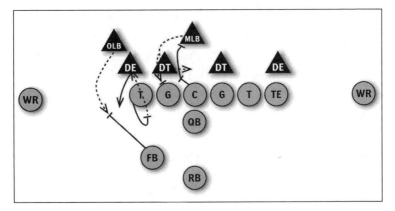

Vince Lombardi's area blocking scheme

as he does in the drive block, will aim for a point which is outside the defensive tackle. If the defensive tackle has an inside charge, the guard immediately releases the tackle, picking up the middle linebacker who would be moving with the key of the fullback toward the hole. The center, since the tackle is moving into him, would pick him off."

The central constructs of zone blocking are solving the problem of stunting and blitzing defenders—really, solving the problem of any sort of personnel advantage on that side of the ball—with a flexible system based on precise coordination as much as sheer physical strength. Lombardi was the main force in bringing that concept into the NFL, but Gibbs would perfect it years later.

Gibbs learned a lot of things from a lot of different people and married them together to create his own unusual but eminently successful approach. During his time at Ohio State from 1975 through 1978, he learned the basics of successful teaching from Woody Hayes—not the crazed coach everyone now remembers, but the freshman English teacher. Hayes had just as much expertise with the language arts as he did with the game. Gibbs learned about dealing with players and maximizing their potential from Bobby Bowden during their time together at West Virginia in 1973 and 1974. Georgia coach Vince Dooley taught him the value of organization during his time there in 1982 and 1983. By the time Gibbs became the Denver Broncos' offensive line coach in 1984, he not only had his blocking system together, but he also had a concrete way of making people understand and execute what he wanted.

Gibbs ran elevated versions of the inside zone and outside zone throughout his career. Zone blocking at any level requires linemen to first determine whether they are covered or uncovered and then help the man next to them if they're not. It's a rough-neck ballet at 100 miles per hour with all kinds of checks and responsibilities. The strength comes in the group and it starts from the inside. "When I coach the center, I tell him that if he is not tough enough to block the nose guard, he is not tough enough to block for me," Gibbs said at one coaching clinic. "If the nose guard is close to the center, the center has him. If he is close to the guard, the guard calls the center into the combination. The nose guard may make the play, but if the center can flatten the defender out of the line of scrimmage, we can be successful."

Perhaps the most impressive distillation of that plan came in Super Bowl XXXII, when Gibbs' Broncos upset the Packers 31–24 behind the MVP performance of Terrell Davis. The running back overcame a severe migraine to rush for 157 yards and three touchdowns, but it was Gibbs' line—without a 300 pounder in the bunch—that negated 350-pound tackle Brown and held left end Reggie White, perhaps the greatest defensive end in NFL history, without a sack. White put up three sacks in Green Bay's Super Bowl XXXI win against the New England Patriots the year before, but the Broncos—primarily right tackle Tony Jones—kept him quiet, and the Denver blocking plan is worth reviewing.

So it went through the line, and Brown found himself winded while White was negated by Jones, who played the game of his career. John Elway grabbing his first Super Bowl win was the lead story, and Davis' strength to overcome a migraine in the game was a marvelous ancillary tale, but it was the guys upfront who defined that win while being led by their at times intractible line coach. "He's got the ability to be tough and demanding, but he cares about his players and he looks after them, which gives him the ability to be extra tough and extra demanding because the players know he cares about them," then-Broncos head coach Mike Shanahan said in 2000. "And there's a fine line right there. There are so many coaches who wind up being buddy/buddy with a player, but they can't be tough on their guys because they get too close to them. Alex has been a guy who is as demanding a person as any I've been around, but he knows how to put his arm around people and let them know he cares about them. It takes a unique guy to be able to do that."

Of course, as Gibbs might himself say, none of that happy horseshit matters if you don't have a plan. And the plan must be based around the right kind of personnel. "[Finding his ideal sort of lineman] is a very hard thing to do because IQ is not what I'm talking about," Gibbs told *The Denver Post*. "Test scores are not what I'm talking about. It's communication skills, the ability to come in each week and change things, and talk a different language, and make quick decisions, and solve problems. That's a smart player to me. I don't look at that like other people do. I look for the smart guys because that is as important to me…almost as important to me as skill. You have to have guys that can put the fires out real fast."

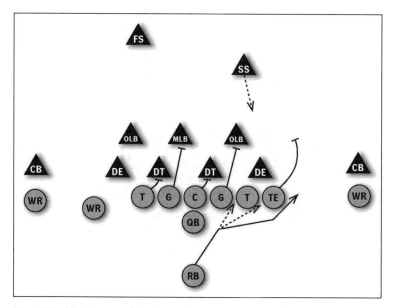

Alex Gibbs' inside zone blocking scheme

Gibbs didn't just coach his line. He also took charge of the backs in his overall philosophy because if the backs weren't reading zone the right way, nothing else mattered. What he coached—and what lasts in today's NFL—is the inside (or tight) zone and the outside (or wide) zone. In inside zone the blockers are directed to push their blocks to the gaps nearest to them, and the back is directed to read the gaps (either play-side or back-side). In outside zone blockers await the defenders who appear in their gaps, and the back takes the outside gap, whichever one opens up. Gibbs saw a defense as a collection of seven men to block with an eighth man as the potential tipping point. When there are nine men to block, as Gibbs has always said, that's when it's time to scrap the gameplan and throw the damned ball. "The tough thing about the Broncos' running game is the way they block," New York Giants linebacker Carlos Emmons said. "The way they block as a unit, if one defensive guy misses a gap, you're dead."

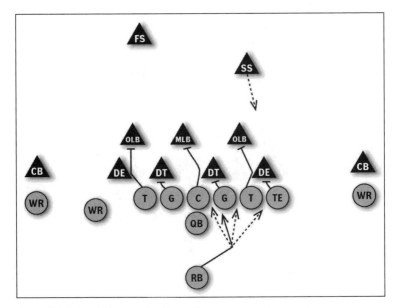

Alex Gibbs' outside zone blocking scheme

When Gibbs joined the Atlanta Falcons' staff as an assistant head coach/offensive line coach/consultant in 2004, he was dealing with a different kind of quarterback and new personnel overall. Quarterback Michael Vick was perhaps the most athletic player at his position in NFL history, and the backfield of Warrick Dunn and T.J. Duckett combined with Vick to produce a rushing attack that led the league all three years that Gibbs was in charge of the line. "I steal everything I've ever used," Gibbs said. "I've never invented anything. I've never developed a play. I've never developed an offense. I've stolen everything I've gotten from players and coaches and film. Everything. I have never, ever invented a thing. All I do that's a little special is I teach different than other people teach. And that's what we are. We're teachers. And people lose perspective of that. I'm not as good with gameplans as a lot of guys. I'm not as good with strategy as a lot of guys. But I'm real good at teaching."

The Greatest Show on Turf

Dick Vermeil retired as the Philadelphia Eagles' head coach after the 1982 season, citing burnout. Football, the game he loved, had taken too much of a toll. He stayed away for 15 seasons and, when he returned to become the St. Louis Rams' head coach in 1997, many wondered why he bothered. The Rams hadn't had a winning season since 1989 and they'd never had one in St. Louis, where the franchise moved from Los Angeles in 1994. The quarterback, Tony Banks, was a developmental player who never developed. The running back, Lawrence Phillips, was a problem child who would soon find himself out of the league and in prison. Isaac Bruce was a young receiver with a lot of potential but very little around him.

Vermeil suffered through two seasons in which his Rams won a combined nine games. Then, in three fell swoops, the coach and the team put together the offense that would shock the world. There was the trade for Indianapolis Colts running back Marshall Faulk before the 1999 draft, giving up second and fifth-round picks for a back who would ride his new team's offense to a Hall of Fame induction. The Rams signed free-agent quarterback Trent Green to a four-year, $17.5 million contract in February of 1999, and the thought was that Green would be the future of the franchise at that position. But the Rams had also taken a flyer on a former Green Bay Packers camp body quarterback named Kurt Warner, and it was Warner who took over when Green suffered a knee injury in the 1999 preseason.

The real key to St. Louis' offensive turnaround, though, happened in a Mobile, Alabama, hotel room in January of 1999. There, during the Senior Bowl, Vermeil interviewed Mike Martz as a potential offensive coordinator. And it was Martz who would show Vermeil, the Rams, and the rest of the NFL the next wave in the philosophy of the vertical passing game. As a kid in San Diego, Martz had watched Sid Gillman coach the Chargers and he had a bright set of ideas as to how to merge Gillman's version of the West Coast Offense with the more standard and popular version set forth by Bill Walsh in the 1970s and beyond. "He is bright, extremely bright," said Vermeil while describing Martz to ESPN.com. "He has a great natural feel for the game and a great feel for the players and what they can and what they can't do. I think he has an even greater feel when he analyzes a defense and what they do not do well and how to go about attacking them at their weakest points. He can exploit a defensive football team. The other thing is he's a courageous play-caller. He can scare you to death when you're on the other end of the headset. Once you get used to his aggressive approach and working with him as a team, I don't think there's any better."

Martz wasn't about balance in the traditional sense. He frequently put his quarterbacks in more peril than other coaches by refusing to cede blocking roles to tight ends. And though the Rams used a fair set of three to five-step drops in their passing game, the time taken by receivers to run deeper routes meant that Warner would be providing his own protection to a point. The Martz offense has been a recipe for implosion when employed by less aware quarterbacks, but Warner had an innate sense of timing in the pocket and the perfect physical gifts to make this offense go.

Adding Faulk in the trade with the Colts was the other keystone in what would become the first truly explosive offense of the new millennium. Faulk was a perfect back for the mixture of the two West Coast Offenses. Not only was he a powerful, fast, and shifty back, but he could also catch passes from anywhere in the formation, block adeptly when asked, and perfectly grasp the offense. From 1999 through 2001, Faulk put together one of the most impressive timelines of sustained excellence for any back in NFL history. In 1999 he became the second back to gain more than 1,000 yards rushing and 1,000 yards receiving in the same season. He neither ran for fewer than 1,359 yards in any of those seasons nor totaled less than 765 receiving yards. As it was for Gillman's and Don Coryell's offenses, those allegedly high-flying offenses with very little in the way of a running game, total balance was actually the key.

However, like his hero Gillman, Martz saw no intrinsic reason for the run to set up the pass—he wanted to be aggressive from the opening play of the opening drive and force defenses to make them let up. With the Washington Redskins, Martz had head coach Norv Turner tell him that he liked the third-down stuff he had installed but wondered why the Redskins couldn't put that more aggressive mind-set to work on early downs. That was Martz's epiphany, and he was able to convince the far more traditionally-minded Vermeil that the Rams had the personnel and vision to make it work. Vermeil did some data crunching with the help of the Elias Sports Bureau and discovered that such aggressiveness could be rewarded. "We looked at every team in the NFL," Vermeil told *Sports Illustrated* in 2000, "and we found that the best offenses in the league last year, Denver and Minnesota, actually threw the ball much more in the first quarter than they ran."

Vermeil told Martz to go run his offense, and the effect on the rest of the league was instant. The Rams ranked 24th in points and 27th in yards in 1998; they ranked first in points and yards in each of the next three seasons. Vermeil retired after the Rams won Super Bowl XXXIV at the end of the 1999 season—a decision he has regretted since—and the team started to lose its personnel touch, but through those three years, the offense Martz designed and implemented was as tough to stop as any in NFL history.

Martz's offense had its antecedents, but at its most effective, it was an interesting hybrid of stuff. He employed the base three-digit system used by everyone from Gillman to Coryell to Joe Gibbs, but he added a lot of different route options for Faulk and an elevated percentage and awareness of option routes for his receivers. Martz had little nuanced changes in route concepts for his receivers based on the coverage—slide your route under against retreat zone coverage, flare it out against retreat man, adjust based on the defender's movements against aggressive press coverage, and so on. Martz's system thusly combined the vertical offense of Gillman and Coryell with the running back-friendly concepts favored by Walsh and the elevated option routes of the Run-and-Shoot. The idea at its apex was to have as many as five potentially open targets on any given play by extending splits and routes beyond the breaking point of any defense.

Everyone was tasked to make it succeed, but the pressure it put on Warner was staggering. Not only did Warner have to master the playbook and attune his own mechanics to this system, but he also had to time his acuity to the various options. And when it came to quarterbacks, Martz could be a fairly daunting taskmaster. When it came to offensive lines and protections, Martz seemed to be less so, which tended to result in a fairly short run for his signal-callers. "I can't blame it all on personnel," Faulk said in 2010. "It's up to what you want to do and what you want to get accomplished, and that's about the quarterback...If you hold on to the football, you are going to get hit in the NFL. In that offense you need to let it go because there's always an opportunity...a hot read of some sort. You can get rid of it, but some guys just hold on."

Warner was up to the challenge until injuries started to take their toll; he was gone from the team by 2004. Faulk retired after the 2005 season, but, effectively, his time as a top-tier back ended in 2002. There were no clear replacements for anyone—Warner, Faulk, all-time left tackle Orlando Pace, Bruce, Torry Holt—who made that offense go. Martz, too, would move on to systems with less talent, and it would take its toll on him and his players. The Greatest Show on Turf Rams had a brief time in the spotlight, but their era truly ended when they went up against the underdog New England Patriots in Super Bowl XXXVI.

The Belichick Hybrid Defenses

After Jimmy Johnson made the one-gap attack defense *de rigueur*, it stood to reason that another man would take one-gap and two-gap concepts and marry them successfully on the same front. And that man was Bill Belichick. By the time Belichick made his way to Foxboro, Massachusetts, as the New England Patriots' head coach in 2000, he had both learned and taught a lot about defense. Belichick's father Steve, an assistant head football coach and longtime scout at the U.S. Naval Academy, was regarded in his time as one of the best personnel evaluators at any level of football and was his son's greatest influence in that regard.

From a coaching perspective, though, Belichick probably learned more from Bill Parcells than from anyone else. Parcells replaced Ray Perkins, who hired Belichick as a special teams coach and defensive assistant in 1979. Belichick became Parcells' defensive coordinator in 1985, and the New York Giants won two Super Bowls with Parcells and Belichick running the defense and outside linebacker Lawrence Taylor wreaking havoc on every offense he faced. When Belichick took over the defense, he devised new ways for Taylor to beat the constant double teams he faced, and Taylor responded with 20.5 sacks in 1986, the first of the Giants' two Super Bowl seasons under the Parcells/Belichick brain trust. Both men had a hand in making Taylor the first true outside linebacker pass rusher in a 3-4 base defense, and while the Giants had other defenders who sported their own Hall of Fame credentials, Taylor was Belichick's first stab at the concept of a hybrid defender—and a hybrid defense.

Belichick would take that strategy to Cleveland in 1991 as the Browns' head coach, but between his own inflexibility, a lack of equitable personnel, and the franchise's move after the 1995 season to Baltimore, the whole thing seemed ill-fated from the start. Fired in February of 1996, he re-joined Parcells—first in New England and then with the New York Jets. The original plan was for Belichick to succeed Parcells as Jets head coach, but a last-minute change of heart on Belichick's part had him instead taking over the Patriots. In that first year, Belichick tore apart a roster that was old, ineffective, and overpaid but had some good starters on the defensive side, including safety Lawyer Milloy, linebacker Tedy Bruschi, defensive end Willie McGinest, and cornerback Ty Law, and it was up to Belichick to maximize the pieces he had and add to the mix in his own way.

This time he had learned enough to understand how to take a team and remake it in his own image. The Patriots went 5–11 in his first season but rebounded nicely in 2001, going 11–5 in the regular season and working their way through the playoffs to face the St. Louis Rams in Super Bowl XXXVI. Belichick's team was a severe underdog; few knew how well they could play just yet. Quarterback Tom Brady was a first-year starter, and the Rams were at the peak of their "Greatest Show on Turf" efficiency.

Belichick's strategy in that game wasn't simple, but it was decidedly old-school—the Patriots would smack St. Louis' playmakers in the mouth over and over before those beautiful routes could develop. They played the Rams' receivers, including running back Marshall Faulk, much tighter and more aggressively than other defenses did and wore them out with this physical approach. The strategy, which helped the Pats beat the Rams 20–17, was rooted in the previous matchup between the teams during the regular season.

The Rams only scored 24 points in that regular-season game. "But I never really felt like we had control of the game," Belichick recalled in *The Games That Changed the Game*. "It seemed like every time they needed a pass, they hit one. We thought going in that night we couldn't just let St. Louis settle in and throw. We wanted to get them out of their rhythm, put pressure on [Kurt] Warner, force incomplete passes. So, we blitzed—a lot."

By Belichick's count, the Patriots blitzed the Rams 43 times in the earlier game, but Warner did a great job of adjusting to those pressures, using quicker passes, and the Rams' line turned in a tremendous effort. In the Super Bowl, the strategy was different. New England barely blitzed at all, instead coming with a wide array of coverage looks and prioritizing that Faulk must be neutralized at all costs. They focused on jamming the receivers and Faulk at the line of scrimmage with just enough pressure to further disrupt the timing of the Martz/Warner passing game. It worked for the most part and served as one of the first famous examples of Belichick's discovery that it is far more important to tailor your system to your opponent than to move into every game with a static set of schemes that are easier to counter.

The only constant in Belichick's defensive strategy has been change, and that change has been defined in part by the *Moneyball* principle, which states that you will derive more value from your roster if you figure out different ways to utilize undervalued assets. In Belichick's case those assets were players who worked better in, say, the 3-4 when fewer teams were running it. Belichick optimized his early Patriots rosters around players who were on the outside looking in from a schematic sense. "When we put in the 3-4 in 2000–01, there were three teams running it," Belichick told Comcast SportsNet New England in late December of 2014. "So, if you wanted a nose tackle, there were plenty of them out there. If you wanted a 3-4 outside linebacker, there were plenty of them out there. Guys like—[Rosevelt] Colvin was a good example at Chicago, or even [Mike] Vrabel, those 3-4 outside linebackers, but there's nowhere to go. New England was a good option for both of them because the guys Mike was playing behind [in Pittsburgh with a more traditional 3-4 defense]. Rosie was trying to play a 4-3 walked-off-the-line linebacker to a defensive end in sub situations. But it wasn't really a clean fit for him. So he had a much cleaner fit in the 3-4."

When the 3-4 craze came back in the 2000s (brought about to a large degree because of New England's success with it), Belichick zigged as everyone else was zagging and transitioned to a 4-3 look. "You look back five, six years ago and you've got 16, 17, 18 teams playing 3-4," he said. "You go to the draft board and think, *Here's a nose tackle. Who needs a nose tackle?* Well, eight teams in front of you need a nose tackle, and there's two nose tackles. It's something you have to figure out where you can get the players to play in your system. Sometimes you just can't get them, so either you have to change your system or modify it or play with lesser players if you want to maintain the system. That's definitely a challenging part of it—keeping up with that, trying to stay at least even with it. Hopefully ahead of it, but at least even, but it's a lot easier said than done."

Belichick's primary gambit to stay ahead of the game was to redefine the gap principles of the defensive line. Before he started tinkering with his fronts, defensive linemen were generally one-gappers or two-gappers. They either held the point so other defenders could flow through (two-gappers), or they attacked right off the snap, intending to create chaos (one-gappers). Teams would generally define their lines around one or the other, but Belichick decided that the best way to optimize his talent was

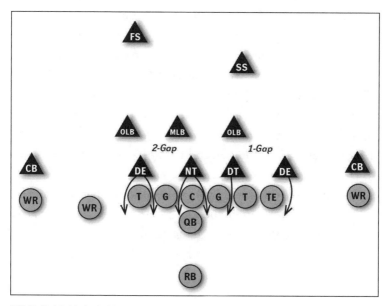

Bill Belichick's hybrid defensive front

to mix the two in hybrid form. This had been done to a degree in other ways—Pete Carroll always preferred a 4-3 over/under defense with a hybrid linebacker, and Wade Phillips liked to use a 5-2 base look, in which his players are actually one-gapping in a traditional two-gap format—but Belichick took it to another level by redefining the idea of the "one-or-the-other" player.

In Belichick's new hybrid fronts, an over concept might assign the nose tackle and strong-side ends two-gap responsibilities, leading to potential blitz possibilities to that side. On the weak side, the three-technique tackle and rush end might be one-gapping and attacking, leaving the front with the best of all possible worlds. Belichick could define his fronts by the mismatches they would potentially create because he wasn't stuck with one philosophy or the other.

In an under, hybrid concept, the numbers favor the weak side, and the players might shift their responsibilities. These weren't the high-flying multi-front defenses brought by Dick LeBeau and Dom Capers with the Pittsburgh Steelers. It was more of a stream of simple concepts strung together in ways nobody had seen before. "We can switch up and give you all kinds of different looks," McGinest told the *Orange County Register* in 2004 just before New England beat the Carolina Panthers 32–29 in Super Bowl XXXVIII. "They might think I'm coming, but I'm actually dropping back into coverage. Or it might be [linebacker Tedy Bruschi] who's coming, and I'm doing something else. I like it. It makes the games enjoyable."

"You have to be flexible enough to learn when you play on this team," Bruschi said in 2004. "I'd been a defensive lineman all my life, and when I got here, they asked me to drop back and used some terminology I'd never heard before. I had to ask an assistant, 'What's that?'"

And "that" was the whole point. If Belichick's players had to come to terms with their terminology and their place in the defense, imagine how confusing it would be for their opponents? By delving into the college ranks, Belichick would further lead the revolution into the next millennium.

CHAPTER 8

BACK TO SCHOOL
The NFL in the 2000s

> *"I don't want to be a product of my environment.*
> *I want my environment to be a product of me."*
> —Jack Nicholson as Frank Costello in *The Departed*

After the Run-and-Shoot died out in the NFL in the 1990s, the thought of bringing elements of a spread-out, quick-tempo collegiate passing game to the NFL was put on hold for a number of years. But as the new millennium took shape, the proliferation of spread offenses in the NCAA caused a number of inventive and frustrated NFL coaches, scouts, and executives to take a second look at hybrid possibilities.

There was Steve Spurrier, who tried iterations of the Fun-and-Gun offense he ran at Florida when he was the head coach of the Washington Redskins from 2002 through 2003. Spurrier went 12–20 in those two seasons, though his failure was less systemic than operational. He famously liked to knock off early for a round of golf while his contemporaries were burning the proverbial midnight oil, and after a few successful outings (Washington beat the Arizona Cardinals 31–23 in Spurrier's first Redskins game, and Shane Matthews completed 28-of-40 passes for 327 yards, three touchdowns, and one interception), things fell apart. The story goes that the rest of league figured out that Spurrier's self-lethal combination of simplistic concepts and rudimentary protection schemes—Patrick Ramsey was sacked 30 times in 327 dropbacks in 2003—was better off in college. And that's where the NFL sent it; Spurrier retreated to South Carolina for the 2005 season.

In truth Spurrier's offense was less option-like than people think. He did have tight ends along the formation to block, he did use power running concepts such as the wham and lead draw, and he presented enough NFL route concepts to make the thing work in theory. The problems with Spurrier's tenure in the nation's capital centered around other issues. The Redskins were subpar in their personnel at just about every spot in the roster, and Spurrier lacked the vision to do what every successful NFL head coach must do: imprint his philosophy on his team in ways that work over time. Put simply, Spurrier was not an NFL CEO. He was able to appear more successful in the preseason, running up the score because the defenses the Redskins faced weren't throwing the whole playbook at him. "When I left Florida after 12 years, I thought I was going to coach in the NFL five or six years and retire to the beach and play golf a bunch and travel around," Spurrier told the *Tampa Bay Times* in 2014. "But that was a bad plan. It was. Later you found out that was not a real good idea. But that's the way I was thinking back then."

The way Spurrier was thinking did not work. But other teams were about to take college concepts and, with a surer combination of inventiveness and elbow grease, change the way the NFL was played in a major fashion.

The Vick Factor

Michael Vick will forever be known for the federal dogfighting charges that landed him in prison for 21 months and forced him to serve two more months in home confinement from 2007 through 2009. But for our purposes and setting those weighty legal and moral issues aside, Vick can be seen as the first player who proved that—in the right system and with the right player at the helm—a base option offense could succeed wildly in the modern NFL. Selected with the first overall pick in the 2001 draft by the Atlanta Falcons out of Virginia Tech, Vick started just two games in his rookie year but unleashed himself upon the league in his sophomore campaign.

Vick's first real coronation as a factor in the future of NFL offenses came in the wild-card round of the 2002 season, when the Falcons traveled to Lambeau Field and handed the Green Bay Packers their first home postseason loss in the franchise's long and vaunted history. Vick's stats weren't world-beating—he completed 13-of-25 passes for 117 yards and a touchdown, adding 64 yards on 10 rushing attempts—but the injured Packers couldn't contain him, and the snowstorm the Packers hoped would slow Vick down never ensued.

But it was two seasons later at the start of the 2004 campaign when Vick's palette of tools was completely and fully integrated into an NFL offense. Atlanta led the NFL in rushing yards and yards per rushing attempt every season from 2004 through 2006, and Vick was the pointman in a read-option offense that also featured two running backs—speedy water bug Warrick Dunn and power back T.J. Duckett. In 2006 Vick became the only true quarterback of the modern era to top 1,000 rushing yards in a single season, running for 1,039 yards on just 123 carries for an incredible 8.45 yards per carry average. That season the NFL's average yards per carry total was 4.2.

Vick's most impressive rushing performance of that season came against the New Orleans Saints in Week 12, when he gained 166 yards on the ground, setting his own regulation single-game record and coming ever so close to the NFL mark he had set against the Minnesota Vikings in 2002 with 173 yards, including a 46-yard game-winner in overtime. That said, the Saints game also portended the limitations of a base option offense without a true receiving threat because Atlanta lost that game 31–13. Falcons receivers couldn't hang on to the ball, and Vick finished his day 9-for-24 for 84 yards. "He's changed the game," Vikings linebacker Henri Crockett told ESPN.com after Vick set that rushing record against Minnesota. "There are going to be no more pocket passers anymore."

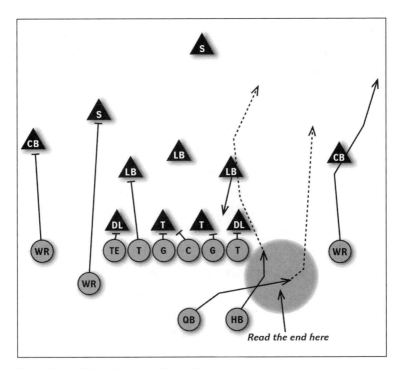

The Atlanta Falcons' read-option offense

That wasn't quite true, but Vick had set a course in motion that others would follow in different ways. Vick's incarceration put an end to that iteration of the read-option, but Philadelphia Eagles defensive coordinator Jim Johnson had established a template to counter the Falcons' multi-faceted run game in the 2004 NFC Championship Game. Instead of having his ends follow the run action and guessing wrong no matter what they did, the blitzingest coach in the NFL went completely against type and directed his defenders to back off and react.

In theory, opposing defensive coordinators could find themselves in a number of strategic holes. Blitzing would have left gaps open for the one-cut zone-blocking style favored by Falcons offensive assistant Alex Gibbs. Vick's instructions were simple: check the reads as fast as you possibly can and, if things aren't to your liking, turn on the jets. His speed made blitzing doubly frustrating. And bringing eight to the box left your defenders caught up in the wave that was Gibbs' zone concept, and the linebackers were washed out as the cutback went away from them.

Edge rushing from a front three or five and leaving a spy for Vick in the middle didn't really work either because Gibbs and offensive coordinator Greg Knapp had a kink in the outside zone that further deployed Vick's speed—a simple option read that kept the end on a string. So the rushing/run-stopping end could either blow right by the running Vick, breaking his own ankles trying to recover, or he could head outside to anticipate the pitch to the back as Vick cut inside and headed upfield. And if the end brought help in the form of a linebacker—in the "scrape exchange," the end covers the back, and the linebacker deals with the quarterback—that left coverage spots open for Vick to throw to tight end Alge Crumpler, his favorite target at the time. It was simple, brutally effective, and brought the Falcons to Philly. A week after gaining 327 yards on the ground against the St. Louis Rams in the divisional round in the friendly confines of the Georgia Dome, the Falcons would have to deal with zero-degree windchill and gusts of up to 35 miles per hour, putting even more pressure on the running game for a win.

Johnson had a different plan to stop the go-go Falcons, which goes with the theme of this book: great coaches don't stick with their trademarks on a no-matter-what basis; they constantly go back to the drawing board, finding new ways to set up their personnel for optimal success. Johnson knew where the traps were and, armed with a map of the minefield, effectively won the game in the first three Atlanta drives.

Although other coaches directed their defenders to overpursue Vick at their peril, Johnson used his linebackers to spy zones and gaps instead. He understood that the cold weather and biting wind would take the pass away to a point and thus treated Atlanta's offense as if it were a 30-year-old Wishbone. Blitz looks were just that—looks for the most part—and those extra defenders would pull back to read and cover at the snap. Ends Jevon Kearse and Derrick Burgess were directed to read and wait instead of pursuing from the start, and Crumpler had to pinball his way through multiple Eagles just to get open. Middle linebacker Jeremiah Trotter was the scud missile inside, the one who had to find the open gap and kill it. The supposedly blitz-happy Johnson succeeded by going against schematic type.

On the third play of Atlanta's first drive, the Falcons went shotgun with two backs, but Johnson countered with an overload left, bringing Dhani Jones and Brian Dawkins up to stop the option to Vick's right. Checkmate. Vick called timeout. Take Two saw the same Falcons formation and an overload look from the Eagles, but only four rushed at the snap. As Vick tried to gain ground upfield, he was accosted first by Dawkins and then Corey Simon, gaining only two yards. In one simple three-and-out,

Johnson showed the Falcons that no matter what variant of their run-based (and admittedly weather-limited) offense they went with he had an answer. Dawkins didn't really move in coverage on the third-down stop; he simply waited for the play to come to him. Faced with a defense that didn't bite on the first move he made, Vick lacked productive options.

Despite Vick's eventual flameout, there were those in the league who believed that a more developed and integrated version of the spread could work in the NFL—or, at least, that the NFL was going to have to take a smarter and more opportunistic look at the players using it in college. Chief among them was Scot McCloughan, who came up as a scout with the Packers in the 1990s and an executive for Mike Holmgren's Seattle Seahawks from 2000 through 2004.

In 2005 McCloughan became the vice president of player personnel for the San Francisco 49ers and he selected quarterback Alex Smith of Utah with the first pick overall in the 2005 draft. Smith came from an option system that was simpler than the NFL required, but it was run-based. (Head coach Urban Meyer would take that system to Florida in 2005, engendering a long history of success with Tim Tebow as his most famous running quarterback.) Smith was upended for years by his own limitations and the 49ers' habit of changing offensive coordinators every year, but, as McCloughan told me in 2007, NFL teams were going to have to change their thinking about players in college offenses for one simple reason—the *Moneyball* concept of finding hidden value in underrated assets and bringing the intrinsic value of those assets to the forefront of your business. It was no different in professional football than it was in baseball, or the stock market, or any other professional system in which the meaning of value had changed.

The structure was nascent, but the belief system was coming. The apex of that belief system in the NFL occurred when the NFL's most successful head coach over the past decade reached out to a college head coach who was about to turn the league on its ear with his own philosophies. Before that could happen, Belichick was upended by an object lesson in option football. Not that Belichick was averse to new offensive trends—the 2007 Patriots were the first team in NFL history to run more than half its plays out of the shotgun formation and set scoring and yardage records that won't be broken for a good long time—but first a series of gadgets worked ever so well for a short while.

The Wildcat

In August of 2007, Arkansas offensive coordinator David Lee drew up three plays for CBS Sports Network, in which the ball was snapped directly to running backs in his offense. Darren McFadden was the point man on these plays, and as Lee said in the video, there were three base run plays out of what he called the Wildcat package:

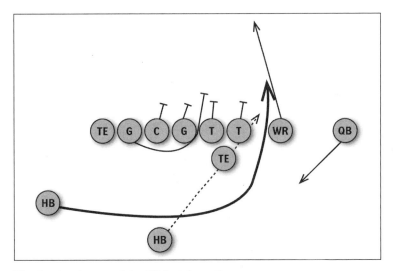

The *Steeler* play out of the Wildcat formation

Steeler had the running back move from left to right after the snap and take the ball from the quarterback (in this case McFadden). The running back then would blast off to the right behind a pulling left guard, an unbalanced offensive line, and an H-back either between and behind the two right tackles or just outside the right tackle to block.

In *Power* the fake to the running back in the *Steeler* formation leaves the quarterback to (hopefully) blow through any one of four different holes to the right behind an unbalanced offensive line with two right tackles.

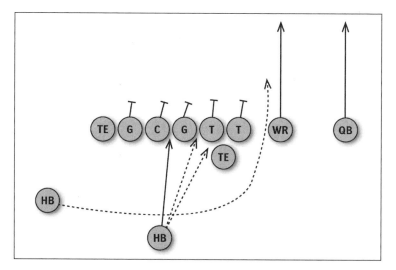

The *Power* play out of the Wildcat formation

In *Counter* the fake leaves the defense biting on *Power* and has them watch helplessly as the quarterback (McFadden in this case) runs left through a huge open cutback lane. McFadden could cut back and make gains through a number of gaps left by a defense overpursuing to the strong-side. "Darren McFadden is such an extremely unique player in his versatility in the Wildcat, putting

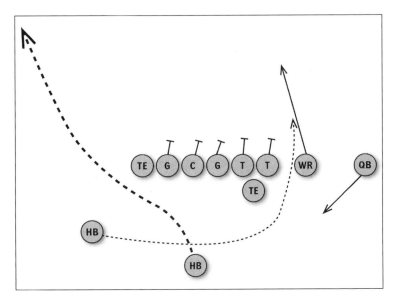

The *Counter* play out of the Wildcat formation

him in the shotgun and letting him play quarterback," Lee said at the time. "He could throw it, run the counter, or the power, or the outside zone. His versatility is something we'll miss when he's no longer a Razorback."

McFadden was selected fourth overall in the 2008 draft by the Oakland Raiders. After the 2007 season, Lee also left Arkansas to become the quarterbacks coach for the Miami Dolphins and he took the Wildcat concepts with him. Something was desperately needed to put the Dolphins, who finished 1–15 in 2007, back on the right track. They began the 2008 season with an 0–2 record, and the inspiration (read: desperation) for change came on the flight back from Phoenix after rookie head coach Tony Sparano had seen his team receive a 31–10 beatdown at the hands of the Arizona Cardinals. Miami had two talented running backs in Ronnie Brown and Ricky Williams, but they combined for just 53 yards on 22 carries out of more conventional formations against

Arizona's defense. "We were all miserable at that point," Sparano told *USA TODAY* in December of that year. "I didn't feel like we had an identity in the run game. I also felt it was getting harder to put Ronnie Brown and Ricky Williams in the game at the same time and get them touches."

Sparano, a former offensive line coach and tight ends coach with several NFL teams and currently the Minnesota Vikings offensive line coach, had done enough vetting with Lee to understand that there was a different option with some potential. "I called David to the front of the plane and said, 'Here's what I want: tomorrow when we get back, I want three runs, maybe a pass out of this Wildcat package. We need to find something we can put our arms around as an offense that can create space.'"

Sparano, Lee, and offensive coordinator Dan Henning worked on the *Steeler/Power/Counter* package through the week with the goal of unleashing it against the New England Patriots at Gillette Stadium. The Patriots had lost Tom Brady for the season to a knee injury in the season's first game, but they were still a formidable team (they went 11–5 with Matt Cassel at quarterback) with an outstanding defense. Still, the Miami Wildcat cabal saw some vulnerabilities in the Patriots and were able to exploit them in a 38–13 win, in which Brown ran for four touchdowns and threw for another. The Dolphins ran six direct snap plays against the Patriots on that afternoon, and they're worth reviewing.

The first *Power* play came with 2:32 left in the first quarter and the Dolphins at the New England 2-yard line. Miami lined up in an unbalanced right line with left tackle Jake Long outside right tackle Vernon Carey. Tight end David Martin served as the H-back behind and between Carey and Long. Ricky Williams was in the left slot, and Chad Pennington was split wide to the left. At the snap Williams ran a sweep/reverse look, Brown faked the handoff to him, and left guard Justin Smiley pulled right between

Carey and Long. The two tackles had opened up a huge hole, and Smiley busted through to take linebacker Jerod Mayo out of the play to the left. Brown had a truck-sized lane to run through. Later in the game, the Dolphins ran this play again.

Steeler play No. 1 came with 4:54 left in the first half; this was the first of three in the second quarter. It had the same formation, same basic personnel. The Patriots appeared to at least recognize the formation this time, but the left side of their secondary—cornerback Deltha O'Neal and safety Rodney Harrison—played back about seven yards. There was little in the way of pre-snap adjustment. As a result the handoff to Williams left the Pats with a blocking mismatch, as Long and Martin sealed off Mike Vrabel, and running back Patrick Cobbs chipped Harrison upfield. The only thing that stopped Williams from a long gain with a quick cut upfield was a stumble and fall. Vrabel was credited with a perfunctory tackle.

Williams recouped those yards on first and 10 with two minutes left in the first half. This was the second *Steeler*. It had the quick cut inside that Williams missed before. Pennington was lined up wide right this time. Other than that, it was the same personnel grouping. Vince Wilfork came through late on the backside. Martin engaged Vrabel decisively with a great moving block, while Long and Carey slipped to the second level and demolished New England's linebackers. Williams got past O'Neal and was finally tripped up by Harrison 28 yards downfield at the New England 17.

The third and final Wildcat play of the second quarter was probably the backbreaker. Miami was at the Patriots' 5-yard line, and Pennington went wide right again with Cobbs in the right slot. The scoring play was *Power*, but the Dolphins had a touchdown if they wanted it with Williams running wide in the *Steeler* as well. Now, the unmentioned adjustment New England made this time was to spy Ellis Hobbs on Williams as he ran left to right for the fake. But Hobbs focused entirely on Williams and bit too hard. By the time Hobbs realized the ball was coming inside, he couldn't reverse his direction and get his bearings. All he could do was to grasp at air as Brown went by. Brown's escorts were dominant once again, as Long, Carey, and Smiley each got a hat on a hat. Brown had little interference on his way to the end zone, and the Patriots had no answer whatsoever for the inside run on the fake. The score at halftime? The very confident Dolphins 21, the extremely confused Patriots 6.

Wildcat No. 5 was the *Counter*, which featured an aerial option wrinkle. The Dolphins faced third and 3 from the New England 19 with 5:51 left in the third quarter. They employed the same base personnel with Pennington wide right. This time the Pats brought six to the line and essentially eight in the box. At the snap all heads went toward Williams; you could almost *feel* 11 Patriots biting in that direction, and this left all action open for the *Counter*. Tight end Anthony Fasano ran a seam route from the far left spot in the line right past Mayo and safety Brandon Meriweather. Brown ran the counter option left and threw up a lefty pass to a wide open Fasano for the touchdown. If the previous plays were physically dominant, this one was downright embarrassing. At this point the Dolphins had the vaunted New England defense on a string.

The final Wildcat formation at the beginning of the fourth quarter did in the Patriots. It was first and 10 from the Miami 38 with the same personnel and same basic formation except with Pennington back to wide left. Brown started to look counter after the fake to Williams but saw a *Power* lane between Long and Carey (again) while Smiley was at the second level ready to decimate anyone in his way (again). Brown just outran everyone to the end zone, putting the cap on his own great day, an incredible performance by the offensive line, and a real validation for the Miami Dolphins' coaching staff.

Other teams took notice and adapted the Wildcat to their own devices, as will happen in the NFL; one of the most time-honored truisms is that it's a copycat league. The Kansas City Chiefs had rookie tailback Jamaal Charles pitch to receiver Mark Bradley and throw a 37-yard touchdown pass to quarterback Tyler Thigpen. The Cardinals, whose head coach Ken Whisenhunt had run option plays with receivers Antwaan Randle El and Hines Ward as the Pittsburgh Steelers' offensive coordinator a few years before, had receiver Anquan Boldin running the "Pahokee" package named after Boldin's Florida hometown. The Cleveland Browns ran several iterations of the option with receiver and return specialist Josh Cribbs, who played quarterback at Kent State. Some teams ran the same kinds of blocking concepts that Lee imported from Arkansas, while others thought that a direct snap to a non-quarterback was all they would need to set defenses on edge.

The latter didn't generally work too well, and the Wildcat's success rate was about to plummet. The fundamental issue with the Wildcat against NFL defenses was that it wasn't variable enough to grow over time. Soon enough, enemy defenses shut it down, starting with the Baltimore Ravens—three games and four weeks after the Wildcat's triumphant NFL debut. In a 27–13 loss, the Dolphins had to keep their guards in to deal with Baltimore's physical defensive line, and the linebackers had the range and aggression to deal with the misdirection aspects of the system. Miami was outnumbered by a personnel disadvantage and had no counter as a result.

Outside of *Steeler, Power, Counter,* and a few other wrinkles, this 'Cat didn't have enough different stripes to fool the NFL over time. The 2008 Dolphins ran a total of 965 plays for 5,529 yards, a 5.7 yards-per-play average, and 38 offensive touchdowns. Of those plays 91 were run out of the Wildcat formation—the actual Wildcat, not a read-option or shotgun draw misclassified as such—for 580 yards, a 6.7 yards-per-play average, and eight touchdowns. But after that first blush against the Patriots, it was all diminishing returns. Still, as those two remnants of the game were going through their life cycles, another college coach was working with a concept that would have a lot more staying power in the pros.

The Pistol Offense

"When I presented this to my staff, they looked at me as if I had lost my marbles." According to the *2010 Coach of the Year Clinics: Football Manual*, that was the reaction to the birth of the Pistol offense, which was created in 2005 by Nevada head coach Chris Ault, who was trying to strike a balance between the shotgun spread concepts he was increasingly seeing in the NCAA and the vertical running game he deemed crucial to success at any level. Ault was a quarterback at Nevada from 1965 to 1968, and his offensive theories helped make him one of five FBS coaches with more than 200 wins during his tenure.

"I coach the quarterbacks at the University of Nevada and I love to throw the football," Ault said. "From 1993 through 1996, we led the country, one way or another, in throwing the football." That said, Ault had to bring it back around. "We have always been a north and south running game offense." The vehicle Ault would use for this radical transformation came to him in early 2005, and he implemented it that year. "I brought the staff together and I told them that this is what I want to look at during spring practice," Ault told his fellow coaches. "I want to move the quarterback 4.5 yards off the ball in the shotgun set. We want our deep back to line up seven to 7.5 yards from the center. I wanted to know if we could move the quarterback off the line and still be able run our offense."

The thought process behind the distance from center of the skill players became clear to Ault as he worked with the formation through those first practices. "I started calling the offense the Pistol—the quarterback was the trigger, and the deep back was the hammer of the pistol," he said. "We took the kids out on the field and ran all the tests on the depth of the back. We lined the tailback up three yards behind the quarterback [who was then 7.5 yards behind center]. It was difficult to see the running back directly behind the quarterback three yards away. At five yards away, the linebackers could see the running back better. By having him seven yards deep, we can get the ball to him deeper than we would if the quarterback was under center."

Ault's new offense really hit the big time when a lightly recruited quarterback named Colin Kaepernick took it over in 2007 as a true freshman and eventually became the first quarterback in NCAA history to throw for more than 10,000 yards and rush for more than 4,000 yards in his collegiate career. Still, Kaepernick had to answer the same old questions about his ability to operate in a traditional, dropback offense behind center. "I don't think our offense will directly translate, but I think we do a bunch of things as progressions and protections that are similar to what NFL teams do, and we just call them something different," he said at the 2011 Scouting Combine. "Picking up on terminology will be a big thing for me, learning what those mean as opposed to what we call things."

But there had been a minor Pistol revolution going on the NFL a few years before Kaepernick made himself available for the NFL, and the terminology was about to come far more his way than the other way around. In 2008 the Kansas City Chiefs were struggling mightily on offense. Their top two quarterbacks, Damon Huard and Brodie Croyle, were out with injuries, and their star running back, Larry Johnson, had been deactivated by the team (and later the NFL) for a number of violations of team and league code. Offensive coordinator Chan Gailey had a hard row to hoe, but he had seen what Ault had been doing in Nevada and he imagined that he could find success with third-string quarterback Tyler Thigpen—an athletic, second-year castoff from the Minnesota Vikings—who had played an iteration of the spread at Coastal Carolina. "It was kind of an adjustment on the fly," Thigpen said in 2010. "The main reason we went to the Pistol offense in Kansas City was Larry Johnson. He was more of a downhill back, not an offset guy in a shotgun, doing zone runs. So, that was the main reason we were doing that kind of stuff. It allowed us to open up a lot of things because you could go with regular personnel and still fool the defense. It was hard for the defense to

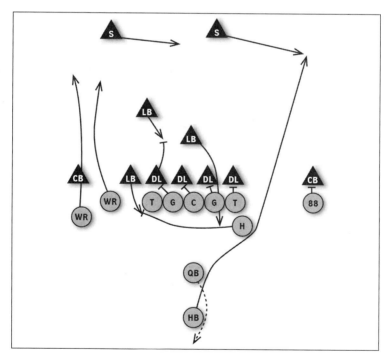

The Kansas City Chiefs' Pistol offense

see the ball, whether you were handing off or faking it and it really allowed us to do a lot of different things."

Gailey implemented the shotgun as a primary concern during Kansas City's Week 7 game against the Tennessee Titans. After the Chiefs had lost 34–0 to the Carolina Panthers the week before, there was little left to lose. Johnson returned to action in Week 11 against the Titans, and that's when Gailey really unleashed the Pistol's potentially lethal combination of formation versatility and traditional power in the running game. "Once that suspension was up, and Larry was back in the lineup, that's when we went more to the Pistol offense," Thigpen said. "[Running backs] Kolby [Smith] and Jamaal [Charles] were used to that zone type of running, where you press the side and make a cutback—or whatever the case may be—whatever lane they've got. We tried running that offense for one or two weeks when Larry came back and then we realized, 'Hey, he's not that kind of back.' That's when we changed to the downhill kind of running. The Pistol is really like an I formation, whether you put the back in the near set or the far set."

Johnson's 15-yard run with 2:25 left in the Week 13 win against the Oakland Raiders was a good example of how the Pistol cut defensive read time, especially when any sort of delay was involved. On this play Thigpen took just an extra moment before handing the ball to Johnson, which had linebacker Thomas Howard overpursuing inside as Johnson bounced outside right. Thigpen told me that there were all kinds of effective schematic combinations. "Whether it was a quarterback draw, a misdirection with a one-back offset, having the back go to the left and bringing him back to the right, it would look to the defense like a zone left run instead of a cutback to the right," he said. "The play-action was really good because you couldn't see the back and whether he had the ball or not with the offensive line up front. I remember a couple times, just running boots and faking to [the back], and it was just wide open when I came out on the boot. It was tough for the defensive end, when he's coming off the edge, to see whether you gave it or not. Normally, he has that advantage when you're coming out from under center to see—whether you're close to the back or not—what kind of fake it is."

And that's what made the Pistol more versatile, universal, and transferrable than the Wildcat had been. The Wildcat was a series of three base plays with room for a few new wrinkles, while the Pistol was a larger mold coaches could use to pour their own specific knowledge into.

The San Francisco 49ers selected Kaepernick in the second round of the 2011 draft, but it wasn't until his second season that he got more than a few looks in what offensive coordinator Greg Roman later called "the Colin Package." Long before this, though, Roman, who worked with head coach Jim Harbaugh at Stanford and then at San Francisco, had traveled to see Ault and explore the possibilities inherent in the Pistol concept. "About three years ago, (I) made the trek to Nevada and visited with him and his staff," Roman told NBC Sports Bay Area in December of 2012. "That was very valuable time spent. He was very accommodating, and it was very interesting as a coach to go really learn something totally new. And he's a very good football coach."

Roman was then looking to implement Pistol play designs at Stanford, where he and Harbaugh had the kind of power/counter run game and variable passing game that would seem to be a perfect fit. When Kaepernick became the starter in Week 7 of the 2012 season after Alex Smith suffered a concussion, Roman had worked enough with Kaepernick to make it fly. What Roman called the Q formation (so named because the 49ers preferred to keep their play calls to one syllable) became the 49ers' base quarterback formation, and the 49ers did all kinds of different things with it. They put multiple backs around Kaepernick—one behind him in the traditional Pistol spacing and one to each side—in a full-house power package. They used offset Pistol with a back to Kaepernick's left or right side (the offense's strong or weak-side) and they ran a lot of highly effective play-action out of the Pistol. In 2013 Kaepernick's first season as an NFL starter, he completed 61.3 percent of his passes out of play-action with 11 touchdowns and one interception—as opposed to a 57.2 completion rate, 10 touchdowns, and seven interceptions without play-action.

But what made the Pistol work for the 49ers—and provided a guide to future use—was how well they integrated it with traditional football concepts. Every aspect of the Kaepernick option

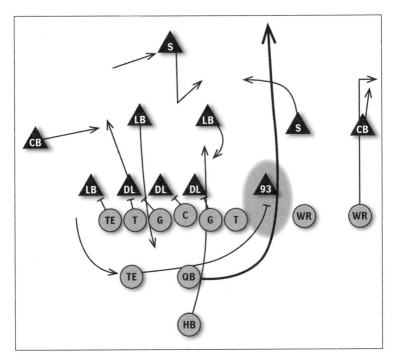

San Francisco 49ers quarterback Colin Kaepernick's 56-yard touchdown in the 2012 NFC Divisional Playoff Game

game had its antecedents—from the old-school Wishbone, to the trap blocks favored by the Pittsburgh Steelers of the 1970s, to the counter plays defined by the Washington Redskins of the John Riggins era, to the read-option, to the Pistol. But the ways in which the 49ers put it together were very different and quite befuddling even to NFL defenses that were primed to stop just about anything.

The most compelling example of the 49ers' Pistol offense came in the divisional round of the 2012 playoffs, when Kaepernick broke Michael Vick's single-game rushing record for a quarterback with 181 yards as San Francisco beat the Green Bay Packers 45–31. Harbaugh and Roman understood and exploited a kink in Dom Capers' defense. Because the Packers' cornerbacks played a high percentage of press-man coverage, lining up as close to the receivers as possible and turning their backs to run with those receivers, Kaepernick had more room and a higher percentage of outside rushing lanes.

Kaepernick's 56-yard touchdown run in the third quarter of that game was an object lesson in how the Pistol—and the run-based deception it produces—can leave aggressive defenses in a major hole. On this play the 49ers lined up with two tight ends to the left, and outside tight end/fullback Bruce Miller motioned into the backfield. This offset Pistol formation set the edge for Kaepernick's run because Miller moved across the formation at the snap and blocked left outside linebacker Erik Walden (93) to help give Kaepernick a lane in the middle of the formation. The Packers had three defensive linemen stacked in the middle of the line, but San Francisco's power blockers took them out, and the inside linebackers bit on the play-action fake to halfback LaMichael James. San Francisco had two receivers to the right—Michael Crabtree to the inside and Ted Ginn, Jr. to the outside—and they blocked out Green Bay's attempt to counter

Kaepernick with a two-deep safety look converted by motion to a single-high concept. "We didn't make any adjustments," Packers defensive back Charles Woodson told NFL.com after that loss. "I just think when the game is going the way it is, you've got to try something different. It's hard to just continue to do the same thing over and over again and continue to get burned…We need to figure out: could we have done something differently as far as our gameplan was concerned?"

Whatever that something different may have been, it didn't show up in the 2013 season opener. This time Green Bay had its forces arrayed against San Francisco's running game, and Kaepernick responded by completing 27-of-39 passes for 412 yards, three touchdowns, and no interceptions in a 34–28 victory. Using the old adage that if you want a running quarterback to stop running, you hit him hard enough to make him do something else, the Packers tried to intimidate Kaepernick. Much to Green Bay's dismay, receiver Anquan Boldin, who the 49ers acquired in a trade from the Baltimore Ravens after Baltimore had beaten them in the previous Super Bowl, outmuscled the Packers' defense for 13 catches, 208 yards, and a touchdown. Tight end Vernon Davis added six catches for 98 yards and two touchdowns of his own. The Kaepernick 49ers eventually came into disrepair due to personnel mismanagement and power struggles up top. But for a brief moment in time, Kaepernick looked to be the next evolution in quarterbacking.

Belichick and Kelly: The Student Becomes the Teacher

The NFL embraced the speed no-huddle offense as never before in 2012, when the New England Patriots ratcheted the tempo of their game to previously unforeseen levels. Bill Belichick's team changed its play-calling and schematics to force defenses to bend to their will, something that Bill Walsh had predicted years before. In his seminal 1998 book, *Finding the Winning Edge*, Walsh said that:

Teams will only huddle when the clock is stopped.

Teams will use single-word offensive audibles.

The timing between the quarterback and the receiver will be more defined.

The quarterback will receive direction from the coach at the line of scrimmage. Because the ball can be put into play at any moment, the defense must commit itself with its front and coverage.

Belichick had already adopted certain aspects of a wide-open offense that his forbearers refused to take on. The 2007 Patriots were the first NFL team of the modern era to run more than 50 percent of their plays in the shotgun. They set a league record with 589 regular-season points, breaking the record set by the 1998 Minnesota Vikings, who had Randall Cunningham—a "converted" running quarterback—under center. In 2008 three teams—the Patriots, Kansas City Chiefs, and Arizona Cardinals—went shotgun more than half the time. By 2014 that figure had grown to 26 of the 32 NFL teams, and the Philadelphia Eagles led the league with an NFL record 86 percent of their plays with their quarterback away from center. The 2014 Eagles were coached by former Oregon head man Chip Kelly—it was his second year in the NFL—but Kelly had already had a fairly major effect on the pros, and Belichick was the conduit.

Belichick reached out to Kelly, and the then-Oregon head coach visited the Patriots' facility in 2010 to discuss an offense that had taken the Pac-12 by storm with its speed concepts, run/pass equality, and ability to force opposing defenses to stay in their base formations. "I was interested to hear how he did it," Belichick told *The Boston Globe* in 2012. "I would say he expanded it to a different level, and it was very interesting to understand what he was doing. Certainly, I've learned a lot from talking to Chip about his experiences with it and how he does it and his procedure and all that."

The Patriots started to adapt their playbook to a new level of simplicity in 2011 under then-offensive coordinator Bill O'Brien. A play that may have been called *0 Flood FAP—SP 238 MAX Z Cross X V* in 2004 was now called much more quickly. Quarterback Tom Brady might utter one word after a play was over to signify the details of a new play, and his teammates would understand what to do and where to go with opposing defenses unable to adjust.

In 2012 Belichick's team set another record. This time it was the number of offensive plays in the regular season (1,191). They also led the league in points with 557, but they did it in a different fashion—by dialing their percentage of shotgun down to 48.2 percent, 14th in the league. Other teams used no-huddle more often than New England did, but no team used the hurry-up with greater effectiveness because the Patriots still put a full array of plays and personnel on the field. It was spread speed with traditional depth, and defenses simply didn't know what to do. No surprise that Kelly's Eagles ramped up their own tempo, registering 1,054 plays in 2013 (Kelly's first season) and 1,127 in 2014.

How did defenses adjust? By running far more nickel and dime defenses (five and six defensive backs on the field) and drafting lighter, quicker linebackers who were more half-field defenders than old-school thumpers. From 2011 through 2014, the number of base NFL defensive plays with five or more defensive backs increased from 40 percent in 2011, to 44 percent in 2012, to 49 percent in 2013, to 60 percent in 2014. The

effective elimination of substitution advantage forced desperate teams to re-jigger their personnel strategies, and eventually
more traditionally-minded coaches would follow suit. "There's
been so much passing game in the last 10 years, and I think the
nickel—it's half the game," Pete Carroll said in 2014. "Half the
game, you're in nickel or some kind of substitution defense. So,
it's whichever way you want to look at it; maybe that's base, and
the other part is substitution now. We're divided about 500 plays
year in and year out, and it's a big deal. That's why [on defense],
we have more than 11 starters. We've got 15 to 16 starters that
we see, and you can tell, depending on the opponent and the
situation in the game, how many of those guys we'll move in and
out and feel comfortable doing that."

Carroll was USC's head coach from 2001 through 2009,
a position he took after a long history as a successful defensive
coordinator and a less notable head coach with the New York Jets
and Patriots. Carroll was a prolific winner with the Trojans and
he ran a series of run-heavy, traditional offenses with quarterbacks
from Carson Palmer to Mark Sanchez. When he returned to the
NFL in 2010 as the head coach of the Seahawks, it appeared to be
business as usual. In that first season, Carroll's Seahawks ran the
ball frequently and used the shotgun in just 38.2 percent of their
plays. But by 2014 that shotgun percentage had increased to 69
percent, and Seattle ranked just 10th in that statistic.

The difference was quarterback Russell Wilson, a highly
mobile and productive player who ran a West Coast Offense at
North Carolina State and a two-back power zone system for a
season at Wisconsin. In that regard Wilson was the perfect field
general in an offense that ran two-back power zone with West
Coast passing principles, but the force multiplier came when
Carroll and offensive coordinator Darrell Bevell turned Wilson
loose as an option factor. All of a sudden, defenses didn't know

how to deal with the duality of Wilson crashing the edge as a runner and Marshawn Lynch bowling through defensive fronts as the best pure runner in the league.

Carroll adapted his offense even more than his defense, and he did so predominantly because of one quarterback—Robert Griffin III of the Washington Redskins, the second overall pick in the 2012 draft. Wilson was taken 73 picks later. In his rookie season, Griffin took elements of the offense he ran under Art Briles at Baylor (shotgun, spread concepts, hurried tempo) and married it to those presented by Washington head coach Mike Shanahan and offensive coordinator Kyle Shanahan (Mike's son). The Shanahans added the Pistol to the zone-running scheme the elder Shanahan had espoused for decades—the same one Alex Gibbs employed that benefitted Michael Vick with the Atlanta Falcons years before—and turned Griffin into a rookie revolution.

It was Griffin, not Wilson or No. 1 overall pick Andrew Luck, who won the AP Offensive Rookie of the Year award, completing more than 65 percent of his passes for 3,200 yards, 20 touchdowns, and five interceptions. Griffin added 815 yards and seven touchdowns as a rusher, and the combination of Shanahan's zone blocking and the stress presented to any defense by Griffin's pure speed turned sixth-round rookie Alfred Morris into a 1,600-yard back in his debut season. "I was impressed with how much they got out of it," Carroll said in November of 2012. "They're way ahead of everybody else in terms of their commitment to a college style of offense, and it's been very effective…It was a good move for me and it's helped us a little bit. I was influenced a little bit more than I thought when I first looked at. You see some of our stuff coming to life, and it's helping us."

It helped out with Wilson in part because he was perfectly attuned to the West Coast Offense passing game with a two-back power ground attack that Bevell wanted to run. As Wilson told me in his rookie year, the formations and terminology were so similar to his college offenses that the learning curve was not nearly as steep as he might have imagined.

The NFL undervalued Wilson because he stood 5'10", but he beat out high-priced free-agent quarterback Matt Flynn in his first training camp and was named the Seahawks' starter before he was out of his first preseason. And in some ways, Wilson has been the ideal mixture of dynamism and efficiency many were eventually hoping to see from a mobile quarterback. His 161/56 touchdown/interception ratio through the 2017 regular season gets a bit lost in the fact that the Seahawks buttressed him with a great running game and the league's best defense, but as much as Lynch opened things up for Wilson by forcing defenses to cheat up to stop him, Wilson opened things up for Lynch and the rest of the Seattle offense with his own rushing ability. It's been said that Wilson had to go to the NFL to play in a college offense, and that's generally true of the transition that the Seahawks—and many other teams—have undergone. Even the staunchest traditionalists have turned around.

Mike Holmgren, who coached the Green Bay Packers and Seahawks to a 161–111 record over 17 seasons, was a Bill Walsh acolyte. And Walsh believed that although several things could happen in a shotgun-heavy offense, most of them were bad. There's little doubt that if Walsh was alive and coaching today, he'd find a way to not only change his thinking in that regard, but also put himself—and his quarterbacks—at the head of the pack. That's what the great innovators do, especially when they're playing from behind.

With all that said, the question *still* remains—is there a repeatable way to make a quarterback dependent on a "college system" successful at an elite level in the pros? Vick had a brief redemptive curve with the Eagles. Colin Kaepernick regressed when defenses assessed that the best thing to do was to wait him out and force him to rely on a limited palette of field-reading abilities. Griffin succumbed to injuries and a new head coach in Jay Gruden, who seemed uniquely put off by his skillset. Cam Newton, who was productive early on with the Carolina Panthers when his coaching staff merged the system he ran at Auburn with the one he would use at the next level, is still a work in progress. "There is a transition," Holmgren said of Oregon quarterback Marcus Mariota on Seattle radio station KJR in April of 2015. Mariota, a graduate of Kelly's Oregon system, who became the Tennessee Titans' starting quarterback. "There is a learning curve there. And I go back to Alex Smith when he was at Utah with Urban Meyer, and Scotty McCloughan, who worked for me in Seattle, was now the San Francisco general manager. He phoned me up and said, 'We're going to take Alex Smith. What do you think?' And I said, 'Well, he was the youngest guy in the draft that year—like 20 years old.' So, he was young and he came from a systems offense, which was even more unique then than it is now. So, there is going to be a longer learning curve to play the position—what they ask him to do in the NFL. Having said that, he's a phenomenal athlete and a great kid. If everyone's on board in knowing that it's going to take a little time, it'll work."

It didn't work for Smith for years because the fix the 49ers were in through his early days; he was more successful when he was Kaepernick's predecessor under Jim Harbaugh and then under Andy Reid in Kansas City. Aaron Rodgers was taken 24th overall in that same draft by the Green Bay Packers and completed just 35 passes in his first three NFL seasons as he sat behind Brett Favre. In the end the time served was good for Rodgers. He used it to develop an understanding of what the NFL required.

Even those coaches and general managers who are convinced that the new wave of quarterback mobility and offensive multiplicity is the way to go will tell you that there's more expected of NFL quarterbacks if they ever want to ascend to the highest level the position allows. John Schneider, Seattle's general manager and the man who banged on the table for Wilson, remarked at the 2015 Scouting Combine that the transitional evaluation of these types of quarterbacks isn't getting any easier. "It's so unique seeing those guys go into the Senior Bowl and seeing those guys under center," Schneider said. "You've got guys moving around, how they move in the pocket, how they adjust. It's harder now. When you watch college football, you see those guys looking to the sideline, and I know me, personally, I've made several mistakes in that regard. You may question the guy's decision-making. You may value it higher—his intellectual level or what a good football guy he is—but you don't truly know because [he is] looking at the sidelines at cards. It's just a process that we have to continue to work through and evaluate. Like any other position, we evaluate all the way through the spring. It's really about figuring out how the guy processes. Can he get the information? Can he express it to his teammates? Can he read a defense? What those guys do…I mean, that's pretty intense stuff. It's like learning a whole language."

CHAPTER 9

THE NFL'S FUTURE
The Genius of Adaptation

> *"Many before have hailed the end of history;*
> *none have ever been right."*
> —author Jonathan Wilson

The final chapter of this book begins with the final words in Mr. Wilson's outstanding book, *Inverting the Pyramid,* because the history of soccer tactics helped inspire *The Genius of Desperation.* Professional American football has been a tough sport to accurately and chronologically chronicle. The quarterback sack only became a statistic in 1982, and the advanced metrics that came to baseball in the 1970s with Bill James and his acolytes have only really touched the NFL over the last decade. Things like defensive hits, hurries, and coverage numbers beyond interceptions and pass deflections are available to the public but are generally limited to the charting staffs of NFL teams or subscription services whose systems are not standardized. The schemes that have defined the game over the decades are generally attributed to more than one person—or not at all. I wanted to bring an order of time to the game's schematic innovations and uncover some of the brilliant men who have forwarded them.

Looking to the future, there are a few things we can deduce for certain. More than one NFL coach and general manager has told me that the modern NFL is more a matchup league than ever before, and what they generally mean by that is that there are far fewer static positions and more players who can fill multiple hybrid positions with their specific attributes. The theory is that when you align the scheme to the player, as opposed to the other way around, you have players more attuned to their responsibilities—and schemes that are more versatile based on the skills of your players.

The linebacker position, for example, has changed drastically over the last decade. Although Tampa-2 schemes, requiring a middle linebacker who could drop into coverage, used to be *de rigueur*, the NFL's modern defenses have smaller, faster linebackers inside and outside for the most part. Your old-school thumpers are run specialists at best; now, the advent of three and four-receiver base offenses require linebackers who can retreat into zone and man coverage as if they were safeties.

In some cases those linebackers once were safeties, and their positional responsibilities have changed to adjust to the modern passing game. The Tampa Bay Buccaneers selected Alabama safety Mark Barron with the seventh overall pick in the 2012 draft. Barron was limited as a traditional strong safety both in run defense and pass coverage, but the then-St. Louis and now Los Angeles Rams saw the potential for something else. They traded for Barron in October of 2014, and when speed linebacker Alec Ogletree suffered an injury in 2015, defensive coordinator Gregg Williams took the 6'1", 213-pound Barron and made him a linebacker in space. Having Barron at the second level of the defense allowed Williams to put different looks on the field, especially in his frequent dime packages.

The Arizona Cardinals made a similar choice in Washington State safety Deone Bucannon, who was selected with the 27th overall pick in the 2014 draft. Bucannon was a rangy pass-defend-ing safety who could run up and hit at the line of scrimmage, but the Cardinals had other ideas for him. Bucannon played strong safety in all but one of 18 games in his rookie campaign—he started at free safety against the San Francisco 49ers in Week 3—but with so much depth at the safety position and a clear need for a hit-and-cover linebacker as Daryl Washington remained on indefinite suspension for various off-field incidents, head coach Bruce Arians and defensive coordinator James Bettcher decided to make Bucannon an inside linebacker, for all intents and purposes.

Thus, Bucannon became the only 210-pound inside line-backer in the NFL and a valuable force inside. He's learned to deal with rushing gaps and expanded his repertoire as a box player while maintaining his ability to cover. The Cardinals referred to him as their "Moneybacker" in their dime-based defense, and he's listed as an $LB on the team's depth chart. After he amassed 11 tackles and returned an interception for a 39-yard touchdown against the Philadelphia Eagles in Week 15 of the 2015 season, he was named the NFC Defensive Player of the Week. Not bad for a guy who would have stuck at strong safety and left it right there for a lot of teams. "Deone was one of those guys that was a tall, active safety we needed to match up on tight ends and running backs," Arians said in late 2015. "We lost Daryl Washington, so there was a void up front. We put him in the nickel package, and he really took off. He was too good to take off the field, so we basically kept our nickel package in and adjusted it to play against regular [personnel]. It's always been that way and it goes back to when I was a head coach at Temple. We'd recruit skinny defensive ends, hoping they'd grow into tackles. Outside linebackers would grow into defensive ends, and safeties that would grow into outside line-backers. It's one of those things that…the more position-flexibility you have, the more valuable you are to us."

I mentioned to Arians that this was the same philosophy Jimmy Johnson used to build the great Dallas Cowboys defenses of the early 1990s—take smaller, faster guys and make them bigger and faster—and he laughed. "Yeah, Jimmy and I grew up around the same time, so it's pretty similar," he said.

At the 2017 Scouting Combine, Cardinals general manager Steve Keim said that this hybrid philosophy worked at several position groups on Arizona's roster. "It's important to have hybrid players at all levels whether it is your defensive line, your linebacker, or secondary. Because when you do things like we do—multiple fronts, multiple coverages—you have that position flexibility where you can play inside, you can play outside. You've got Deone from a matchup standpoint who can potentially cover tight ends, can cover at times slot receivers to an extent. To have a guy like Tyrann Mathieu who can invert, play in the slot, play in the nickel for you, the more flexibility you have, the more you can do. Those guys have become so valuable because this game has become a matchup situation."

Selected in the third round of the 2013 draft, Mathieu became Arizona's Swiss army knife in the secondary, playing effectively everywhere from outside cornerback to free and strong safety. The Cardinals have a very specific philosophy regarding positional versatility, but they're hardly the only team doing so. You can expect that to continue. NFL teams select receivers and cornerbacks—and will continue to—specifically for their ability in the slot. Slot cornerback and slot receiver are positions that were relative afterthoughts a decade ago, but in today's NFL, they're starter positions.

In a larger sense, we can point to the idea that more than ever those coaches and play-designers and executives, who stay ahead of the curve by adapting to their environments and realities, are the ones who will find consistent success. Bill Belichick is the obvious iteration of this idea, but there were two contrasting ideologies I saw in Week 16 of the 2015 season that point to the NFL's primary requirement these days: adapt or find yourself on the outside looking in.

In the second half and overtime of the Denver Broncos' Monday night win against the Cincinnati Bengals that ended that Week 16, head coach Gary Kubiak surprised me. Throughout his long career as an offensive coordinator and head coach in the NFL, Kubiak stuck with a few basic offensive concepts: the inside and outside zone running game, multiple tight ends deployed as route-runners, and a passing game that's built off of play-action and boot-action as much as any in the league. At times he had tied himself to his schemes to a fault. (I've talked to players around the league about the predictability of Kubiak's passing concepts and how easy they are to read and react to.)

With Peyton Manning as his quarterback, Kubiak stubbornly stuck to his ideas in the face of clear evidence that Manning worked better in other schemes. It's not that Manning's clear regression was exactly Kubiak's fault—there are a host of reasons for that—but this seemed like yet another example of Kubiak's insistence that his players fit his concepts, no matter what. And that's generally a recipe for disaster unless the players happen to fit what the coach wants.

But down 14–3 to the Bengals at halftime, Kubiak did adapt to the benefit of quarterback Brock Osweiler. His late-game offense increased the tempo, allowed Osweiler to react to what he saw on the field, forced Cincinnati's defense into its base formations, and exhausted the Bengals' defense with a higher play volume. The Broncos had 63 total plays in the game, but 47 came in the second half and in overtime. Denver gained just 89 yards in the first half and finished with 390 for the game.

Similarly, Broncos then-defensive coordinator Wade Phillips veered away from his first-half strategy of playing his cornerbacks in aggressive man coverages and used more zone concepts in the second half. Bengals receiver A.J. Green was toasting Denver's excellent cornerbacks just as Pittsburgh Steelers wideout Antonio Brown had the week before. But after Phillips' adjustments, everything changed. Backup quarterback A.J. McCarron was more flustered by the zone concepts, and his deep throws started to wane. After the game McCarron admitted that the errant snap exchange that sealed Denver's win in overtime was due to his need to scan the protection a bit too long. Cincinnati gained 204 yards in the first half and only 90 yards thereafter.

Denver's adjustments made all the difference. "It's something we felt like we needed to do because we had no possessions," Kubiak said about the decision to adjust the tempo. "In the first half, we had three. I don't know if I've ever been a part of that. We had to do something to create some tempo and some plays before the day is over. You've got to sit there and say, 'Okay, we had 16 snaps.' We were well on our way to about 40 in there for a while. We had to do what we had to do."

NFL coaches have to adjust and adapt. Any coach who tells you that it's all about execution, and his players just need to play better…well, he's either lying to himself or lying to you and he probably isn't long for the job.

Fired by the Philadelphia Eagles after the 2015 season, Chip Kelly was famous for throwing a similar line out there. Whenever opponents are saying publicly that they have your system figured out before the plays happen, as was happening to the Eagles early that season, that's big trouble. In Kelly's three NFL seasons, he hadn't expanded his palette enough, and the league caught up to him. It always does. When Kelly was taken out of his own tendencies and was instead asked to present a system that could defeat NFL defenses past their initial adjustments, it didn't work. It didn't work any better when the San Francisco 49ers hired Kelly in the 2016 season and relieved him of his duties after just one season.

"You know when a team is in Tampa-2 [coverage], they're going to slant their 3 and 7 technique [defensive linemen]," Kelly told Philly.com in September of 2015 after Josh Huff, one of his own receivers, claimed that Cowboys defenders were calling out plays before the Eagles ran them. "When they do it, it's not a surprise to us. Everybody has predictabilities and tendencies going into every game. That's just part of the game. Everybody kind of does what they do…We need to execute."

Part of the problem in Philadelphia was that with Kelly's breakneck tempo, the quarterback didn't have time to call audibles. Basically, he would head to the line, read what he saw as well as he could, and the offense would have to hope for the best. If the pace didn't break the defense, that strategy would collapse in on itself and eventually it did for Kelly.

Head coach Mike McCarthy has presided over a passing game in Green Bay that had relied too much on the superhuman efforts of Packers quarterback Aaron Rodgers for years. Generally, McCarthy and his staff would prefer to run a bunch of isolation routes over and over without presenting Rodgers with better openings instead of "scheming guys open" in NFL parlance. But if you ask the coach about the system, he'll point back to the players. "The reality is: we're not that far off," McCarthy said the day after Rodgers completed 22-of-43 passes for 202 yards, one touchdown, and one interception against the Chicago Bears in a 17–13 Thanksgiving night loss in 2015. "It's the attention and the details. Our issues are technique and discipline in the technique, and quit worrying so much about the plays. Just win the route or win the play called."

McCarthy has uttered several different iterations of this over the years. Green Bay's offensive inflexibility really came home to roost when Rodgers missed several weeks in the 2017 season with a broken collarbone. The Packers lost eight of their last 11 games and missed the playoffs for the first time since 2008. Backup Brett Hundley, a mobile quarterback with a limited ability to read the field and digest more advanced passing concepts, was hung out to dry as Green Bay's coaching staff was slow to adjust their offense to fit what Hundley could likely do—succeed marginally with run-pass options and routes that provided easy first reads.

Systems come and go. Belichick has become the foremost and most successful proponent of the philosophy that you don't go into a game or a season with a definitive system or scheme—instead you design and vary your concepts to best meet your opponent. That's why you've seen the Patriots run everything from pure inside power runs to three-tight end sets as a base package to spread sets with a tight end flexed out on offense, and it's why the Pats tend to switch from a 4–3 to a 3–4 as a base defensive concept every few years. It not only throws a different wrinkle into the gameplan, but also keeps them ahead of the NFL's trends to produce a corresponding personnel advantage.

And just to keep everyone guessing, Belichick will throw a new wrinkle in there now and again. Although most coaches preach the importance of continuity along the offensive line, Belichick and his coaching staff have been known to put different line combinations on the field not only for each game, but also for each *drive*. These things don't always work, but they are examples of one coach's need to stretch past the constraints of any one system at any time.

The RPO and Super Bowl LII

Ohio State (and former Utah and Florida) head coach Urban Meyer told Mike Kuchar of X & O Labs that by 2014 the run-pass option would take over college football as more and more teams used RPOs as a base strategy in their offense. That's proven to be true. At the high school and college levels, the RPO has become a base construct of offenses all over the country. It's an excellent advantage to be gained when you're dealing with high player turn-over and relatively limited time with your players on the practice field and in the film room.

In a nutshell the RPO allows the quarterback to adjust his strategy after the snap based on the movement of an unblocked defender. There's an element of read-option here, but the RPO allows for more diverse passing concepts than the simple short stuff found in most basic option offenses. It also works for quarterbacks who aren't mobile, which makes it more of a multiple passing concept than the standard read-option. The idea is not for the quarterback to take off running; it's to give him the flexibility to pass or run based on the scope of the defense.

NFL teams started using RPOs more and more in recent years; according to Pro Football Focus, the average NFL game had about five such plays in 2016, and that number went up, as did the awareness of the concept at the NFL level, when the Philadelphia Eagles implemented it with backup quarterback Nick Foles, who became the starter after Carson Wentz suffered a torn ACL against the Los Angeles Rams in the 13th game of the 2017 season. Wentz had become the epicenter of Philly's offense in only his second NFL season because of his ability to combine precision passing with toughness and mobility, and the injury would have felled a team with a less creative coaching staff.

Instead, head coach Doug Pederson, offensive coordinator Frank Reich, and quarterbacks coach John DeFilippo turned to Foles and gave him the RPO as an easy way to get what were essentially free yards against defenses who couldn't help but guess wrong. "I just think the RPO game is a unique way to put stress on different defenders," Reich told me in the week leading up to Super Bowl LII. "Usually, the stress you're trying to put on a defender [at the line of scrimmage] is to push them around. In the RPO game, sometimes that involves not blocking a defender and putting stress on him, like, 'Why is no one blocking me? What am I supposed to do? Should I run after the ball carrier or should I stand here and try to guard the receiver who's coming into this area?' That's some of the uniqueness of the RPO game, and when you get a quarterback who can read that unblocked defender quickly and deliver the ball with accuracy at different arm angles, it can be a very dangerous weapon."

Foles isn't as dynamic or mobile as Wentz nor does he have his arm or accuracy, but the RPO—and the threat of it—helped him exponentially. The Eagles may have only run it a few times per game, but they ran the concepts so well as an integration to their base offenses that opponents never really knew what to focus on. "It's a run, but it's also a pass if the quarterback decides to throw it and read it," New England Patriots safety Devin McCourty told me. "Very tough defensively because every guy has a job and a role on our defense, and you have to do that. If you play the run when you're supposed to be playing the pass and they throw it, that's going to be a big gain. If you play the pass and they run it, that hurts you, too. We can't have guys doing things that don't fit the defense."

What makes the RPO potentially more long-lasting in the NFL is the stress it puts on defenders on every play—and the levels to which it can be implemented. This isn't a three-play Wildcat that defenses were able to figure out in half a season or a basic read-option that can be countered with spying linebackers. The RPO concepts may not be advanced enough to be a base offense in the pros, but as an adjunct system to gain an advantage, it's the kind of thing every defensive coordinator is looking to snuff out as quickly as possible. Getting embarrassed on a repeat basis by a "high school" offense doesn't look good on your resume. "You can just never have a good call," Eagles defensive coordinator Jim Schwartz said. "You can have a defense that's great against the run, and they have a run called, and the quarterback pulls the ball and throws it. So, it really takes away the play-calling a little bit from the defense. If you have something that's really good against the pass, and the quarterback sees it, he can just hand the ball off. If you have something that makes it very difficult to run the ball, he can keep the ball and end up throwing it. It's just another layer—you add the RPO along with read-option stuff; it's made it really difficult for defenses. You have to have multi-dimensional players and you have to be sound straight across the board. You have to defend the width of the field and the length of the field, run and pass, on every single play."

As then-Patriots defensive coordinator Matt Patricia noted to me a couple days before the Eagles beat New England for their first Super Bowl title and Foles threw three touchdown passes and caught another from tight end Trey Burton, Philly's use of the RPO allowed Foles to put his mind at ease regarding easy yardage in crucial situations by reacting to—and exploiting—the empty part of the field laid bare by the unblocked defender. "The RPO is a small part of what they do," Patricia said. "They do a lot, so you have to read your keys and be disciplined and handle all of it because it is going to change based on the down and distance and situation. We've got to defend everything they do, not one specific thing. It's the combination that makes them so successful. They do a great job of understanding what you're in defensively and putting their guys in position. They run great routes and they do a good job of what I'll call 'taking the profit.' If someone is open right now, they're going to get the ball out quick and let them run. As much as they can get the ball in the hands of their skillplayers in space and allow them to make plays, that's what they're going to do."

The Eagles took a play concept from the high school and college ranks, dressed it up to beat opponents at the highest levels of the game, and deployed those innovative concepts when they would have otherwise been outgunned and outmanned. In the modern NFL, any coach, who doesn't adopt that mind-set and thinks his precious system will magically take the NFL by storm any longer than it takes the rest of the league to figure it out, is halfway to his own professional execution. As the NFL progresses, imagination will be a key attribute. Adaptability will be an absolute necessity. And when you see a new scheme or concept infiltrate the league seemingly out of nowhere, you likely can assume that it was due to the desperation of one play-caller, and because of the genius of him and his staff, he was able to think outside the box and find a new way.

- ACKNOWLEDGMENTS -

This book would not exist without Mike Tanier, who kicked my ass when I didn't believe I was the one to do it, and Laura Fritts-Drew, who offered her love, her support, and her awesome Whidbey Island cabin as the perfect writer's retreat when deadlines were looming. My gratitude knows no bounds.

Louis Riddick, for your time and great words.

Michelle Bruton, Jeff Fedotin, Josh Williams, and everyone at Triumph Books for the opportunity to make this project a public endeavor.

Aaron Schatz, Matt Ryan, Tom Mantzouranis, Chris Stone, Ben Eagle, Melissa Jacobs, Ian Kenyon, and Collin McCollough for editorial wisdom through time.

Everyone who's been a part of the NFL1000. When you're an old guy with half a clue, it's crucial to learn from young and hungry talents who can show you different ways to think.

Peter King, Greg Cosell, Jim Trotter, Mark Pesavento, Matt Ryan, and Mike Freeman for your mentorship and generosity of spirit.

The book's "beta readers"—Brian Billick, Chris Brown, Greg Cosell, Mike Freeman, Tony Khan, Amy Trask, Jim Trotter, Trey Wingo, Dave Zirin. Your insight is greatly appreciated.

Local inspiration: everyone who is grinding away at Hedgebrook and Hugo House and all the writers' groups and colonies in and around Seattle. I'm blessed to live in a literary city with infinite creative energy. Liz Matthews, Ian Furness, John Clayton, Stephen Cohen, and everyone in the Seattle football media.

- SOURCES -

Parts of the author's following articles are used in this book with permission

"The Miami Wildcat, and Other Tall Tales," Football Outsiders, September 24, 2008

"Cover-3: Saturday Night Special," Football Outsiders, October 6, 2010

"Cover-3: Way of the Gun," Football Outsiders, October 13, 2010

"Option Routes, and Why They Drive Some Receivers Crazy," Yahoo! Sports, June 24, 2012

"Off the Grid: The Death of Execution, Deone Bucannon Q&A, and more," SI.com, December 28, 2015

Books

Arnsparger, Bill, *Arnsparger's Coaching Defensive Football*, St. Lucie Press (1999)

Atwood, Gretchen, *Lost Champions*, Bloomsbury (2016)

Bennett, Tom, *The Pro Style*, Prentice-Hall (1976)

Billick, Brian and MacCambridge, Michael, *More Than A Game*, Scribner (2009)

Blount, Roy, *About Three Bricks Shy of a Load*, Ballantine Books (1974)

Brown, Chris, *The Essential Smart Football* (2012)

Brown, Chris, *The Art of Smart Football* (2014)

Brown, Paul with Clary, Jack, *PB: The Paul Brown Story*, Atheneum (1979)

Cantor, George, *Paul Brown: The Man Who Invented Modern Football*, Triumph Books (2008)

Carroll, Bob, Gershman, Michael, Neft, David, and Thorn, John, *Total Football II*, Harper Collins (1999)

Clary, Jack, *Great Teams' Great Years—The Cleveland Browns*, Macmillan (1973)

Clary, Jack, *Great Teams' Great Years—The San Francisco 49ers*, Macmillan (1974)

Cohen, Rich, *Monsters—The 1985 Chicago Bears and the Wild Heart of Football*, Farrar, Straus, and Giroux (2013)

Coryell, Don with Stein, Joe and Clark, Diane, *Win With Honor* (1976)

Daly, Dan, *The National Forgotten League*, University of Nebraska Press (2012)

Daly, Dan and O'Donnell, Bob, *The Pro Football Chronicle*, Macmillan (1990)

Danyluk, Tom, *The Super '70s,* Mad Uke Publishing (2005)

Ellison, Glenn, *Run-and-Shoot Football—The Now Attack,* Parker Publishing (1965)

Frommer, Harvey, *When It Was Just a Game,* Taylor Trade Publishing (2015)

Golenbock, Peter, *Cowboys Have Always Been My Heroes,* Warner Books (1997)

Greenberg, Murray, *Passing Game,* PublicAffairs (2008)

Gruver, Ed, *The American Football League, a Year-By-Year History,* McFarland & Company (1997)

Harris, David, *The Genius,* Random House (2008)

Henderson, Frank and Olson, Mel, *Football's West Coast Offense,* Human Kinetics (1997)

Holley, Michael, *War Room,* Harper Collins (2011)

Horrigan, Jack and Rathet, Mike, *The Other League,* Follett Publishing (1970)

Huff, Sam, and Shapiro, Leonard, *Tough Stuff,* St. Martin's Press (1988)

Jaworski, Ron, with Cosell, Greg and Plaut, David, *The Games That Changed the Game,* Ballantine Books (2010)

Johnson, James, *The Wow Boys,* University of Nebraska Press (2006)

Johnson, Jimmy, *Turning the Thing Around,* Hyperion (1993)

Katzowitz, Josh, *Sid Gillman—Father of the Modern Passing Game,* Clerisy Press (2012)

Kirwan, Pat with Seigerman, David, *Take Your Eye Off the Ball 2.0,* Triumph Books (2015)

Landry, Tom, *An Autobiography,* Harper Collins, (1990)

Layden, Tim, *Blood, Sweat, and Chalk,* Sports Illustrated Books (2010)

Lombardi, Vince, edited by Flynn, George, *Vince Lombardi on Football,* Galahad Books (1973)

Maraniss, David, *When Pride Still Mattered,* Simon & Schuster (1999)

Maxymuk, John, *NFL Head Coaches, a Biographical Dictionary,* 1920–2011, McFarland & Company (2012)

MacCambridge, Michael, *America's Game,* Random House (2014)

Miller, Jeff, *Going Long,* McGraw-Hill (2003)

Millman, Chad and Coyne, Shawn, *The Ones who Hit the Hardest,* Gotham Books (2010)

Newhouse, Dave, *Founding 49ers: The Dark Days before the Dynasty,* Kent State University Press (2015)

Palladino, Ernie, *Lombardi and Landry,* Skyhorse (2012)

Pomerantz, Gary, *Their Life's Work,* Simon & Schuster (2013)

Ribowsky, Mark, *The Last Cowboy—A Life of Tom Landry,* W.W. Norton (2014)

Riger, Robert and Maule, Tex, *The Pros,* Simon and Schuster (1960)

Ryan, Rex and Walker, Jeff, *Coaching Football's 46 Defense,* Coaches Choice (1999)

Shula, Don and Sahadi, Lou, *The Winning Edge,* Dutton (1973)

Smith, Robert, *Illustrated History of Pro Football,* Grosset & Dunlap (1977)

Sporting News Selects Pro Football's Greatest Quarterbacks, Sporting News (2005)

Steidel, Dave, *Remember the AFL,* Clerisy Press (2008)

Steidel, Dave, *The Uncrowned Champs: How the 1963 San Diego Chargers Would Have Won the Super Bowl,* Carrel Books (2015)

Walsh, Bill, and Dickey, Glenn, *Building a Champion,* St. Martin's Press (1990)

Walsh, Bill, with Billick, Brian and Peterson, James, *Finding the Winning Edge,* Sports Publishing, Inc. (1999)

Whittingham, Richard, *What a Game They Played,* Harper & Row (1984)

Zimmerman, Paul, *The New Thinking Man's Guide to Pro Football,* Simon and Schuster (1984)

Websites

Newspapers.com

NFL Films

Scribd.com

SIVault.com

YouTube.com